Leadership

Fr. Kevin,

May you be blessed
in all you do!

Deacon Dan

Leadership

The Wisdom of the World and the Beatitudes

DANIEL LOWERY

WIPF & STOCK · Eugene, Oregon

LEADERSHIP
The Wisdom of the World and the Beatitudes

Published with ecclesiastical approval granted on OCTOBER 12, 2021.

Wipf & Stock
An Imprint of Wipf and Stock Publishers
199 W. 8th Ave., Suite 3
Eugene, OR 97401

www.wipfandstock.com

PAPERBACK ISBN: 978-1-6667-3252-8
HARDCOVER ISBN: 978-1-6667-2633-6
EBOOK ISBN: 978-1-6667-2634-3

DECEMBER 8, 2021

Contents

List of Figures

Foreword

WHILE SERVING AS A board chair for a Catholic social agency some years ago, I was in the habit of meeting once every month with our executive director over breakfast. We found this to be a useful way to maintain communications outside of the highly structured confines of the boardroom. One such occasion stands out in my memory. Our executive director was anticipating a very difficult day due to the need to lay off two of the organization's long-term employees because of budget constraints. It happens that both the executive director and I serve as deacons in the Roman Catholic Church. After a long and rather sobering conversation, the executive director looked up and said: "This sure doesn't feel diaconal, Dan." As someone who had long served in management and administrative positions of various kinds, I knew exactly what he meant; and, if he had used the term "Christian" instead of "diaconal," I would have understood that as well.

Management in organizations of all kinds—private, public, nonprofit, and ecclesial—is difficult. There are great joys in serving in these capacities, but this kind of work can be a burden, too. Managers confront daunting challenges on a day-to-day basis, and they have to make decisions that can sometimes leave them ill at ease or isolated. At times, conflicts can arise between a manager's responsibilities on the job and her faith commitments, and reconciling these discordant notes can lead to frustration or even to a bifurcated existence in which the manager lives one life during the workweek and another on Sunday. Further, too few first-time managers receive any kind of formal training or formation in the lived experience of management. As a result, they may not have access to conceptual frameworks that could help them negotiate the exigencies associated with their new roles and responsibilities.

This text addresses this concern. We will examine the complex interface that exists between a manager's faith commitments on the one hand and the exercise of her responsibilities as a manager on the other. More specifically, we will bring the wisdom of the world concerning management into conversation with the wisdom of God as it is reflected in the Beatitudes proclaimed by Jesus in Matthew's Gospel. Given the concerns expressed by so many managers I have encountered along the way and what many perceive to be a crisis of leadership in our world, there is a clear need for a reflection of this kind.

Competent managers are important, but what we really need are true leaders. Indeed, a sharp distinction is drawn in this text between "management" and "leadership." Whereas "management" can be understood as the responsibility for and performance of any one or more of several organizational or societal functions, e.g., planning, organizing, staffing, directing, coordinating, reporting, and budgeting, in a manner oriented to ends external to the manager, "leadership" can be understood as the balanced exercise of these same responsibilities in service to a broader array of stakeholders in a manner that is constrained by the leader's internalized virtues and informed by values and intellectual commitments drawn from a larger belief system, but oriented, nonetheless, to ends sanctioned by the organization or by society. Leadership can thus be distinguished from management in four important ways: first, leadership is oriented to service; second, it involves an array of stakeholders; third, its exercise is constrained by virtues internal to the leader; and fourth, its exercise is oriented to values and intellectual commitments drawn from a larger belief system. For faithful disciples of Jesus, this involves Christian values and Christian intellectual commitments.

Several editorial decisions have guided this effort. First, although I serve in ordained ministry in the Catholic Church, this text is not written from a denominational perspective. It should prove helpful to managers and nominal leaders from a variety of Christian traditions and those from other faith traditions as well. At the same time, I have not shied away from the Catholic intellectual tradition. And at points in the analysis at which denominational perspectives may be pertinent, differences are noted and the assessment of the question at hand is left to the reader.

A second editorial decision pertains to the critical stance adopted with respect to the world's wisdom. Our understanding of the social world is often stunted by unreflective thinking. We tend to accept the world as it is presented to us: "It has always been this way, and it will always be so." In his seminal work *The Making of the Self*, Charles Taylor argues persuasively that our understanding of ourselves and the social world in which we live are constructs. To a considerable extent, they are the products of our own time and place. This includes our received understanding of management and leadership. To our great misfortune, the narrowness of this unreflective view—a view now so very prevalent— separates us from other understandings that are, nonetheless, part and parcel of our historical and cultural patrimony.

A third editorial decision pertains to the kinds of scholarly sources tapped for the purposes of this analysis. As we shall see, a number of academic disciplines, including, most notably, sociology and the management sciences, focus considerable attention on the nature and functions of management. Unfortunately, however, for many of us who labor in the field, each of these academic disciplines tends to be committed to its own very particular understanding of human nature, to its own underlying meta-theory, to its own research agenda, and to its own vocabulary. They present themselves as incommensurate systems. To further complicate the matter, knowledgeable practitioners have added their own diagnoses and prescriptions as well. The result is a virtual Babel of insights pertaining to the management challenges we face in our increasingly complex world. With respect to the twin topics of management and leadership, there is as much of a need to bring our academic disciplines into conversation with each other on the one hand and the collective wisdom of the academy with the wisdom of knowledgeable practitioners on the other, as there is to bring the wisdom of the world into conversation with the wisdom of Scripture and the broader Christian tradition.

This is why the review of management theory and practice in chapter 2 is somewhat lengthy. More detail is provided than might be expected in a text concerning moral and just behavior. My own experience suggests, however, that few who labor in contemporary organizations are fully cognizant of the managerial "language games" within which they labor, and this includes graduates of MBA and MPA programs. That being said, readers who are well acquainted with the development of management theory and practice over the course of the last century may want to leap over the perspective-by-perspective account unfolded in chapter 2, skipping, instead, to the two meta-criticisms advanced with respect to these language games in the final four pages of the chapter.

A fourth editorial decision pertains to citations. An interdisciplinary work such as this necessarily summarizes settled information drawn from this or that field of study. This is certainly so in this instance with respect to management theory, existential thought, Enlightenment moral philosophy, and Catholic social teaching. I have footnoted lightly on these topics, reserving citations—for the most part—to foundational texts, non-canonical questions, and quotations, of course. Readers are referred to any number of academic textbooks on these topics for more detailed information.

A fifth editorial decision pertains to the citations of certain seminal thinkers. This study is not intended for an academic audience familiar with decades of scholarly discourse. All such contributions enter into a stream of conversation engaged in by other scholars and practitioners over the course of many generations. To provide some context in this regard, the original publication dates of key texts are cited and the birth years and the years in which key contributors to this ongoing conversation died, if applicable, are noted as well. This should provide some sense of the overall flow of the larger conversation concerning management and leadership into which we are entering. In some instances, these key contributors are or were well-aware of each other; in others, they are not or were not. They are all, nonetheless, party to a broad stream of thought that extends far beyond their own unique contributions.

A sixth editorial decision pertains to the exemplar who is featured in chapter 11: Dag Hammarskjöld, Secretary General of the United Nations from 1953 until his untimely death in 1961. It could be argued that the world does not need another older, albeit now deceased, white exemplar who hailed from the Northern Hemisphere. In our own time, we have come to know a wider variety of virtuous men and women from across the globe. Several attributes recommend Hammarskjöld, however. First, he died almost sixty years ago, and the public's memory of him has faded to a considerable extent. He is thus something of a "fresh face" in our own time and place. Second, Hammarskjöld left a remarkable journal behind, a diary of sorts that chronicles his journey of faith in considerable detail. We are thus in a position to correlate key events in Hammarskjöld's very public life with his private reflections pertaining to his self-identification as a disciple of Jesus. Finally, Hammarskjöld worked "in the world." Mother Teresa left a remarkable journal behind, too, but she labored in and for the church. We hope to convey the need for virtue oriented to Christian values and to Christian intellectual commitments to a wider audience. Hammarskjöld may thus be more accessible to some than Mother Teresa or any other "religious" exemplar.

A seventh editorial decision pertains to academic discourse. Scholars, in general, resist pigeonholing. This is particularly so in the case of existential philosophers and theologians. A number of existential themes are addressed in this text. To the extent possible, the several works of scholars associated with these themes will be referred to as "existential" with no suggestion that the authors themselves should be categorized as "existentialists." That being said, the broad outlines of an existential perspective are developed in chapters 3, 4, and 5.

An eighth editorial decision pertains to the extensive appeal in part II to the work of the early church fathers, a diverse collection of holy men who wrote and preached across a broad geographic area over a period of several centuries. There is no single patristic perspective as such. Nevertheless, the sense of the Beatitudes conveyed in their work differs rather dramatically from the view that clearly dominated moral thinking in the post-Tridentine or modern era, a perspective that still resonates in some circles, even in the wake of the Second Vatican Council. Further, the early church fathers had no access to the thinking of the many seminal spiritual writers who followed them, including, for instance, Thomas Aquinas, Thomas à Kempis, Ignatius of Loyola, and, most importantly for our purposes, a number of theologians and spiritual writers from the twentieth century who were so profoundly influenced by existential thought. These thinkers privileged the contributions of the early church fathers, but extended it, as well, in new and fruitful directions. Our intent, therefore, is not so much to replicate patristic thought with respect to the Beatitudes, as to employ the insights of the early church fathers, most notably Augustine and John Chrysostom, in asserting the enduring value of the Beatitudes for all Christians, all of whom are called to holiness.

Most of the quotations of the early church fathers included in this text are drawn from an anthology masterfully assembled by Philip Schaff in *Nicene and Post-Nicene Fathers*, which was originally published in 1888 by the Christian Literature Publishing Company and subsequently republished by Catholic Way Publishing in 1914. In a few instances in which the literary style of nineteenth-century piety impedes easy comprehension, translations drawn either from the 1975 translation of the *Liturgy of the Hours*, which was drafted by the Catholic Church's International Commission on English in the Liturgy, or from Kevin Knight's edited transcription of Schaff's work, which is available at www.newadvent.org/fathers/1601.htm, are employed instead.

The biblical references cited throughout the text are drawn from the New American Bible. This is of particular importance at just one point in the text, however: our examination of the fourth Beatitude, i.e., "Blessed are they who hunger and thirst for righteousness . . ." Some translations of the Bible use the term "justice" in place of "righteousness," which, as we shall see, coveys a very different meaning to contemporary ears.

A final editorial decision pertains to gender, a perennial challenge when drawing on works written when different writing conventions prevailed. To offset the all too frequent use of masculine pronouns in the quotations incorporated into this text, feminine pronouns will be employed in the original portions of the narrative.

I have approached this project as a teacher, as a practitioner, and as a Christian disciple. As an undergraduate, I majored in philosophy and history. I hold master's degrees in business administration and pastoral studies and a PhD in public administration. Over the course of my academic career, I have taught business management, public administration, and theology classes at both the undergraduate level and the graduate level. As a practitioner, I worked as a manager in the federal government for two decades. I also consulted with management teams and boards of directors in the private sector, labored in several administrative capacities in higher education, and served as an executive director or board chair for a number of civic and nonprofit organizations, too. Finally, I am an ordained deacon in the Roman Catholic Church and continue—in retirement—to manage a leadership formation program in my home diocese.

I am what the social sciences refer to as a "boundary spanner," a technical term, perhaps, for someone who is considered a "jack of all trades, albeit, perhaps, a master of none." At different points in my journey, my feet have been planted in any number of very different worlds. As a result, I have experienced management and leadership in a variety of contexts. I have attempted to bring these several perspectives to bear in this project, hopefully, to good effect.

Following an introductory chapter laying out the nature of the management challenge we sometimes face as committed Christians, part I will focus on the "wisdom of the world" as it pertains to management and leadership. In this portion of the text, we will bring four very different perspectives into conversation with each other: first, alternative understandings of management and leadership drawn from the secular literature; second, a contemporary understanding of virtue ethics as reflected in the work of Alasdair MacIntyre; third, the existential thought of Karl Rahner and several other existential philosophers and theologians; and, finally, the insights of a number of competing political philosophies. This inquiry will be both appreciative and critical. Appreciative inquiry focuses on that which adds value for those who are impacted by the phenomenon or the experience under investigation.

Chapter 2 will examine a number of the more influential management theories and models of the last century. Chapter 3 will focus on servant leadership, an antidote of sorts to two deep-seated flaws shared by the theories and models examined in chapter 2. Although servant leadership represents a notable step forward, it, too, will be found lacking. Chapter 4 will make the case for a traditional understanding of virtue as *the* missing ingredient in the servant-leader model. This is the point at which the distinction noted above between management and true leadership will be further developed. In chapter 5, the foregoing analyses will be applied to the public square.

In part II, we will introduce the Beatitudes as proclaimed by Jesus in chapter 5 of Matthew's Gospel. The eight Beatitudes will be presented as an ideal path of formation for all Christians, including managers and nominal leaders who aspire both to a more integrated experience of life and to true leadership in the organizations they serve. The historical development of the church's understanding of the Beatitudes will be examined and a perspective celebrated by several of the early church fathers will be introduced in the overview to part II. Servais Pinckaers, a contemporary scholar, will serve as our primary guide. In effect, the several different perspectives on management and leadership examined in part I of the text will be brought into conversation with a privileged understanding of the Beatitudes.

In chapters 6 through 10, each of Matthew's eight Beatitudes will be examined in some detail. Key themes explored in parts I and II of the text will be brought together in chapters 8, 9, and 10. To further integrate parts I and II, Dag Hammarskjöld, an exemplar, will be introduced in chapter 11. Finally, a select set of societal implications will be examined in chapter 12.

Two appendices are shared as well. The first graphically displays the information introduced in chapters 2 and 3 concerning the most influential management theories and models of the last century. The second includes personal reflection questions applicable to Matthew's Beatitudes.

It is quite unusual in academic work to bring such very different literatures into conversation with each other. Our tendency in academia is to stick to our knitting. As academics, we like to stay in our respective lanes. Something more is required, however, when the many challenges associated with management and leadership, more specifically, are viewed from the individual or phenomenal perspective of the manager or the nominal leader as a person of faith. As we shall see, an existential focus of this kind requires a more integrated or holistic approach.

I am grateful for the support provided by my wife Barbara and my children, Katie and Christopher, as I have negotiated—sometimes successfully and sometimes not—the vicissitudes of management, leadership, and discipleship, too, over the course of a lifetime. I have also benefited greatly from the examples provided by effective and faithful leaders in a number of institutional settings.

I would be remiss, however, if I did not call special attention to the many students I have encountered along the way. As every teacher knows, one never fully understands the material being shared until it is tested in the crucible of the classroom. I have benefited greatly from the insights contributed by the many students with whom I have shared a classroom at Indiana University Northwest and Calumet College of St. Joseph and in the Diocese of Gary, too. In gratitude, I dedicate this text to them.

Chapter 1

The Management Challenge for Christians

WORK CAN HOLD GREAT meaning in our lives. There is broad agreement on this point. The existential psychologist Viktor Frankl (1905–97) argued, for instance, that work and other kinds of creative acts represent one of three ways in which individuals can experience a profound sense of meaning.[1] The Lutheran theologian and philosopher Paul Tillich (1886–1965) pointed to work as one of several opportunities for "spiritual self-affirmation."[2] The existential psychiatrist Karl Jaspers (1883–1969) referred, instead, to "productive affairs"[3]; and the philosopher Charles Taylor (b. 1931) introduced the more general term "practice" and defined it as "any more or less stable configuration of shared activity whose shape is defined by a certain pattern of dos and don'ts."[4] As a particular venue in which we can exercise our creativity, work can, indeed, engender a profound sense of meaning.

This is particularly so in the case of managerial work. The rich combination of mission, strategy, team-building, and problem-solving can serve as a vibrant pallet from which we can draw in crafting a meaningful life. It is no wonder then that we invest so much of our time, talent, emotional energy, and effort in this defining aspect of our lives.

1. Frankl, *Psychotherapy and Existentialism*, 115.
2. Tillich, *The Courage to Be*, 46.
3. Jaspers, *Reason and Existenz*, 123.
4. Taylor, *Sources of the Self*, 204.

Management can be debilitating and destructive, too, however. Indeed, it is remarkable how many managers leave their employment relationships under less than ideal circumstances. In far too many instances, a manager's career ends with an unanticipated summons to the human resources office and an escort out of the building. In others, careers in management wind down in disappointment, disillusionment, or bitterness. At best, it seems, careers in management tend to end as "unfinished symphonies," a turn of phrase the great Jesuit scholar Karl Rahner (1904–2004) applied to life more generally.[5]

It is remarkable, as well, how often careers in management can be experienced as sources of spiritual discontent. This can range from low-level discomfort to a disconcerting sense of dissonance or guilt over decisions made and actions taken. Careers in management can even be experienced as the locus of existential crisis. Indeed, work—most notably, managerial work—is a frequent topic in spiritual direction. This should not be surprising in the case of committed Christians. As affirmed by William A. Barry, "for Christian believers, any experience can have a religious dimension because they believe that God is not only transcendent to, but also immanent in, his created universe . . . Because I believe in God, I discover in my experience more than what, at first blush, seemed to be there and name that mysterious 'more' God."[6] As affirmed by St. Paul, committed Christians hope to experience God as "all in all" (1 Cor 15:28), and this includes our work.

This text is written with this concern in mind. It is written for Christians who are searching for a way to better integrate their faith commitments and their work as managers and nominal leaders. As we shall see, this requires virtue, a moral concept that has been substantially de-valued in recent centuries. Virtue is presented in this text as the privileged means through which managers can become true leaders. An argument for virtue is laid out in part I, and a tried-and-true path for forming oneself in virtue is presented in part II.

Our purposes in this chapter are more circumscribed: first, to describe the nature of the problem before us in experiential terms; second, to share a useful way of thinking about management problems; third, to examine some of the very different and sometimes conflicting ways in which the Christian tradition has regarded secular work; and, fourth, to

---

5. Rolheiser, *The Holy Longing*, 156.
6. Barry, *Spiritual Direction*, 25–26.

consider whether or not it is even possible for today's managers to think about work as a spiritual concern.

The argument advanced in part I of this text is based substantially on the work of Alasdair MacIntyre (b. 1929), a moral philosopher whose seminal work *After Virtue* (1981) has contributed significantly to the revival of virtue ethics over the course of the last thirty to forty years. In this text, we are focused more narrowly on managerial work and will draw more explicitly on Christian values and Christian intellectual commitments, but the basic argument is the same: a sustained commitment to moral virtue is needed if our work in organizations is to be experienced as an integrated whole.

After Virtue begins with a powerful critique of all kinds of contemporary organizations. According to MacIntyre, organizations are oriented today to instrumental ends. There is no place in most of them for any consideration of ends external to the organization. This includes a concern for people as anything other than inputs, constraints, or variables; and it pertains, as well, to any moral thinking that extends beyond that which is legal. According to MacIntyre, there is little room in the boardroom or the management suite or on the shop floor, for that matter, for any consideration of moral virtue.

MacIntyre's critique is quite broad, indeed, and extends to all aspects of modern life, including the public square. Because of the developments he cites, lives are increasingly experienced as fractured or compartmentalized. "Modernity partitions each human life into a variety of segments, each with its own norms and modes of behavior . . . And all these separations have been achieved so that it is the distinctiveness of each and not the unity of the life of the individual who passes through those parts in terms of which we are taught to think and feel . . . Life comes to appear as nothing but a series of unconnected episodes—a liquidation of the self."[7] As a result, those who serve in organizations experience their professional lives as roles or as characters, "a very special type of social role which places a certain kind of moral constraint on the personality of those who inhabit them."[8] MacIntyre argues further that the identities we take on in contemporary organizations include not just moral constraints, but moral imperatives, too, all of which are oriented to the

7. MacIntyre, *After Virtue*, 204.
8. MacIntyre, *After Virtue*, 27.

instrumental ends of the organization. Indeed, "characters are the masks worn by moral philosophies."[9]

According to MacIntyre, this can engender considerable dissonance and considerable dysfunction, too. "[E]ach of us is taught to see himself or herself as an autonomous moral agent; but each of us also becomes engaged by modes of practice, aesthetic or bureaucratic, which involve us in manipulative relationships with others. Seeking to protect the autonomy that we have learned to prize, we aspire ourselves not to be manipulated by others; seeking to incarnate our own principles and stand-point in the world of practice, we find no way open to us to do so except by directing toward others those very manipulative modes of relationship which each of us aspires to resist in our own case. The incoherence of our attitudes and our experiences arises from the incoherent conceptual scheme which we have inherited."[10]

According to MacIntyre, there is little room in contemporary organizations for a consideration of virtue, and this can be experienced as a great loss, indeed, as a kind of rending of the true self. "The liquidation of the self into a set of demarcated areas of role-playing allows no scope for the exercise of dispositions which could genuinely be accounted virtues . . . For a virtue is not a disposition that makes for success only in some one particular type of situation."[11] As a result, those who labor in contemporary organizations can be cut adrift from any deeper sense of meaning, including any sense of meaning anchored in one's faith.

According to Charles Taylor, this existential drift can be amplified in those who are not grounded in any substantial way in a faith tradition. "What does it mean to say that for me fullness comes from a power which is beyond me, that I have to receive it, etc.? Today, it is likely to mean something like this: the best sense I can make of my conflicting moral and spiritual experience is captured by a theological view of this kind. That is, my own experience, in prayer, in moments of fullness, in experiences of exile overcome, in what I seem to observe around me in other people's lives—lives of exceptional spiritual fullness, or lives of maximum self-enclosedness, lives of demonic evil, etc.—this seems to be the picture that emerges. But I am never, or only rarely, really sure, free of all doubt, untroubled by some objection—by some experience which won't

---

9. MacIntyre, *After Virtue*, 28.

10. MacIntyre, *After Virtue*, 68.

11. MacIntyre, *After Virtue*, 205.

fit, some lives which exhibit fullness on another basis, some alternative mode of fullness which sometimes draws me back, etc. This is typical of the modern condition, and an analogous story could be told by many an unbeliever."[12]

MacIntyre's critique is powerful, indeed, but it is presented in phenomenal terms. To this point, it describes "how it feels" to be ensnared in a complex web of organizational objectives and norms. In this sense, it is philosophical in nature. To this point, it can even be described as "emotivist," a dismissive term MacIntyre himself applies to a broad range of philosophical frameworks. Further, MacIntyre's critique is not framed in the language of management. It makes no use of examples drawn from the lived experience of managers or nominal leaders.

Given this, four management scenarios follow, each of which is intended to locate the challenge portrayed by MacIntyre in a managerial setting. Each of these scenarios can be described as layered. The metaphor of an onion or of a set of *matryoshka*s or Russian dolls can be helpful in this regard. In the first layer, two or more organizational ends or objectives compete for attention. To the extent that a conflict emerges in this initial layer of analysis, it typically involves two or more competing "decision frames," all of which are sanctioned, at least to some extent, by the organization. More often than not, a choice is made between the competing decision frames and the analysis is brought to a close. On occasion, however, the impacts or possible impacts of a decision on a person or on any number of persons will emerge. (As we shall see in chapter 4, the term "person" holds particular significance.) The foregrounding of a concern for a person as a person—as opposed to an input, a constraint, or a variable—can be considered a second level of analysis. On rare occasions, a third level of analysis will impose itself on the manager. This third level of analysis engages the manager's faith commitments and her other non-instrumental intellectual commitments. For a Christian manager who takes her faith seriously, this can produce considerable dissonance if the decision conflicts with her religious or spiritual beliefs.

A first-level analysis will be presented initially for each of our four scenarios. We will then introduce a concern for "persons" in each of the examples as an alternative decision frame. Finally, we will illustrate the cognitive dissonance that can result when Christian values and Christian intellectual commitments are introduced into the equation.

---

12. Taylor, *A Secular Age*, 10–11.

In our first scenario, a credible accusation of sexual harassment is lodged by a low-level employee against the executive director of a nonprofit organization. The executive director is highly regarded and is himself a prominent member of the community. He is also a longtime friend of the board chair. The clients served by the nonprofit organization are themselves vulnerable individuals, and the organization is heavily dependent on the financial support of the community. In the first level of analysis, three possible decision frames could compete for attention. The problem could be viewed as a public relations problem, a potential legal problem, or a matter of human resources policy. Whichever of these decision frames is ultimately foregrounded will likely determine the course of action to be followed by the board chair.

In our second scenario, a chief executive officer has concluded that a certain product is approaching the end of its life cycle and that the firm may soon be forced to abandon or significantly reengineer the product in question. In the first level of analysis, at least three possible decision frames could compete for attention. The problem could be viewed—first and foremost—as a matter of "harvesting" whatever potential profits might be generated by the product before it is eliminated altogether from the firm's product line. Second, the matter could be perceived as a re-engineering challenge. Third, it could be framed as an opportunity to cut costs if the production of the product can be moved offshore, thus obviating a high-cost union contract and, thereby, extending the life cycle of the product in question.

In our third scenario, an otherwise highly regarded and productive employee has transgressed an organization's attendance policy on multiple occasions. Progressive discipline has been applied, and the employee is now facing termination. She asks for forbearance, noting the need to attend to the health and wellbeing of her aging parents on a daily basis. At least two decision frames could initially come into play in a situation such as this. The operations supervisor to whom the employee reports could argue for an exception to the policy in question on the grounds that the offender is her most productive employee and that her dismissal would have an adverse impact on staff morale. Alternately, the firm's attorney and its human resources director could argue that making an exception in this instance could set a dangerous precedent that would likely undermine the enforcement of the organization's attendance policy in the future.

In our fourth scenario, a new executive director of a nonprofit organization has learned that her board chair's company has long been party to a noncompetitive contract with the nonprofit organization for an array of professional services. The executive director could view this matter through a political lens. She could hope simply "to live to fight another day." At least two other decision frames are possible, however. The matter in question could be viewed as a violation of a board member's duty of loyalty, a legal doctrine that proscribes board members of nonprofit organizations from subordinating the interests of the organization they serve to their personal or professional interests. Alternatively, it could be viewed as a matter of policy that needs to be addressed by the board itself, perhaps in consultation with the board's attorney. Again, the decision frame that is ultimately foregrounded will likely determine the executive director's response.

The decision frames featured in these four scenarios are all instrumental in nature. They are oriented to the needs of the organization in question. To this point, no formal consideration has been given to the many other people—as persons, in fact, rather than as inputs, constraints, or variables—who could be impacted by the decisions to be made or the actions to be taken.

This second level of analysis will be described in more detail in chapter 3. For now, it is sufficient to note that all kinds of people are impacted by all kinds of decisions made and by all kinds of actions taken by those who serve in management positions. Some of these people are impacted directly and others indirectly, including the family members of those who are impacted directly by a decision or by an action and members of the local community as well, to the extent that disparate treatment, collateral damage, or a societal externality of one kind or another might be involved. Indeed, a catalogue of primary, secondary, and tertiary impacts on people can be lengthy in some instances. Figure 1 is by no means exhaustive in this regard.

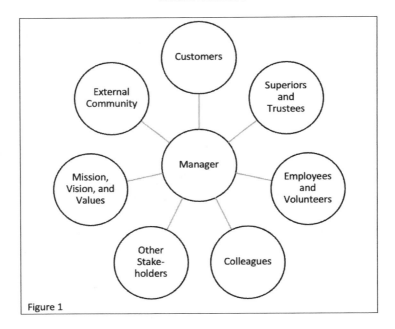

Figure 1

This secondary level of analysis rarely comes into play on its own, however. More often than not, it requires a voice external to the organization that refuses to go unheeded, an insistent advocate from within the organization, or the threat of an embarrassing story in the media that cannot be ignored. The decision frames employed in most of today's organizations involve first-level analyses.

Further, when this second level of analysis is triggered, it is typically because the individual in question has taken on the identity of a person as opposed to that of an input, a constraint, or a variable. The individual previously recognized solely as a customer, client, subcontractor, employee, supplier, complainant, union member, or resident takes on the identity of a person whose story has unique and enduring value, value that extends well beyond their functional or transactional relationship with the organization. This is the sense in which MacIntyre defines persons—first and foremost—as "story-telling animals."[13] As Hannah Arendt (1906–75) observed, "*who* somebody is or was we can know only through knowing the story of which he is himself the hero—his biography, in other words; everything else we know of him, including the work

13. MacIntyre, *After Virtue*, 216.

he may have produced and left behind, tells us only *what* he is or was."[14] We have now moved far beyond the transactional nature of relationships that more typically concern most of today's organizations.

Even if one is open to the need for a second level of analysis, little will likely change unless this newly attained recognition is processed through a robust set of values or intellectual commitments. A gestalt-like epiphany in which a manager recognizes a broad array of stakeholders as persons, each with his or her own unique story, is certainly possible. These stakeholders will likely acquire little or no additional standing with respect to the decision to be made or the action to be taken, however, unless this recognition is informed by a tradition oriented to action on their behalf. This is the point at which a perceived "problem" can take on a moral dimension.

From this personalist perspective, the moral can be understood as how one thinks about and acts toward oneself and toward others as persons. Further, just behavior can be understood as a particular kind of moral behavior that pertains to how life's benefits and burdens are shared among individuals recognized as persons and communities comprised of persons. This third level of analysis is clearly distinct from the prior two.

With respect to this kind of moral analysis, some of today's Christians look to the Old Testament prophets's condemnation of idolatry and the indifference exhibited by the people's leaders to the plight of those who lived on the margins of life, i.e., the *anawim*, to the Beatitudes in chapter 5 of Matthew's Gospel, to the parable of the sheep and the goats in chapter 25 of Matthew's Gospel, and to the commandment to love one another in chapter 13 of John's Gospel. These are not the only lenses through which to interpret the Christian *kerygma*, to be sure, but they align well with a personalist perspective and reflect a coherent and faithful understanding of Jesus' teachings. Together, they function as Christian values and as Christian intellectual commitments, a perspective that will be further developed in chapters 8 and 10.

The problem, of course, is that a third-level analysis grounded in Christian values and in Christian intellectual commitments can lead to very different conclusions than those derived exclusively from a first-level analysis. The committed Christian can hear messages from the pulpit on Sunday morning that are very much at odds with the decision frames available to her on the job.

14. Arendt, *The Human Condition*, 196.

Consider, again, the four scenarios introduced above. In the case of the sexual harassment complaint, little thought is given in the level-one analysis to the unique story of the person who filed the complaint or to the needs of the social agency's vulnerable clients. A second-level analysis could expand the field of interest considerably, but it is only when it is filtered through a Christian lens that the insufficiency of the level-one analysis is revealed. Consider, for instance, Matthew 18:6: "Whoever causes one of these little ones who believe in me to sin, it would be better for him to have a great millstone hung around his neck and to be drowned in the depth of the sea." This teaching should engender discomfort in the mind of the board chair if she is, in fact, a committed Christian. This is the sense in which a robust third-level or moral analysis can create a disconcerting level of dissonance in the mind of a committed Christian.

In our second scenario, a product is rapidly approaching the end of its life cycle. The first-level analysis is focused exclusively on the organization's instrumental ends. A second-level analysis could potentially broaden the range of factors to be considered to include the firm's employees and their families. It is unlikely that this will make a difference, however, unless this expanded focus is filtered through a robust set of values and intellectual commitments. Consider, for instance, the generosity displayed by the landowner in Matthew 20:1–16. He hired laborers at daybreak, at nine o'clock, at noon, at three o'clock, and at five o'clock, and then paid them all a full day's wage. "Are you envious because I am generous?" the landowner asks. This provocative story alludes to a relationship shared by the landowner and the laborers as persons, and it speaks to a certain level of moral accountability as well. The chief executive officer who is exclusively accountable to a board of directors may not be able to do anything with a third-level analysis of this kind, but it cannot help but give pause to a Christian who is serious about her faith.

In the third scenario, a dispute over a firm's attendance policy is being contested by an operations supervisor who is primarily concerned about productivity and staff morale on the one hand and the firm's attorney and human resources director on the other. The employee's difficulty with respect to her aging parents is foregrounded in neither of their respective positions. If they could be awoken to the need for a level-two analysis—that is, to the need to attend to the employee as a person who is experiencing a great deal of stress in managing her familial responsibilities—conceptual space could be created in which a level-three analysis might be possible. Consider Jesus' condemnation of the scribes and

Pharisees in Matthew 23:13–26: "They tie up heavy burdens and lay them on people's shoulders, but they will not lift a finger to move them . . . Woe to you, scribes and Pharisees, you hypocrites. You pay tithes of mint and dill and cumin and have neglected the weightier things of the law: judgment and mercy and fidelity."

Our fourth scenario involves a board chair's long-standing, non-competitive contract with the nonprofit organization he serves. A second-level analysis would likely disclose the interests of individual clients who are served by the organization. However small the amount might be on a per capita basis, these clients are certainly being cheated out of funds that could otherwise be allocated to the services they receive from the organization. The same could be said of the pay levels set for employees of the organization. If this realization prompted a level-three analysis, i.e., a moral analysis, the board chair would likely be associated in quick order with the dishonest steward portrayed in Luke 16:1–14. Jesus' teaching could not be more clear in this instance: "No servant can serve two masters. He will either hate one and love the other or be devoted to one and despise the other. You cannot serve God and mammon."

The point here is not to turn managers into moralists. It is, instead, to reveal ways in which moral considerations and matters of justice can intrude on decision-making processes in contemporary organizations. It begins with a recognition that managerial decisions and actions affect people—persons, in fact—whose own stories are sacred. No particular outcome follows necessarily in any of these scenarios. It is important to note, too, that few managers are entirely free to act on their own. As we shall see, the virtue of prudence is required to discern what may or may not be possible in many kinds of situations. For now, it is sufficient to note that a level-one analysis focused on alternative decision frames of an instrumental nature can be disrupted when a level-two analysis intrudes, and this is especially so when a level-three analysis marshaling the full resources of Christian tradition are brought to bear.

At this point, one could be forgiven for concluding that it is difficult if not impossible to practice a life of discipleship while pursuing a career in management. Indeed, certain teachings in the New Testament pertaining to competing priorities seem unambiguous. Jesus tells his disciples that "every one of you who does not renounce all his possessions cannot be my disciple" (Luke 14:33). As we have seen, a career can be considered a very valuable kind of possession, indeed, one that can contribute significantly to the personal experience of meaning. Elsewhere, however,

Jesus seems—on the surface at least—to sanction the kind of bifurcated existence that so concerned Alasdair MacIntyre: "Repay to Caesar what belongs to Caesar and to God what belongs to God" (Mark 12:17). And elsewhere, Jesus interacts in positive ways with those who clearly hold responsible positions in the world. This includes Nicodemus, a Pharisee and a prominent member of the Sanhedrin with whom Jesus met alone at night (John 3:21), and the centurion whose servant Jesus cured from a distance (Matt 8:5–13). These incongruent stories point to the need for a canonical reading of Scripture, of course, a reading that employs the whole of Scripture as a lens through which to read any particular pericope; but it points, as well, to the complexity of the question that lies before us: Can aspiring disciples of Jesus serve in management positions in the secular world and still remain faithful?

Further, the situation in the earliest days of the church sheds little light on this pressing question. For instance, whether or not Christians could partake of meat sacrificed to pagan gods seems to have been a matter of some concern as Christianity moved into the gentile world (1 Cor 8:1–13). This represented more than a matter of meat; for the people of Corinth, it had more to do with the extent to which they could or could not participate in the social and civic life of the community. Further, although the record is somewhat confused in this regard, it seems that service in the Roman army may have been closed at times to Christians. This likely had more to do with the obligation to sacrifice to the gods associated with particular military units than religious discrimination *per se* or—from the Christian perspective—a commitment to pacifism.[15] Nevertheless, the Roman army was one of the most prominent institutions in the ancient world. A bar to enlistment would have limited opportunities for social advancement in a world otherwise defined by its rigid class structure. Still further, it seems that leadership positions emerged quickly in the church, most notably bishops, presbyters, and deacons. According to the biblical record, charismatic leaders gave way to institutional authority in the first or second generation of Christians. These various developments leave a mixed picture with respect to the church's view of leadership.

The age of martyrdom ended in 313 with the Edict of Milan and the legalization of Christianity throughout the Roman Empire. This precipitated, in turn, a remarkable development. An increasing number of men

---

15. Hall, *Living Wisely*, 98–99.

and women determined that they had been called to abandon the world altogether. This movement began with eremitic monastics who followed the example of St. Anthony (250–355) in retreating to the Egyptian desert in order to live in complete isolation. Later a communitarian form of monasticism emerged in which men and women separated themselves from the world in order to live under a shared "rule," most notably the Rule of St. Basil (330–79) in the East and the Rule of St. Benedict (480–543) in the West. Over time, this created a kind of two-tiered Christianity in which those who abandoned the world were viewed as true disciples and those who remained in the world were thought of as lesser disciples or in some sense less holy.

During the Reformation of the sixteenth century, both the Lutheran tradition and the Reformed tradition rejected this bifurcated understanding of discipleship in no uncertain terms. "Monkish" lifestyles were rejected altogether, and monasteries and convents were disbanded. Martin Luther (1483–1546), Huldrych Zwingli (1484–1531), and John Calvin (1509–64) argued that holiness can be exhibited in married life and in the commercial life of the marketplace, too.

All of this has left something of a mixed picture in our own day. Although widely criticized, the five models of church and their respective stances vis-à-vis the world first articulated by H. Richard Niebuhr (1894–1962) in *Christ & Culture* (1951) remains the starting point for these kinds of analyses. Niebuhr began with what he referred to as the "Christ against culture" paradigm. This view postulates a strict division between the church and the world. Indeed, the world is viewed as fallen and hence unredeemable. "Kingdom values" are understood to be incompatible with the world's values. In the "Christ against culture" paradigm, the church is understood to be countercultural. Although it is all too easy to associate this view with the Amish, the Mennonites, and certain religious cults, this perspective can be found to one degree or another in many of today's Christian denominations.

Niebuhr's second paradigm, "Christ of culture," is positioned at the opposite extreme. According to Niebuhr, Christians committed to this view are perfectly at home in the world as it is. They do not perceive any great tension between the church and the world. Nineteenth-century liberal Protestantism is often cited as a case in point. Christianity and Victorian culture, in particular, were widely viewed as complementary and hence mutually reinforcing. In today's America, the "Christ of culture" paradigm is reflected in the theologies of certain evangelical churches that celebrate the American way of life and view the United States's role in the world as uniquely blessed by God. This perspective is decanted, at times, as a kind of "American exceptionalism." As a result, the prophetic voice tends to be muted in the "Christ of culture" paradigm.

Niebuhr associated the third paradigm, "Christ above culture," with Catholicism, in particular the late medieval Catholicism of the scholastics. According to Niebuhr, Christians who embrace the "Christ above culture" perspective understand human existence as taking place on two distinct levels. The first is the cultural level, i.e., work, education, political life, the arts, etc., or, for our purposes, the life of the world. These dimensions of life are not viewed as fallen as such. In fact, culture can serve as fertile ground for pursuing God's work in the world and can thus be deemed good. The second level is entirely spiritual in nature. In this view, believers are challenged to celebrate both the world and their faith in God.

Niebuhr associated the fourth paradigm, "Christ and culture in paradox," with Martin Luther and the German Reformation. Like the "Christ above culture" paradigm, it posits two levels of existence. In Lutheran theology, this is referred to as the "two kingdoms" doctrine. This paradigm differs from the "Christ above culture" paradigm to the extent that it understands the world as sinful or fallen. In this view, we must live in the world and honor both God and Caesar, but we should never forget for a moment that the world is profoundly corrupted by sin. A believer who holds this view would never confuse patriotism with discipleship. She would never wrap herself in the American flag or in any other flag for that matter. The criticism of this paradigm is that it can be too accepting of the world's power structures. Since they are understood to be essentially and irredeemably corrupt, Christians should invest little time or effort in improving them. The prophetic voice can be somewhat muted in this perspective as well.

The last paradigm, "Christ the transformer of culture," was championed by Niebuhr, who associated it with Protestantism's Reformed tradition. In this view, the church and culture do not stand side by side, as they do somewhat comfortably in the "Christ above culture" paradigm, or as they do somewhat uncomfortably in the "Christ and culture in paradox" scenario. In this paradigm, Christ is hailed as superior to all secular powers and authorities. The world is redeemable, but only so to the extent that it subordinates itself to Christ. Individual Christians see in Christ the ideals and values they need to function as disciples in a fallen world. Some associate this fifth model of church with contemporary Catholicism, too. In making this claim, they point to the church's rich social teaching tradition and the work of the Second Vatican Council.

As the foregoing analysis suggests, the extent to which Christians should or should not involve themselves in the world, including, presumably, the management of secular organizations, remains something of an open question. This is evident, too, in our understanding of "vocation." Indeed, two very different understandings of "vocation" exist side-by-side in today's Catholic Church. The privileged view was embraced during the Second Vatican Council. From this perspective, the idea of *vocare*, i.e., to call or to summon, pertains explicitly to the "universal call to holiness," a foundational belief espoused in such seminal church documents as *Lumen Gentium*,[16] which was promulgated by Pope Paul VI at the close of the Second Vatican Council; Pope John Paul II's apostolic exhortation *Christifideles Laici*[17]; the Catechism of the Catholic Church[18]; and, more recently, Pope Francis's apostolic exhortation *Gaudete et Exsultate*.[19] In this understanding of vocation, work in the world, including managerial work, can be embraced as part and parcel of one's vocation and hence as integral to discipleship.

At the same time, an older, more circumscribed understanding of "vocation" persists in the church. In this more narrow conception, a vocation is understood as a calling to ordained or consecrated life. By analogy, marriage and the single state can also be viewed as vocations. Although this older view was substantially eclipsed in the years following the Second Vatican Council, vestiges pertaining to the priesthood, to married life, and to the single life can still be found in the Catechism of the Catholic Church and in the Code of Canon Law.

As Laurence J. O'Connell has noted, this older understanding of vocation—although not wrong *per se*—"was narrow and exclusive when contrasted with the fuller meaning of call as set down in Scripture and tradition."[20] Significantly, this older view orients marriage almost exclusively to the shared life of the couple and their children, i.e., the domestic church. As affirmed in Canon Law, "the matrimonial covenant . . . is by its

16. Second Vatican Council, "*Lumen Gentium*," 32.

17. Pope John Paul II, *Christifideles Laici*, 16.

18. *Catechism* 2013.

19. Pope Francis, *Gaudete et Exsultate*.

20. O'Connell, "Vocation," 1010.

nature ordered toward the good of the spouses and the procreation and education of offspring."[21] The Catechism of the Catholic Church affirms this orientation as well.[22] A vocational life outside of the immediate confines of one's marriage, including, presumably, managerial work, is not forbidden or discouraged in these citations, but it is certainly not featured or celebrated as a path to holiness in any meaningful sense.

As this somewhat lengthy excursus suggests, the Christian tradition has underwritten a variety of views with respect to work in the world. Nevertheless, the ascendant view in Roman Catholicism, at least, is grounded on the universal call to holiness and is hence reflective of the "Christ the transformer of culture" paradigm articulated by Niebuhr. In this view, Christians are obligated to participate in the life of the world, but they are encouraged to do so assuming a stance that is both critical and appreciative. A critical or prophetic sensibility is thus essential as Christians engage in the life of the world, and this certainly includes their work as managers in contemporary institutions of all kinds.

One question remains: Is it even possible for aspiring disciples of Jesus to marshal a stance in their work that is both critical and prophetic? This cannot be assumed. In philosophical discourse, the scholars of the Frankfort School and Herbert Marcuse (1898–1979), in particular, decried the channeling of individual thought into unyielding pathways carved out by an overbearing social order that includes today's private, public, or nonprofit organizations. According to Marcuse, thinking has been "totalized" in "mimetic" directions.[23] A similar critique has been advanced by an entire generation of postmodern scholars as well.

We need not go quite this far, however. In chapter 4, we will demonstrate the extent to which moral perspectives can be eclipsed at times. Despite this, there is considerable evidence that moral thinking and moral behavior are still possible. Again, a kind of gestalt experience is required. Managers must be provided with "eyes to see and ears to hear," and so be awakened, first, to the interests of persons, i.e., a level-two analysis, and, second, to the demands of Christian discipleship, i.e., a level-three analysis.

Alasdair MacIntyre shared an example of this kind of gestalt experience. "'What is he doing?'" he asked. "'Writing a sentence'; 'Finishing his

21. *Code of Canon Law*, 1055.

22. *Catechism* 1601.

23. Marcuse, *One-Dimensional Man*, 10.

book'; 'Contributing to the debate on the theory of action'; 'Trying to get tenure.'"[24] This progression of ever-deeper meanings is illustrated, too, in the familiar story of the four bricklayers, each of whom was asked what he was doing. The first said that he was laying bricks. The second responded that he was building a wall. The third bricklayer looked around at the construction site and observed that he was building a cathedral. With pride, the fourth bricklayer proclaimed that he was helping to erect the community's collective prayer to God. The first two responses constitute instrumental views of the bricklayers's work. The latter two more clearly illustrate the bricklayers's personal experience of meaning and the craftsman's unique standing in his community.

Conventional research methods can be of limited value in assessing the capacity of today's mangers to foreground a concern for persons and for larger societal, spiritual, or religious purposes. A study I directed in 2000 suggests, however, that these kinds of deeper reflections can be prompted using something other than a quantitative research method that makes use of survey instruments.[25] I conducted four one-hour interviews with five individuals who then served in high-ranking positions in the regional offices of five different federal agencies. A unique qualitative research method was employed: the life story method, in which an interviewee's life is unfolded as a kind of story in a succession of in-depth interviews. The interviewee in this kind of encounter is invited to construct and then claim a certain reality in the narrative of her life.

Somewhat surprisingly, two of the five public administrators who participated in the project affirmed a deep connection between their religious beliefs and their respective conceptions of their professional lives. The research project was not designed to elicit religious or spiritual worldviews *per se*. In fact, two of the other five participants espoused perspectives that can better be described as communitarian or democratic in nature, and the fifth's worldview clearly reflected a stoic perspective.

Most importantly for our purposes, all five of the participants demonstrated a capacity to frame their professional work in contexts that extended far beyond the instrumental goals of the agencies they served. Lengthy quotes from two participants in the study are presented here because they speak to the extent to which high ranking managers and administrators can, in fact, view their secular work in spiritual terms. By

24. MacIntyre, *After Virtue*, 207.
25. Lowery, "Self-Reflexivity."

the third of our four interviews, the chief judge of the Chicago Regional Office of the Federal Merit Systems Protection Board was able to locate his understanding of his work in his Lutheran faith.

> I don't know if this is the old two kingdoms theology of my Lutheran heritage coming out, but the idea of being subject to no one and the freest person of all by virtue of our relationship to our Creator, and then, at the same time, being the most dutiful servant of all, as Luther put it. I think this is a beginning point for discussing what we're called to do in our employment lives and in life in general. That passage from Micah that you should "do justly, and love mercy, and walk humbly with your God" is a starting point. And that's what all of us are called upon to do, not just judges. Everybody should treat each other with justice and courtesy and a level of mercy that maybe we don't think about so often.
>
> I think of vocation all the time. And I think that I can find a sense of calling to every job that I've had. [This sense of vocation] is so central as to be essential. It is simply the way that I understand this employment part of my life . . . Employment is tremendously important. Doing something useful and something that you can believe in is a great privilege. Not everybody has that opportunity in life. And the fact that I've been given that opportunity and have something that I enjoy and can find meaningful to do [makes me feel] very fortunate. So, vocation, yes . . . I suppose if I were driving a cab or still a policeman or something like that, that I would see that as a vocation as well. I'd have to feel some sense of calling to do any job or at least understand my relationship to that employment in order for me to be motivated to get up in the morning . . . To try to segregate religious and theological concepts from the work that I'm called to do, the vocation that I sense in my civil service, would so detract from the richness of the experience, the work experience, that it would make it less meaningful for me to be employed.

Similarly, the commissioner of the Social Security Administration's five-state Chicago Region drew on what he described as his "very traditional" Catholic faith.

> I recognized early on in my career that I brought a very strong value system to most situations. To the extent that I could articulate this value system, I was a valuable person to have around. I do feel a need to challenge and question things that appear not to be mission-related. I feel a need to integrate things into some

overall picture that makes sense. And I think that these qualities were ones that have been valued by my bosses.

It is important [to me] to try to integrate things, to have context, and to have underpinnings to behavior that reflect meaning. And so, I found myself using my position as a subordinate—carefully—to describe meaning, to describe value, or to place context around behavior suggesting that it needs to be motivated by higher ideals . . .

I am not comfortable with the notion of compartments [in describing a life well-lived] . . . Clearly those compartments can cause tensions. But when I'm centered and at my best, they're seamless. I have a much better connection to the flow of life through all of [its various] facets.

Having a relationship with God is extremely fundamental to me, very core. The Catholic Church is my church and I'm in it for the long haul. Yes, there's a lot about Catholicism that I take umbrage with. There're some things about my kids that I haven't always loved, too. But they're mine and I love [them] . . . I am very concerned with spirituality. For me, things have to have a deeper meaning. And so I work actively at that.

My basic sense is that all of life is interconnected. I operate under the sense that there is a plan and that [it's my job] to find and fit into that plan in the right way . . . It goes back to the traditional notion of vocation in a way.

I've never been one of those who could say, "I'm going to be a doctor. I'm going to be a neurosurgeon." I always have to go through a kind of discernment process. For me, this involves listening . . . My spiritual director tells me to "listen for the nudge . . . " Trying to faithfully listen for the nudge, trying to follow the nudge when it comes, and then finding myself in positions that are by and large so enjoyable and so fulfilling makes me feel lucky. It's like, "Wow, how the hell did all this happen to me? This is great!" But the big difference between that and notions that I read about in the literature have to do with being receptive rather than somehow mapping out and pursuing certain goals and achievements. There are life forces [involved]. [In this sense], the management literature just doesn't tell me the truth, at least my truth . . . The older I get, the more my view is that it's all pure gift. [It's my responsibility] to be true to understanding the gift, to using the gifts . . .

Contra Marcuse and many of today's postmodernists, we can conclude from these excerpts that at least some of today's managers are open to the larger purposes that work can play in their lives and that these larger purposes can be religious or spiritual in nature. Given this, moral reflection and moral behavior may be more widespread—or, at least, more possible—in contemporary organizations than we sometimes imagine. Further, as Niebuhr's "Christ the transformer of culture" paradigm suggests, it may be required of aspiring disciples of Jesus who choose to serve in all kinds of managerial and leadership positions.

In the following pages, we will explore the roots of the discomfort so many managers and nominal leaders experience on the job. We will do so under the assumption that those who exercise authority in all kinds of organizations and in the public square, too, are fully capable of moral reflection.

Further, we will abandon the widely-held belief that this kind of dissonance is something to be ignored or medicated or counseled into silence. As will be noted in chapter 3, this kind of discomfort can be part and parcel of a self-reflective individual's search for meaning. Indeed, concerns of this kind tend to be ontological in nature; they do not—in and of themselves—indicate professional failure or the onset of a psychological malady. Angst is not an illness to be overcome. On the contrary, it is an ontological condition that many reflective people share. Indeed, Carl Jung (1875–1961) observed that many of his patients did not suffer from any kind of neuroses or mental illness, but rather from the perceived senselessness and meaninglessness of their lives.[26] Paul Tillich agreed, noting that the experience of anxiety is normal; it is a recognition of our ontological predicament; it is "universal and inescapable."[27] Tillich attributed anxiety to the "possibility of non-being"[28] and the anticipation of death.[29] Jung maintained that the loss of the ideals and the values of "the morning," which often accompanies the aging process, creates this existential anxiety.[30] Together, the universal horizons of life, change, death, and the sense of rootlessness that attends to the human condition engender an understanding of life as a project in which the desired end is the experience of meaning or authentic living. When the pursuit or achievement of this end is frustrated, discomfort, dissonance, and conflict can follow.

26. Jung, *Modern Man*, 61, 103.

27. Tillich, *The Courage to Be*, 41, 70.

28. Tillich, *The Courage to Be*, 35.

29. Tillich, *The Courage to Be*, 142.

30. Jung, *Modern Man*, 106.

Still further, we will examine these kinds of experiences as spiritual phenomena. Indeed, a turn to the spiritual will provide a singular focus in part II of our text. This follows a sense among so many today that our allegiances as Christians must be first to God and then to the integrated expression of our faith in all aspects of our lives, including our professional lives and our lives as citizens, too. We will thus follow Augustine (354–430), a great doctor of the Western church, in this regard. In a prayerful reflection that opens *The Confessions*, his autobiographical masterpiece, Augustine prays: "You have made us and drawn us to yourself, and our heart is unquiet until it rests in you."[31] This does not mean that the wisdom of the world has no value. As we shall see, it clearly does. As committed Christians, however, we believe that a greater wisdom is at work in our lives. Paul put this well in his First Letter to the Corinthians:

> We do speak a wisdom to those who are mature, but not a wisdom of this age, nor of the rulers of this age who are passing away. Rather, we speak God's wisdom, mysterious, hidden, which God predetermined before the ages for our glory, and which none of the rulers of this age knew; for if they had known it, they would not have crucified the Lord of glory. But as it is written: "What eye has not seen, and ear has not heard, and what has not entered the human heart, what God has prepared for those who love him," this God has revealed to us through the Spirit. For the Spirit scrutinizes everything, even the depths of God.
>
> Among human beings, who knows what pertains to a person except the spirit of the person that is within? Similarly, no one knows what pertains to God except the Spirit of God. We have not received the spirit of the world but the Spirit that is from God, so that we may understand the things freely given us by God. And we speak about them not with words taught by human wisdom, but with words taught by the Spirit, describing spiritual realities in spiritual terms. Now the natural person does not accept what pertains to the Spirit of God, for to him it is foolishness, and he cannot understand it, because it is judged spiritually. The spiritual person, however, can judge everything but is not subject to judgment by anyone. For "who has known the mind of the Lord, so as to counsel him?" But we have the mind of Christ (1 Cor 2:6–16).

31. Augustine, *The Confessions*, 3.

PART I

The Wisdom of the World

THE URGENCY OF ALASDAIR MacIntyre's critique and his conception of virtue were affirmed in chapter 1. In truth, this text is an *homage* of sorts to MacIntyre and Robert Greenleaf (1894–1990), the acknowledged father of the servant-leader model. Greenleaf advanced a radical conception of leadership, but fell short in revealing its moral roots. MacIntyre's understanding of virtue fills this need and can thus be viewed as a powerful complement to Greenleaf's work.

Our thesis—as it pertains to the management literature—is advanced in part I of this text. It is presented in the form of four arguments: one, the management theories and models available to us are useful, but deficient, nonetheless, in at least two respects; two, the servant-leader model proposed by Robert Greenleaf addresses these twin concerns, but its claims in this regard are poorly rooted and hence weak; three, these challenges point to the need for virtue and externally anchored values and intellectual commitments as a foundation for true leadership in all kinds of organizations; and four, analogues to the management theories and models now available to us pertain more broadly to the public square, but these analogues are deficient as well. These four arguments will be addressed, in turn, in chapters 2 through 5.

This is the portion of the text in which several incongruous and sometimes competing streams of thought pertaining to management and to leadership more broadly will be brought into conversation with each other. This includes several academic disciplines *vis-à-vis* each other and the collective wisdom of the academy *vis-à-vis* the wisdom of knowledgeable practitioners. In part II, the wisdom of the world will be brought into conversation with the wisdom of the Christian tradition.

A sharp distinction is drawn in this portion of the text between "management" and "leadership." Whereas management can be understood as the responsibility for and performance of any one or more of several organizational or societal functions, e.g., planning, organizing, staffing, directing, coordinating, reporting, and budgeting, in a manner oriented to ends external to the manager, leadership can be defined as the balanced exercise of these same responsibilities in service to a broader array of stakeholders in a manner constrained by the leader's internalized virtues and informed by values and intellectual commitments drawn from a larger belief system, but oriented, nonetheless, to ends sanctioned by the organization or by society. Leadership can thus be distinguished from management in four ways: first, leadership is oriented to service; second, it involves an array of stakeholders; third, its exercise is constrained by virtues internal to the leader; and fourth, its exercise is informed by values and intellectual commitments drawn from a larger belief system.

Some might argue that the distinction drawn here between management and leadership is an arbitrary one. To a considerable extent, the extant literature on these twin topics tends to merge the two concepts. As we shall see, however, leadership reconceived along the lines proposed here—leadership oriented first and foremost to service and leadership that is fully anchored in a Christian conception of virtue and in Christian values and intellectual commitments—can make all the difference for the leader, for the organization she serves, and for the broader community, too.

Chapter 2

Management Theory and Models

THE FIRST OF FOUR arguments to be presented in part I is unfolded here. As we shall see, the management theories and models available to us are useful, but deficient, nonetheless, in at least two respects.

Even the preliminary task of cataloguing the wide-ranging literature pertaining to management can be daunting. This is so for a number of reasons. First, the extant literature is located in very different fields of study. There is less overlap between the academic disciplines of business management on the one hand and public administration on the other than one might expect; and the literature pertaining to church identity, structure, and management, i.e., ecclesiology, is something entirely distinct as well. Second, much of the management literature has been developed by practitioners. The kind of literature reviews characteristic of academic work are rare in the contributions of practitioners. Indeed, there is little effort to connect new theories and new models to the theories and models that preceded them. Research agendas in the academy tend to build on each other. Academic work is cumulative in nature. In contrast, theories and models developed by practitioners tend to strike out more boldly into new territory, and they are typically tethered to personal and institutional intuitions rather than to rigorous research *pe se*. Further, the work of practitioners is rarely subjected to peer review, the gold standard for work in the academy.

As a result, management theories and models are typically presented as self-contained packages. The scientific management theories of Frederick Winslow Taylor, for instance, were presented as all that might be needed by any modern organization. W. Edwards Deming was famously dismissive of any chief executive officer who dared question his near-exclusive reliance on control charts. And Milton Friedman publicly disdained his rivals. Taking some acclaimed theorists at face value, one could easily conclude that any theory or model proposed by anyone else would not be worth the time and effort needed even to peruse it. Indeed, some management theories and models are entirely incommensurate. They reflect very different understandings of the human person and very different understandings of organizations and roles within organizations, too. They employ different control mechanisms and make use of very different methods and technologies as well.

To illustrate this point, imagine a diverse group of consultants called together to tackle a particular problem: a practitioner of scientific management, an administrative management theorist, a human relations scholar, a behaviorist, an operations research specialist, a financial management analyst, a statistician, and a business process engineer. The outcome would likely resemble the experience of the blind men in India who encountered an elephant for the first time. According to the ancient parable, each of the blind men touched a different part of the elephant's body and then described it, in turn, as a snake, a fan, a tree trunk, a wall, a rope, and a spear. Even though our several management consultants might speak the same language, they practice very different "language games," a term coined by Ludwig Wittgenstein. Language games go beyond the words and sentence structures employed in a communication. They include, as well, contexts, underlying values, formal and informal rules of interaction, indeed, entire constellations of meaning. In a very real sense, the different language games undergirding the management theories and models employed in all kinds of organizations over the course of the last century have produced something more akin to the Tower of Babel than a General Assembly meeting at the United Nations in which concurrent translation services are provided for all.

It is useful, nonetheless, for practitioners to acquire some sense of these various language games. Together, they can contribute to the development of a broader range of options for analyzing management challenges and provide a more complete toolbox for addressing these challenges. An expression attributed variously to Abraham Maslow, Bernard Baruch, and others is instructive in this regard: "If all you have is a hammer, everything looks like a nail."

Third, we sometimes forget that the management of large organizations is still a relatively new phenomenon. With three notable exceptions, i.e., the Roman Catholic Church, higher education, and the military, each of which embodies centuries of design, culture, control mechanisms, and disciplinary practice, organizations prior to the industrial revolution tended to be small. In the United States, everything changed after the Civil War. Large steel mills employing thousands of workers quickly replaced small, family-owned foundries. Nothing remotely like General Motors, Standard Oil, or Bell Telephone existed in the United States prior to the latter third of the nineteenth century.

As the world grew more complex, the public sector also evolved. The responsibilities of government expanded rapidly during the Progressive Era, a remarkable moment in time extending from the 1890s to the 1920s, and again during the New Deal of the 1930s. The responsible exercise of a broad array of new public duties put a premium on rationality and competence. As a result, political influence and patronage, long the *sine qua non* for employment in the public sector, fell into disrepute.

In a very real sense, the immediate needs of large organizations preceded management theory. This is why, in part, so much of today's management literature is attributable to practitioners rather than to scholars. Practitioners scrambled through much of the twentieth century to promote efficiency, hoping, thereby, to secure competitive advantage for their firms in the private sector and the ideal of "good government" in the public sector. Given this, we should not be too dismissive of certain older theories and models. From today's perspective, they may seem simple or even naive. They represent, nonetheless, very real attempts to deal with very real challenges that very real organizations—both private and public—faced in their own time and place.

The most influential language games extant in the management literature of the last century are assessed in the following pages: scientific management, administrative management theory, the human relations movement, behavioralism, the functional study of the chief executive and the unity of focus, management science, the maximization of shareholder wealth perspective, and the quality movement. These eight management theories and models differ dramatically and so can seem incommensurate; and they do, in fact, reflect very different perspectives. Moreover, these theories and models do not constitute the full universe of management thought and practice. Other theories and models—behaviorism or operant modeling and professional acculturation studies, for instance—could have been included, but the eight addressed here can, nonetheless, be thought of as the main tributaries in what remains a very wide river system. Each of these eight theories and models will be described in terms of its focus or "unit of analysis," its primary goals and objectives, its signature methods and techniques, and its strengths or enduring value. Key criticisms lodged against each of them will also be noted.

Each of these several language games will be examined both appreciatively and critically with respect to our first argument. As we shall see, considerable "wisdom" can be found in all but one of them. As we shall also see, no one theory or model or collection of theories and models is sufficient—in and of itself—to address the moral challenges so many managers and nominal leaders face in striving to be effective in the exercise of their organizational responsibilities, faithful to their religious commitments, and spiritually accountable in their work lives.

SCIENTIFIC MANAGEMENT

Modern management theory began in the United States with Frederick Winslow Taylor (1856–1915), a mechanical engineer who labored, first as a clerk and then as a foreman in the rapidly evolving steel industry of the 1880s and 1890s. Taylor's understanding of management was detailed in a 1911 monogram, *The Principles of Scientific Management*. This title notwithstanding, "scientific management," or Taylorism, can better be described as a kind of applied engineering than a science *per se*.

Taylor focused almost exclusively on narrowly-defined job tasks performed in manufacturing settings. In Taylor's view, the chief problem facing the emerging industries of his day was "systematic soldiering" or malingering, the ongoing effort of workers to labor deliberately in order to protect their individual and group interests.

To address this challenge, Taylor recommended the use of time-and-motion studies to determine the "one best way" to accomplish any given task, the simplification and deskilling of jobs in order to minimize the use of unreliable "rules of thumb" or heuristics in the performance of any given task, the development of standard operating procedures, the adoption of incentive pay based on the productivity of the "best man" assigned to any given job, and close supervision to ensure no slacking in effort over the course of the workday.

The principles of scientific management were adopted in the early decades of the twentieth century by a number of large companies in the manufacturing and transportation industries. (The development of

Ford's iconic assembly line in the early decades of the twentieth century has been attributed to Taylor as well, even though the extent of his influence in this regard is less than certain.) The principles of scientific management would also prove of great interest to progressives who sought to modernize government in the first several decades of the twentieth century.

Scientific management's legacy persists to this day. Indeed, a number of techniques associated with Taylorism are still in use, including job analysis, time-and-motion studies, and workplace design or ergonomics. Scientific management is widely viewed, too, as the seedbed for a host of other managerial theories and models, all of which can be grouped under the conceptual umbrella of the "efficiency movement." This includes operations management, operations research, industrial engineering, and, more recently, process control, process reengineering, Six Sigma, and lean manufacturing.

From our vantage point in the twenty-first century, it is all too easy to criticize Taylor and scientific management. First, his focus was narrow: the task at hand. Taylor showed little interest in the overall structure of the modern industrial firm or the broader array of responsibilities now associated with management. Second, scientific management sees workers as little more than fungible inputs. In Taylor's view, workers are motivated exclusively by their economic interests and should be understood as such. Third, Taylor believed the goal of management to be the profitability of the firm. He showed little interest in society as a whole. Nevertheless, Taylor was convinced that consumers would benefit over time from the lower cost of manufactured goods that would follow from the widespread adoption of his management principles.

From a moral perspective, the principal defect in scientific management lies in the fact that it is a closed system. When workers are viewed as fungible inputs, human dignity is eliminated as a concern. The personal wellbeing of the worker and the supervisor, too, are of little interest. Further, the intrinsic meaning of work is irrelevant in this understanding of management. Still further, social concerns are of little consequence when the enhancement of the firm's profitability is accepted as the sole criterion of success. Indeed, there is little room in scientific management for the celebration of human dignity or the pursuit of the common good, nor is there any need for the development or exercise of personal virtue.

ADMINISTRATIVE MANAGEMENT THEORY

Administrative management theory developed contemporaneously with scientific management theory. Because these two approaches to management are viewed as complementary, they are sometimes described as parallel manifestations of "classical management theory." Whereas scientific management pertains exclusively on the rational design of job tasks, administrative management theory focuses on the rational articulation and performance of a more comprehensive array of managerial functions. There is a marked correspondence, in fact, between administrative management theory and the several attributes of the bureaucratic form previously detailed in Max Weber's seminal work: a division of labor based on functional specialization, a well-defined hierarchy, a system of rules covering the employment relationship, a system of procedures pertaining to the work to be performed, neutrality in interpersonal relations, and the selection and promotion of employees based on their technical competence.[1]

Henri Fayol (1841–1925) is often identified as the father of administrative management theory. Following a career as a mining engineer, manager, and chief executive officer, Fayol published *Administration Industrielle et Générale* in 1916.[2] In this influential text, Fayol posited five "irreducible" managerial functions, i.e., planning, organizing, commanding, coordinating, and controlling, and fourteen principles: the division or specialization of work; the clear delegation of authority and responsibility; discipline; sufficient unity of command to ensure that each employee reports exclusively to one supervisor; unity of direction or the grouping of related work units under a single manager so that their efforts can be coordinated; the subordination of individual interests to the general interest of the organization; fair remuneration; an appropriate balance between the centralization and decentralization of decision-making; a "scalar chain" that helps employees understand where they are located in the organization's hierarchy; order, i.e., a clean, tidy, and safe workplace; equity or fair treatment; job security so that turnover can be minimized; sufficient freedom of action so that innovation can be pursued; and the development and maintenance of a certain *esprit de corps* among those who work for the firm.

1. Weber, "Bureaucracy."
2. Fayol, *General and Industrial Management.*

Administration Industrielle et Générale would not be published in English until 1946, but Fayol's theories had come to the attention of Columbia University professor Luther Gullick and others in the 1930s. In his "Notes on the Theory of Organization," which Gullick drafted while serving on the President's Committee on Administrative Management or "Brownlow Committee" (1936–37), Gullick drew explicitly on Fayol's work in coining the acronym POSDCORB to delineate the work of the chief executive officer and, by extension, the managers and supervisors who serve under her: planning by purpose, process, clientele, material, or place; organizing; staffing; directing; coordinating by structure or by a common idea or mission; reporting; and budgeting.

Scientific management and administrative management theory both promote rational control: the rational control of job tasks in the case of scientific management and the rational control of the organization in the case of administrative management theory. According to both, the primary goal or objective is a "singleness" of purpose and effort oriented in a direction established by the organization.

To accomplish this singleness of purpose and effort, Gullick recommended the rational division of work, the co-ordination of work either by departmental structure or the "dominance of an idea" reflecting the organization's "singleness of purpose," and a bureaucratic organizational design reflecting the principle of "homogeneity" or like purposes. Whereas incentive pay figures prominently in the case of scientific management, the achievement of a singleness of purpose and effort is achieved in administrative management theory through policy, clear lines of authority, and the promise of career advancement.

Administrative management theory has had a profound impact on the way work is organized and managed in the private sector, in government, and in the nonprofit and civic sectors as well. Following the Second Vatican Council, many of the chanceries in the Roman Catholic Church in the United States also adopted the managerial principles embedded in the POSDCORB acronym. Despite predictions of its imminent demise, the bureaucratic model is alive and well, in fact. It speaks—even today— to the perennial need for order.

Like scientific management, administrative management theory is not without its critics. Most importantly, administrative management theory tends to view organizations statically. Contemporary organizational theories prefer biological metaphors or even chaos theory to the mechanical and architectural metaphors used by administrative management theorists to describe organizations. Further, administrative management theory shows virtually no interest in informal networks of socialization or unsanctioned organizational behavior. Still further, administrative management theory tends to view workers instrumentally. On the surface, it may seem more humane than scientific management. For instance, Fayol emphasized the need for "fairness," "equity," and "*esprit de corps*." Administrative management theory is, nonetheless, every bit as concerned about controlling work and workers for the sake of organizational purposes as scientific management.

Herbert Kaufman's *Forest Ranger* (1960) is a case in point. In minute detail, Kaufman describes the many ways in which the US Forest Service channels and controls virtually every decision made down to the lowest levels of the organization. Interestingly, however, the portrayal of the forest ranger himself is one-dimensional. He comes across as a remarkably bland character, a cipher with no apparent frustrations, aspirations, or dreams. The forest ranger's interest in his family is muted. His involvement in the community is touched on only in passing. For all intents and purposes, he is interchangeable with every other forest ranger.

Dwight Waldo (1913–2000) went further, however. Indeed, his critique was a moral one. In his seminal text, *The Administrative State* (1948), Waldo decried the values undergirding the bureaucratic ideal as "individualist, utilitarian, [and] instrumentalist."[3] According to Waldo, these values are oriented entirely to the end of efficiency. Although his critique is noteworthy, the range of moral foundations Waldo proffered as alternatives was quite limited and entirely secular in nature. "Because of their widespread acceptance by the national community and their obvious influence upon writings in public administration," he examined only five such foundations: "the democratic idea and related ideas such as the 'mission of America,' the belief in 'fundamental law,' the doctrine of progress and 'progressivism,' the gospel of efficiency, and faith in science."[4]

THE HUMAN RELATIONS MOVEMENT

The human relations movement cannot be viewed as a comprehensive theory or model of management as such. In fact, only two of the seven management functions encapsulated in the POSDCORB acronym are

3. Waldo, *The Administrative State*, 71.
4. Waldo, *The Administrative State*, 15.

addressed directly by scholars associated with this perspective: staffing and directing. This approach to human motivation in the workplace is better thought of as a corrective to scientific management and administrative management theory and their manifest failure to fully account for workplace behavior. As explained by Elton Mayo, the "logic of sentiment" is as powerful—if not more so—than the logic of "cost and efficiency" that underlies both scientific management and administrative management theory.

Two foci are typical of work produced by scholars associated with this movement: worker motivation and the interpersonal relations of workers and their supervisors. As we shall see, these twin foci extend well beyond the economic and policy "controls" endorsed by Frederick Winslow Taylor, Henri Fayol, and Luther Gullick.

No single set of management methods and techniques are associated with the human relations movement. Nevertheless, three broad strategies can be discerned: efforts to satisfy the needs of individual workers, needs that go well beyond their economic needs; the promotion of positive patterns of interaction between workers and their supervisors; and the appropriate matching of a supervisor's "management style" to both the economic or policy ends of the organization on the one hand and the psychological and social needs of their subordinates on the other.

The human relations movement is closely associated with Elton Mayo (1880–1949), a Harvard-based psychologist, and the Hawthorne studies described in his groundbreaking text, *The Social Problems of an Industrial Civilization* (1945). Mayo and Fritz Roethlisberger, Mayo's graduate student and lead investigator, were engaged by Western Electric to develop strategies to reduce worker turnover in the relay assembly plant at its Hawthorne Works in Cicero, Illinois. After first establishing both an experimental group and a control group, Roethlisberger and his team adjusted lighting in order to determine its effect on productivity. Surprisingly, productivity went up in both groups. They then manipulated other working conditions, including the length of the workers's rest periods. Again, productivity went up in both groups. Finally, Roethlisberger restored all of the working conditions that had been manipulated to their original conditions. Again, productivity went up!

Mayo determined that neither pay nor working conditions could account for the changes in productivity observed by his team. He concluded, instead, that workers in both the experimental group and the control group had developed positive relationships with various members of the research team. Mayo found that these relationships better explained changes in worker productivity than either pay or working conditions. Contra scientific management, the "logic of sentiment" was deemed at least as impactful as the "logic of cost and efficiency"; and contra administrative management theory, the "informal" structure of the workplace was deemed to be at least as important as pay and workplace design.

Mayo's insights would inform a number of developments over time, all of which fall under the rubric of the human relations movement. In 1943, Abraham Maslow (1908–70) crafted a theoretical framework that still undergirds much of this work. He argued that "human needs arrange themselves in hierarchies of prepotency." Needs lower in the hierarchy must be satisfied to a substantial degree before higher-order needs can fully emerge. This hierarchy begins with physiological needs, and then progresses, in turn, to safety needs, social needs, esteem needs, and self-actualization. As Maslow put it: "For the man who is extremely and dangerously hungry no other interests exist but food."[5]

Other important work in the human relations movement would follow. For instance, Frederick Herzberg's two-factor theory differentiates between variables holding a potential to motivate and variables holding only a potential to de-motivate, i.e., hygiene factors. Douglas McGregor distinguished between two types of managers: "theory X" managers, who view workers as unmotivated, irresponsible, and resistant to change; and "theory Y" managers, who view workers as self-motivated, responsible, and capable of self-direction and self-control. Other scholars in the human relations movement have focused on job design and leadership.

In time, this research would contribute to the development of various "contingency theories" of leadership, all of which acknowledge that there is no one right way, as such, to manage workers. Effective leadership depends on context. In this vein, studies conducted at Ohio State University in the 1950s posited two kinds of management behaviors: "consideration" and "initiating structure." Similar studies pursued by researchers at the University of Michigan's Survey Research Center applied different terms to the same concepts: "relation-oriented behavior" and "task-oriented behavior." In 1970, William Redman drew on this research in describing four distinct management styles, each of which can be performed well or poorly depending on the circumstances in which the manager finds herself: supporting, coaching, delegating, and directing.

5. Maslow, "A Theory," 131.

The human relations movement has made two enduring contributions to management theory and practice. First, it has served as a powerful corrective or counterweight to the management theories and models that preceded it. Scientific management and administrative management theory are reductive. Scientific management reduces human needs and human motivations to the economic, and administrative management theory tends to view workers as automatons whose efforts can be controlled by policy and clear lines of authority. Scholars in the human relations school see workers as individuals who harbor complex needs that are both extrinsic, i.e., pay and working conditions, and intrinsic, e.g., psychological wellbeing, socialization, personal achievement, etc., in nature.

Second, the human relations movement did not isolate itself in an ivory tower. Its impact has been felt well beyond the academy. Most importantly, the human relations movement spawned organizational development (OD), a management sub-discipline that links theory and "action research" to organization-specific change initiatives. Associated with Kurt Lewin (1898–1974), the primary tools of OD interventions include job design and job enrichment, team building, coaching, improved communications, and conflict resolution. OD itself would engender research into the ways in which knowledge is obtained and put to use in organizations. Peter Senge's influential text *The Fifth Discipline: The Art and Practice of the Learning Organization* (1990) is highly acclaimed in this genre.

Work in the human relations movement, most notably Elton Mayo's and Frederick Herzberg's contributions, has been criticized, nonetheless, for a certain lack of scientific rigor. Action research, in particular, is discounted by some because it eschews the disinterested stance of the conventional researcher and disavows the use of hypotheses and fully articulated evaluation criteria.

The limited scope of the human relations movement's reach is problematic for others. Scholarship falling under the rubric of the human relations movement shows little interest in larger societal concerns or a true commitment to the satisfaction of deeper human needs. Indeed, this approach to the study of management is criticized for its overriding focus on productivity. Some critics view it as no less instrumental in its view of workers—albeit with a passing nod to a thin veneer of humanist values— than scientific management and administrative management theory.

BEHAVIORALISM

Herbert Simon (1916–2001) was awarded a Nobel Prize in 1978 for his groundbreaking work pertaining to decision-making. An economist, political scientist, and cognitive psychologist, Simon dismissed the management theories and models promoted through the first five decades of the twentieth century as little more than folklore: "It is a principal defect of the current state of administration that, like proverbs, they occur in pairs. For almost every principle one can find an equally plausible and acceptable contradictory principle."[6]

Simon argued for an alternative focus, one that would enable scholars to test well-defined hypotheses. In his paradigm-shattering *Administrative Behavior: A Study in Decision-Making Processes in Administrative Organizations* (1945), Simon promoted managerial decision-making—rather than individual job tasks, organizational design, or informal networks of relationships—as a more appropriate focus for the rigorous development of testable research hypotheses.

With respect to the goals or objectives of organizations, Simon was something of an agnostic. Indeed, he preferred "purpose" to other, more value-laden terms. In Simon's view, once a purpose is established in an organization or with respect to any given initiative, efficiency should be adopted as the primary criterion of evaluation. "What about the issues of fact that underlie decisions? These are largely determined by a principle that is implied in all rational behavior: the criterion of efficiency . . . The criterion of efficiency is completely neutral as to what goals are to be attained. [It] demands that, of two alternatives having the same cost, that one be chosen which will lead to the greater attainment of the organization's objectives; and that, of two alternatives leading to the same degree of attainment, that one be chosen which entails the lesser cost."[7]

Simon's understanding of efficiency as a criterion of evaluation differs from Frederick Winslow Taylor's, however. Whereas Taylor sought the "one right way" to do any job task in order to optimize performance, Simon theorized that managers use efficiency as a criterion to choose between and among a more limited set of choices. They "satisfice" in a world of "bounded rationality." "Administrative theory is peculiarly the

---

6. Simon, *Administrative Behavior*, 29.

7. Simon, *Administrative Behavior*, 12, 149–150.

theory of intended and bounded rationality—of the behavior of human beings who *satisfice* because they have not the wit to *maximize*."[8]

It is important to note that Simon was concerned with the *study* of management rather than management *per se*. Unlike those whom he criticized, he did not promote a comprehensive set of management principles. For the most part, Simon spoke, instead, to the academy. The scholars who succeeded him would embrace positivism and behavioralism as conceptual paradigms and the use of experimental and quasi-experimental designs on the one hand and the research methods and techniques of the social sciences on the other in seeking to isolate "facts" pertaining to the practice of management.

Although Simon's impact on the study of management in the academic disciplines of management and public administration has been significant, his pivot to positivism accelerated the separation of the academic study of management from the practice of management. Indeed, Simon's legacy with respect to the practice of management is mixed. In the 1950s and 1960s, practitioners would attend more closely to the wisdom of Peter Drucker, whose contributions are examined below, than to the scholarly findings of the management and social sciences.

A second criticism pertains to decisions in which facts, ends, and values are unclear or contested. The extent to which Simon's positivist orientation, his embrace of "purpose" as a singular organizational goal or objective, and his adoption of efficiency as the chief criterion of evaluation has proven helpful has been challenged. Interestingly, Charles Lindblom would later coin a term with respect to the development of public policy—a domain in which facts, ends, and values are often unclear or in conflict—that bears some resemblance to Simon's concept of "satisficing." According to Lindblom, managers in complex policy environments simply "muddle through."[9]

In terms of his moral thinking, Simon dismissed any use of the terms "good" and "ought" as irrelevant to decision-making. In his view, the purpose behind any managerial question or set of questions should be separated entirely from any moral principles or concerns of a moral or ethical nature that lie outside of the organization. "Decisions in private

8. Simon, *Administrative Behavior*, 118.
9. Lindblom, "Muddling Through."

management, like decisions in public management, must take as their ethical premises the objectives that have been set for the organization."[10]

THE FUNCTIONAL STUDY OF CHIEF EXECUTIVES AND THE UNITY OF FOCUS

In the 1950s and 1960s, Peter Drucker (1909–2005) was widely acknowledged as the nation's most influential thinker on the topic of management. A prolific writer, Drucker resists easy classification. Unlike Taylorism and Fayolism, no school of management is associated with his name; and, even though Drucker was affiliated with several institutions of higher learning over the course of his long career, he drew most of his insights from his extensive consulting practice. Indeed, Drucker understood management to be a liberal art rather than a science *per se*, and his work is every bit as "proverbial" as Frederick Taylor's or Luther Gullick's. Still, there is no denying Drucker's influence, beginning with the publication of *Concept of the Corporation* (1946), an comprehensive study of General Motors Corporation, and later *The Practice of Management* (1954).

Drucker's understanding of the organization departed significantly from the static model portrayed, most notably, in administrative management theory. He described organizations in terms that are almost organic in nature. Organizations are born, grow, flourish, and decline.

It is a difficult to isolate any single focus or unit of analysis in Drucker's work. Nevertheless, his extensive consulting portfolio was devoted, in large part, to the work of chief executive officers. Although it is true that Drucker paid considerable attention to decision-making, he is best known, perhaps, for articulating several "practices" that help chief executive officers make sound decisions: effective time management; a sustained focus on results rather than tasks; building on strengths, both the chief executive officer's strengths and those of others in the organization, too; a disciplined focus on a select set of objectives, all of which hold the promise of "results"; and the adoption of a systematic approach to decision-making.[11]

According to Drucker, the chief executive officer's primary responsibility is to develop and maintain a unity of focus with respect to strategic objectives, thereby enabling the organization to achieve results

10. Simon, *Administrative Behavior*, 61.

11. Drucker, *The Effective Executive*, 23–24.

and flourish. According to Drucker, the efforts of all employees in the organization should be directed to this end.

Even though he focused much of his attention on chief executive officers, Drucker's understanding of management and managerial decision-making was expansive. He did not view workers as "fungible" or as "ciphers" controlled by policy or a well-defined career path. According to Drucker, workers in modern organizations should be viewed, instead, as "knowledge workers" who represent the organization's most important resource. The primary task of managers, then, is to harness all the resources of the organization, including its "knowledge workers," toward the achievement of well-defined strategies and objectives, all of which promise to help the organization flourish over time in a highly competitive and uncertain environment.

Drucker dismissed efficiency as an appropriate objective for organizations and hence for managers. In his view, efficiency only makes sense as an overarching goal if the work process in question is stable and permanent. According to Drucker, few work processes meet these criteria, no matter the sector in which they are located, private, public, or nonprofit. Given this, a more appropriate goal for managers in modern organizations is effectiveness or results, more specifically, both of which can ensure the ongoing flourishing of the organization. According to Drucker, "knowledge work is defined by its results."[12]

To develop and maintain a unity of focus oriented to strategic objectives, Drucker recommended a number of techniques, including, most notably, management-by-objectives (MBO) and planning. MBO is used to direct and assess employee efforts with respect to larger organizational purposes in ways that are results-oriented and measurable. In MBO systems, the pursuit of a discrete set of well-articulated objectives is typically incentivized by the promise of pay increases, bonuses, and promotional opportunities. The particular approach to planning recommended by Drucker focuses more on organizational strengths than organization weaknesses, more on the future than the present or the past, and more on the external environment than the day-to-day functions of the firm, unit of government, or non-profit organization. In effect, the clear articulation of goals and objectives from the top of the organization to the bottom, together with planning oriented to results and to the ongoing flourishing of the organization, serve as a control function in Drucker's

12. Drucker, *The Effective Executive*, 7

schema in the same way that standard operating procedures and incentive pay serve as such in the case of scientific management and policy in the case of administrative management theory.

The key strengths of Drucker's work are twofold. First, his views on management were couched in language that chief executives could understand. Whereas Simon spoke to scholars, Drucker spoke to practitioners, many of whom attended closely to his words. Second, Drucker's counsel on the need for forward-looking planning has been widely embraced. Michael E. Porter's "five forces model," perhaps the most highly acclaimed approach to strategic planning now available, fully reflects Drucker's views in this regard. As detailed in *Competitive Strategy: Techniques for Analyzing Industries and Competitors* (1980), Porter's definitive word on the subject, a robust strategic planning process begins with the articulation of an organization's mission, vision, and core values. It then proceeds to the evaluation of the organization's external environment, i.e., the strength of the competitive forces now confronting it, factors driving the industry as a whole, and the competitive "positioning" of the organization's rivals *vis-à-vis* these driving forces, and an assessment of the organization's internal resources and capabilities and the strength of its "value chain" as well. Having completed these analyses, the organization will then be in a position to choose from among five alternative "platforms" on which to compete, i.e., overall low cost, broad differentiation, focused low cost, focused broad differentiation, and best cost. A set of strategic objectives that aligns well with the organization's optimal competitive platform can then be identified.

Three attributes of Porter's approach to strategic planning, in particular, are fully reflective of Drucker's perspective on planning. First, his insistence on the need for a mission statement and a clear articulation of the organization's vision and values are consistent with the way in which Drucker portrayed organizations in biological rather than mechanical terms. People have missions, visions, and values; machines do not. Second, Porter's "five forces model" is focused as much, if not more, on the organization's external environment as on its internal strengths and weakness. Third, Porter's model is forward-looking. It is concerned more about a preferred future than it is the past or the present.

The lack of precision in Drucker's work has proven something of a lightning rod for some scholars, however. Terms such as "effectiveness" and "flourishing" are less precise and hence less measurable than efficiency or compliance with policy. In the view of Drucker's critics,

MANAGEMENT THEORY AND MODELS41

"effectiveness" and "flourishing" can be distilled all too easily into any number of concepts and variables, some of which can undermine or cancel out others.

A second criticism pertains to a lack of empirical support for Drucker's work, a criticism that is sometimes attached to Michael E. Porter's efforts as well. Herbert Simon might well have dismissed much of Drucker's work as "proverbial."

Another more specific criticism pertains to Drucker's endorsement of MBO. There is now a widespread consensus that MBO's promise has never been realized. Some note that certain management responsibilities are difficult to define and hence to measure, for instance, the need to develop and maintain *esprit de corps* and teamwork, both of which were featured as key responsibilities in Fayol's work. As a result, a bias in favor of quantifiable objectives over other important tasks can develop over time. This should come as no surprise, since MBO attaches powerful incentives to the time and attention employees pay to certain objectives over others. The problem is that some of these other responsibilities may be critically important as well. Further, MBO takes no account of the informal networks of relationships or the "logic of sentiment" that proved of such interest to Elton Mayo and others associated with the human relations movement. In MBO systems, the range of incentives usually begins and ends with money and the promise of promotion. Still further, W. Edward Deming and others would excoriate MBO in the 1980s and 1990s for its failure to account for the natural variation characteristic of most work processes. According to Deming, holding employees accountable for results that are more attributable to the work processes over which they have little or no control rather than to their own efforts is absurd. Finally, critics note that few do MBO well. Even if this control mechanism was theoretically sound, it tends not to "play well" in the real world.

At a societal level, Drucker prescribed a more proactive role for organizational leaders and managers than did Taylor, Fayol, Gullick, Mayo, or Simon. "In modern society, there is no other leadership group but managers. If the managers of our major institutions, and especially of business, do not take responsibility for the common good, no one else can or will."[13]

Still, at a fundamental level, Drucker's understanding of "knowledge workers," including the chief executive officer, was largely instrumental

13. Drucker, *The Effective Executive*, 325.

in nature. In Drucker's view, workers should be valued only to the extent that they can contribute to the ongoing flourishing of the firm, the unit of government, or the nonprofit organization for which they labor. In fact, "it is the duty of the executive to remove ruthlessly anyone—and especially any manager—who consistently fails to perform with high distinction. To let such a man stay corrupts the others."[14]

With respect to moral thinking, Drucker's work is also something of a mixed bag. On the one hand, he promoted a high level of employee autonomy and insisted on the need for collaboration and collegiality. On the other, Drucker was more than willing to tolerate a troublesome employee if she was "effective." "The effective executive knows that to get strength one has to put up with weakness."[15]

MANAGEMENT SCIENCE

Management science—not to be confused with scientific management—is associated most closely not with a scholar but with a practitioner, Robert McNamara (1916–2009). McNamara championed this perspective in the private sector during his tenure at Ford Motor Company (1946–60), in the public sector during his service as Secretary of Defense (1960–68), and in the nonprofit world, as well, during his time as president of the World Bank (1968–81).

Management science can best be understood, perhaps, as an interdisciplinary subfield in the academic field of management. Like behavioralism, management science promises analytic rigor. Whereas behavioralism draws on the analytic methods of the social sciences, however, management science integrates applied mathematics, systems thinking, and performance budgeting.

The focus or unit of analysis in management science is decision-making, but not with respect to the organization as a whole. The tools of management science are applied, instead, to decisions pertaining to particular products, processes, and initiatives. Further, the tools of management science are employed to optimize the use of resources so that a select set of clearly defined objectives can be achieved. The overarching goal in each instance is resource optimization.

14. Drucker, *The Effective Executive*, 89.
15. Drucker, *The Effective Executive*, 87.

Initiatives associated with McNamara over the course of his long career illustrate the types of problems typically addressed using the tools of management science. While part of a statistical control group in the Army Air Forces during the Second World War, McNamara and his team were directed to determine if it would be cost-effective to fly bombers from Europe to the campaign in the Pacific after VE Day. Surprisingly, the team concluded that it would be cheaper to build new bombers on the West Coast. At Ford, McNamara led the effort to produce a low-cost vehicle that would appeal to suburban homeowners. The result was the Ford Falcon. As Secretary of Defense, McNamara launched an ultimately futile campaign to degrade the capabilities of the Vietcong in South Viet Nam. To this end, the use of "body counts" was adopted as a singularly important metric. While at the World Bank, McNamara insisted on the use of "systems thinking" to isolate variables that contribute most significantly to third-world poverty, hence the World Bank's focus on population control during his tenure as president. Again, the tools of management science pertain to particular products, processes, and initiatives, and analyses of all such challenges are directed to the optimization of resources in the pursuit of predetermined objectives.

Three methods or sets of methods are uniquely associated with management science. The first set, the various techniques associated with operations research, is drawn from applied mathematics. Linear programming is a powerful tool in which an optimal solution is calculated using mathematically defined objectives, e.g., revenue forecasts, expenses, time, etc., and a select set of mathematically defined constraints. Operations research was used to great effect during McNamara's time with the Army Air Forces during the Second World War and at Ford, too.

Toward the end of McNamara's time at Ford, systems analysis came into vogue. Any system—biological or organizational, for instance—can be conceived of as a process in which inputs are converted into outputs in a series of steps. In time, systems thinking would contribute to the development of various planning and project management tools, for instance, the critical path method (CPM) and the program evaluation review technique (PERT). Each step in a complex process is sequenced in a way that graphically illustrates their relationships. PERT builds on CPM by assigning probabilities to the expected completion date for each step in a project. Cost-benefit analysis was embraced at the same time.

While at the Pentagon, McNamara added at third set of techniques to his toolbox: performance-based budgeting. Traditional accounting methods tally objects, e.g., worker pay, raw materials, rent, tools, machines, vehicles, etc., hence the term "object code accounting." Moreover, object code accounting tends to be departmental rather than programmatic in nature. In a performance-based budget, program objectives are quantified, the various resources needed to achieve these ends across all of the organization's departments are identified, the needed resources are allocated and deployed, and the program in question is evaluated on a regular basis against its predetermined objectives. While serving as Secretary of Defense, McNamara introduced performance-based budgeting as a complement to the Defense Department's use of the analytic tools of operations research and systems thinking.

Management science has had a profound impact on the way some organizations manage their work. For instance, the transportation of goods, i.e., logistics, has been entirely transformed by linear programming and the other tools of operations research; and this development has accelerated exponentially over the course of the last thirty years due to the widespread use of personal computers and the development of the internet. Similarly, many contemporary construction projects would be difficult to manage without the use of CPM, PERT, and other graphical planning tools.

The strengths of management science are twofold. First, the tools of this management subfield add rigor to programmatic decision-making. We have come a long way from the "rules of thumb" discredited by Frederick Winslow Taylor, the "proverbs" dismissed by Herbert Simon, and Peter Drucker's biological conception of the organization. Using the tools of management science, program and project goals are quantified and performance metrics are used to determine success or failure. There is an undeniable rigor in the use of management science's tools and techniques.

Its second strength pertains to its integration of analysis, planning, and budgeting. The tools employed at each step of the decision-making process are powerful in and of themselves. Together, they can contribute to the more rational conceptualization of problems and the identification of possible solutions and, hence, to the accomplishment of important organizational goals and objectives.

As is true of all such language games, management science is not without its critics. First, program budgeting has proven unwieldy. Indeed, one complaint at the Defense Department during Robert McNamara's tenure was that no one but McNamara could understand the reams of spreadsheets that constituted the department's budget. As a result, few were in a position to stand up to McNamara as the Vietnam War expanded. It seems that even senior-level officials were intimidated by the department's budgeting and planning process. This "illusion of rigor" can be particularly problematic in the case of some public and nonprofit organizations in which complex programs and initiatives entail multiple objectives, some of which may defy precise quantification.

Second, sub-optimization can occur if problems are not effectively framed. In 1960, McNamara was hailed on the front cover of *Time* as one of the "Whiz Kids" who had turned Ford's fortunes around. By the middle seventies, however, the years of cost-cutting at Ford had led to unreliable product lines that American consumers were abandoning in favor of Toyotas and Hondas. More tragically, the use of "body counts" as a metric during the later stages of the Vietnam War incentivized wildly inflated counts that proclaimed success even as observers in the field had concluded that the war effort was failing miserably. Both Ford and the Department of Defense learned the hard way that the use of metrics needs to be carefully balanced and that integrity in their use must be ensured if the tools of management science are to prove reliable.

A third criticism pertains to the uncritical acceptance of programmatic goals and objectives. In his memoir, *In Retrospect: The Tragedy and Lessons of Vietnam* (1996), McNamara acknowledged that he had become disillusioned with the war by late 1965. He continued to prosecute it anyway, however, until he left the Department of Defense in 1968. According to McNamara, he refrained from sharing his views publicly out of loyalty to President Johnson. More broadly, the tools of management science—in and of themselves—provide little purchase for the questioning of larger organizational goals and purposes.

A final criticism pertains to the observed tendency among some practitioners of management science to lose contact with a product or initiative as it is experienced on the ground. The numbers on a spreadsheet, the income statement, the process map, and "body counts" can all too easily become more real than the product or the initiative itself. In his devastating account of the decline of the American auto industry, *The Reckoning* (1986), David Halberstam called attention to this blind spot in Robert McNamara's thinking.

> [McNamara] had come in one morning and given Don Frey, who was then one of his top product men, a piece of paper. It was a church leaflet with penciling on the back; McNamara, Frey gathered, had been daydreaming in church. The penciling

described a car. But it was not a sketch of what the car should look like, or a statement about how it should handle, or a notion about what group of customers it should appeal to. It was a series of statistics—what the car should weigh and cost. "Bob," Frey finally said, "you've got everything down except what kind of car you want." "What do you mean?" McNamara asked. "Well, do you want a soft car, a hot, sexy car, a comfortable car, a car for the young, or a car for the middle class? Whose car is it, what does it feel like?" "That's very interesting," McNamara said. "Write down what you think is right."[16]

There is an undeniable tendency in management science toward "bean-counting." To paraphrase Oscar Wilde, some who practice management science "know the price of everything and the value of nothing," it seems.

THE MAXIMIZATION OF SHAREHOLDER WEALTH

The maximization of shareholder wealth perspective emerged in the late 1970s as a powerful lens through which to understand the responsibilities of the chief executive officer and, through her, other managers in the firm. This remarkably simple idea holds that the chief executive officer has but one responsibility: to maximize shareholder wealth or the wealth of the firm's owners in the case of a privately held corporation. The kind of worker needs addressed by scholars associated with the human relations movement, for instance, count for little in this view beyond the extent to which meeting workers's needs might contribute to higher stock prices. Societal needs count for even less.

Like most of our managerial language games, the maximization of shareholder wealth mantra has many fathers. It was articulated in a particularly powerful way, however, by Milton Friedman in an article that appeared in the *New York Times* on September 13, 1970.[17] Over time, this truncated understanding of management would also become associated with Jack Welch and his tenure as chief executive officer at GE during the last two decades of the twentieth century.

Maximizing shareholder wealth can be understood as a direct repudiation of Peter Drucker's management philosophy. Whereas Drucker understood the chief executive officer to be accountable to the

16. Halberstam, *The Reckoning*, 209.

17. Friedman, "Social Responsibility."

organization and to its ends, Friedman argued forcefully that the chief executive officer is accountable solely to shareholders. Whereas Drucker described organizations in biological terms and oriented the behavior of the chief executive officer to the flourishing of the organization over the long-term, Friedman oriented the behavior of the chief executive officer to the short-term financial gain of shareholders. And whereas Drucker viewed the chief executive officer as a moral agent who is responsible to society as well as to the organization, Friedman eschewed any such role for the chief executive officer.

As a management philosophy, the maximization of shareholder wealth is reductionist in the extreme. First, it eviscerates the idea of the private firm as a "legal person," reducing it, in effect, to the status of a money-making machine. Although the firm still enjoys standing in the law as a "legal person," this identity is circumscribed, and any sense that the firm is a moral construct is abandoned altogether. Second, it diminishes the standing of the chief executive officer to that of a fiduciary agent. Third, it reduces moral behavior on the part of the management team to that which is legal.

The focus of the chief executive officer and the management team in this remarkably thin understanding of management is quite simple: asset valuation. The singular goal of the management team is also clear: to increase dividend payouts and stock price, and, of these, the latter is by far the more important.

With respect to its methods and techniques, maximizing shareholder wealth as a management philosophy is quite eclectic. It is equally amenable to methods of control associated with scientific management, administrative management theory, the human relations movement, management science, and even total quality management, which is discussed below, as long as these methods promise to increase shareholder wealth in the near term.

Three distinctive strategies have emerged in the wake of the widespread adoption of this approach to management, however. First, executive compensation has shifted from the payment of salaries to the distribution of equities. This more closely aligns the interests of the management team to the interests of shareholders. At the same time, boards of directors have dramatically increased the overall financial value of executive compensation packages in order to incentivize decision-making serving the short-term interests of shareholders. According to one report, the ratio of compensation packages for chief executive officers to the pay of the "typical worker" in the firm jumped from twenty-to-one in 1965 to fifty-eight-to-one in 1989 and to more than two hundred-to-one in 2018.[18]

Second, deregulation at the federal and state level has been aggressively pursued by firms and private sector consortia as well. Regulations have the effect of constraining certain executive behaviors in order to promote competition or for some other larger societal purpose. In the view of some firms, laws and regulations increase costs and so hamstring the firm's ability to compete in an increasingly global marketplace, hence the dramatic expansion of lobbying efforts in Washington, DC and in statehouses in recent decades, much of which has been focused on deregulation.

Third, the popularity of leveraged buyouts has increased. By one account, the number increased from four in 1980 to 410 in 1988. Whereas venture capitalists tended to focus on start-up firms in the 1960s and 1970s, debt-financed takeovers of existing firms ballooned in the 1980s and 1990s. Low debt ratios achieved over the course of many years had left some long-established firms vulnerable to corporate raiders.

The maximization of shareholder wealth perspective was embraced in the 1980s and 1990s as *the* way to understand management responsibilities in the private sector. It was quickly adopted a kind of mantra in business schools across the country. Indeed, the overriding duty to maximize shareholder wealth has now been inculcated into several generations of MBA students. Affirming its widespread adoption, the influential Business Roundtable embraced the maximization of shareholder wealth as its official view of the private sector firm's purpose in 1997.

Two developments ensured the rapid adoption of this management philosophy. First, deregulation at the federal level was launched in the late 1970s under Jimmy Carter and then accelerated to a considerable extent under Ronald Reagan in the 1980s. This greatly expanded money-making opportunities for private firms. Second, mutual funds grew dramatically in the 1980s and 1990s as organizations moved from defined-benefit to defined-contribution retirement plans. As a result, individual stocks would come to be viewed more as wealth-generating commodities than as certificates of ownership in particular firms. In effect, the promise of short-term gains supplanted long-term value as an investment goal.

---

18. Mishel and Wolfe, "CEO Compensation."

In fact, the maximization of shareholder wealth perspective has three compelling attributes: it is easy to understand; it is easy to communicate; and success or failure in this regard is easy to measure. Those who promote the maximization of shareholder wealth as a management philosophy also claim that society as a whole benefits because increases in wealth in the aggregate "trickle down" to all over time. This is an empirical question, of course; and, as we shall see, the evidence in this regard is less than convincing.

At least five criticisms have been leveled against this understanding of management. First, the underlying philosophy that animates the maximization of shareholder wealth mantra often goes unexamined. Milton Friedman was a libertarian. Moreover, he advocated the libertarian perspective on teleological rather than deontological grounds. For Friedman, freedom—personal or economic—was never an end in itself. He believed, instead, that libertarianism produces better personal and societal results. This conclusion is debatable, of course, but is rarely reflected upon by those who promote the maximization of shareholder wealth as *the* exclusive way in which the duties of the chief executive officer and, through her, the firm as a whole should be understood.

Second, in conflating moral behavior and legality and by so powerfully incentivizing short-term financial gain, the maximization of shareholder wealth perspective has induced wave after wave of scandal in the corporate world, engulfing, for instance, such well-known firms as Worldcom, Enron, Arthur Anderson, and Lehman Brothers. As the fictional character Gordon Gekko—played to such great effect by Michael Douglas in the 1987 film *Wall Street*—declared: "Greed is good!"

Third, the maximization of shareholder wealth perspective disdains philanthropy and social investment of any kind. In Friedman's view, this kind of spending "steals" money from shareholders who are in a better position to decide which, if any, philanthropic causes warrant their consideration. Any sense that the firm is a member of a larger community or a potential catalyst for social change is thereby abandoned.

Fourth, it is not at all clear that the maximization of shareholder wealth perspective has produced the kinds of results promised in the late 1970s and 1980s. By one account, "the rate of return on assets and on invested capital of US firms declined from 1965 to 2009 by three quarters."[19] It is perhaps not surprising, therefore, that the Business Roundtable

19. Denning, "The Origin."

abandoned its embrace of the maximization of shareholder wealth mantra in August 2019. Its "Purpose of the Corporation" statement now recognizes five categories of "stakeholders": customers, employees, suppliers, the communities in which firms are located, and shareholders as well.[20] By 2009, even Jack Welch had repudiated his association with this management philosophy: "On the face of it, shareholder value is the dumbest idea in the world. Shareholder value is a result, not a strategy . . . Your main constituencies are your employees, your customers, and your products. Managers and investors should not set share price increases as their overarching goal . . . Short-term profits should be allied with an increase in the long-term value of a company."[21]

Fifth, the understanding of the firm's purpose on which the maximization of shareholder wealth perspective is premised can exact considerable damage when it is transferred to the public sector. This conclusion may not seem apparent at first glance since public sector organizations do not produce wealth in a direct way. It is so, nonetheless, in at least three respects. The first, deregulation, has already been noted. The second pertains to the conflicted missions of certain governmental agencies. For instance, does the Department of Energy work for energy producers or for those who need to be protected from the unregulated exploitation of public lands? Similarly, should the Department of Education focus on the needs of public schools or should it underwrite the efforts of those who seek to privatize public education? Public policy can be warped when the weight of government is brought to bear on behalf of those in the private sector who seek primarily to maximize shareholder wealth. The third way in which the maximization of shareholder wealth philosophy has infiltrated the public sector pertains to the tendency, in some circles, to see the Dow Jones Average as a singular proxy for the state of the economy as a whole. As a measure of performance, it is easy to understand, but it oversimplifies the economy in an irresponsible and dangerous way.

THE QUALITY MOVEMENT

The quality movement encompasses a number of approaches that go by various names: total quality management, total quality control, Six Sigma, lean manufacturing, and process reengineering. It is associated with

20. Business Roundtable, "Our Commitment."
21. Denning, "The Origin."

a number of practitioners and consultants as well. At the same time, it has made surprisingly few inroads into the academy. Key thinkers associated with the quality movement include W. Edward Deming (1900–93), the author of *Out of the Crisis* (1982); Joseph M. Juran (1904–2008), whose work is detailed in Frank Gryna's *Juran's Quality Control Handbook* (1951); Armand V. Feigenbaum (1922–2014), the author of *Total Quality Control* (1951); and Kaoru Ishikawa (1915–89), who promoted the "seven tools of quality management."

Deming, Juran, and Feigenbaum garnered considerable attention in the 1980s and 1990s because of their work in post-war Japan. All three had been engaged by Japanese firms to help get them back on their feet after hostilities had ended. The Japanese learned their lessons well. By the mid-1970s, Japanese products—most notably cars and trucks and a whole host of electronic products, too—had come to be recognized as superior in both quality and price to products produced in the United States. In response, American businesses clamored to know more about the "total quality" techniques employed in Japan. The Japanese pointed to Deming, Juran, Feigenbaum, and Ishikawa. As a result, the quality movement quickly emerged as a trendy albeit somewhat eclectic approach to management.

The quality movement can be viewed as a reaction against the several management theories and models that preceded it. Although some expressions of the quality movement highlight the importance of standard operating procedures, most emphasize the need for worker autonomy. Scientific management's focus on narrowly defined job descriptions was thus abandoned. Fayol's hierarchical order and "scalar chain" were also disavowed in favor of cross-functional teams. The "logic of sentiment" and the mix of psychological and sociological factors associated with the work of scholars in the human relations movement were eschewed in favor of a more circumscribed understanding of worker motivation. The quality gurus suggested somewhat obliquely, to be sure, that all workers—including managers—can discover a deeper "meaning" in their efforts when they are assigned responsibility for the processes with which they work. Deming, in particular, excoriated one of Peter Drucker's signature contribution to management theory and practice: MBO. Deming's "fourteen points" ridiculed the very idea that employees should be held accountable for outcomes produced in work processes over which they have little or no control. Finally, the several quality gurus viewed management science—especially its unrelenting focus on cost reduction—as responsible for the precipitous decline of the manufacturing sector in the United States in the 1970s and 1980s.

The foci or units of analysis in the various expressions of the quality movement vary. Methods associated with Deming and Ishikawa were oriented to the control of individual work processes. Juran's interests and Feigenbaum's, too, were broader. Juran's "quality trilogy," for instance, addresses three broad tasks: quality planning, quality control, and quality improvement. And Feigenbaum promoted clearly defined specifications employed throughout the production process, beginning with the product's design and extending through to the point of final inspection.

The goal that unites these several approaches to management is customer satisfaction. Even Feigenbaum's focus on conformance to specifications is oriented to this overarching goal. The specifications he celebrated are determined by the customer, not the firm *per se*. Further, the concept of the "customer" is broad in the quality movement. It includes not just external customers, but anyone inside the organization who is dependent on another worker, work unit, or department for a service, a benefit, direction, or information.

Several strategies and techniques are associated with the quality movement, most importantly a commitment to continuous improvement, i.e., *kaisen*. Deming drew on the work of Walter Shewhart in promoting the plan-do-check-act quality cycle as a way to engage workers in the incremental improvement of any product or service in order to enhance the overall satisfaction of the customer.

Variation across a broad array of quality characteristics, i.e., performance, features, reliability, conformance, durability, serviceability, aesthetics, and perceived quality, is viewed as a key problem in all work processes. Several statistical and non-statistical techniques can be employed to tease out sources of variation so that they can be eliminated or their impacts minimized. Process control charts are thus recommended for any discrete or continuous variables deemed relevant to customer satisfaction. Unlike some statistical methods, process control charts are easy to use and interpret. Other simple analytic tools are recommended as well, most notably, cause-and-effect or fishbone diagrams, check sheets, histograms, pareto charts, scatter diagrams, and flow charts.

Teams are viewed as essential in every expression of the quality movement. In the view of the several quality gurus, workers are positioned closer to work processes than anyone else and so know best how to improve them. The Japanese executives interviewed by representatives of

American companies in the 1970s and 1980s celebrated the use of "quality circles," i.e., self-directed work teams that meet regularly to analyze and improve the work processes for which they are responsible. This was something of a revelation for American companies whose leaders never imagined, it seems, that frontline workers could serve in this capacity. The Japanese also promoted the use of cross-functional teams to break down decision-making silos and the prospect of sub-optimization at the departmental level.

Award and certification programs are also associated with the quality movement. The Malcolm Baldrige Quality Award was created by the federal government in the late 1980s to promote quality improvement. And the International Standard Organization's ISO 9000 family of quality standards has dramatically changed the way in which quality is promoted in a number of industries. ISO 9000—and other industry-specific standards modeled on the design of ISO 9000—are based on best practices. First released in 1987, the ISO 9000 standards are not product- or industry-based. They are generic in nature and pertain equally to manufacturers and service providers in both the private sector and government. ISO 9000 audits are conducted to confirm the health of an organization's internal control mechanisms. Three topics are addressed in these wide-ranging audits: the organization's quality policy, i.e., objectives that pertain to such concerns as product or service "fitness for use," performance, safety, and reliability; the organization's approach to quality management, i.e., the various management functions that establish and sustain an organization's quality policy; and the organization's quality system, i.e., the structures, responsibilities, procedures, processes, and resources used to implement an organization's quality program.

Other strategies and techniques are sometimes viewed as successors to the quality movement. This includes process and business reengineering, Six Sigma, and lean manufacturing. Keen observers view these several strategies and techniques as logical developments in the quality movement, however. Reengineering is thus needed when a process, a product, or a service is approaching the end of its life cycle. It may be prudent at this point to "reengineer" the item of concern. *Kaisen* can then begin anew. Similarly, Six Sigma can be understood as a rigorous approach to process control. And lean manufacturing can be viewed as a tool for tailoring a product or service to an individual customer's quality specifications.

The quality movement has exhibited three enduring strengths. Whereas Peter Drucker focused on the need for forward-looking plans, the quality movement tends to stick to the challenge at hand, i.e., work processes already in place. The near collapse of the manufacturing sector in the United States in the 1970s and early 1980s amply demonstrated the need to attend to the present as well as the future. Second, the quality movement celebrates customer satisfaction as *the* standard—as opposed to an organization's policies in the case of administrative management theory or its financial targets in the case of the maximization of shareholder wealth perspective—against which performance should be measured. Third, workers are viewed somewhat differently in the several expressions of the quality movement than they are in any of the other managerial language games examined to this point. Indeed, the quality movement embraces what Douglas McGregor described as the "theory Y" view of workers, i.e., as self-motivated, responsible, and capable of self-direction and self-control. Beyond this, the quality movement holds that workers can experience a deeper meaning in their work. They can experience "pride of workmanship," according to Deming, hence the motivating potential of job enrichment and the full engagement of workers in developing the processes with which they work.

Two criticisms attend to the quality movement. First, some assert that it is every bit as instrumental in its view of workers as scientific management, administrative management theory, management science, and the maximization of shareholder wealth perspective. The quality movement may tap more deeply into a worker's experience of meaning, but it is oriented to the very same end as other management philosophies: the profitability of the firm, in the case of the private sector, or certain policy ends in the case of governmental entities and nonprofit organizations.

Others note that the quality movement is only tangentially connected to an organization's strategic planning processes. In this view, firms committed exclusively to one or more of the several expressions of the quality movement can be blinded to the external environment in which they compete. Similarly, public agencies can become oblivious to the public policy and political environments in which they function. The kind of multifaceted strategic planning process recommended by Michael E. Porter, for instance, is viewed by these critics as a much-needed complement to an organization's quality improvement program.

Value can be found in seven of the eight language games examined in this chapter. The maximization of shareholder wealth perspective is the notable exception. The job analyses and workplace design still employed by organizations can be traced back to Frederick Winslow Taylor and scientific management. The rational order promoted in administrative management theory has contributed to greater efficiency in the workplace. The tools of OD have engendered better workplace communications. Herbert Simon's behavioral critique has isolated decision-making as *the* defining responsibility of management. It has also encouraged several generations of scholars to study how knowledge is acquired, used, and shared in organizations. Peter Drucker's focus on unity of effort has engendered a lasting appreciation for long-term planning. Management science has introduced rigor in decision-making pertaining to certain classes of management problems. The gurus of the quality movement prompted a much-needed pivot away from an exclusive focus on the needs of the firm to the needs of customers. It affirmed, as well, that work can engender the personal experience of meaning, an experience that goes well beyond the "logic of sentiment" or the promise of a safe and harmonious workplace. Even the maximization of shareholder wealth mantra deserves some credit for having demonstrated the utter folly of employing any single measure of organizational performance to the exclusion of all others.

Our appreciative inquiry into each of these several language games suggests that none of them need be embraced to the exclusion of the others. Elements from at least seven of these eight sets of management theories and methods can be effectively included in the manager's toolbox of strategies, methods, and techniques.

We have also addressed a number of deficiencies that pertain uniquely to each of these language games. An overarching critique is needed, too, however. Lacking an overarching critique encompassing all eight of these language games, we could all too easily conclude that it is just a matter of selecting the right mix of strategies, methods, and techniques. We could all too easily forestall our search for something more satisfying at the level of the individual or something more faithful to our religious and spiritual commitments, too.

In fact, two overarching criticisms are in order. The first pertains to human motivation. This concern is essentially ignored in the case of administrative management theory and management science. In keeping with the positivist epistemology that undergirds their work, behavioralists do not promote any particular theory of human motivation. This concern is viewed as entirely economic in nature in the case of scientific management and in the maximization of shareholder wealth perspective, too. This narrow understanding of human motivation is implicit, as well, in Peter Drucker's endorsement of MBO. The gurus of the quality movement hint at the intrinsic "meaning" of work, but fail to develop this concept in any substantial way. They certainly show no awareness of thinking on this topic originating from any other fields of study or practice. For the most part, the language games examined in this chapter do not address human motivation in any substantial way.

It could be suggested that the human relations movement—most notably, with respect to Maslow's hierarchy of needs—may represent an exception to this overall conclusion. Again, however, the human relations movement is interested in human motivation because its techniques represent powerful means to an end that is properly oriented to organizational purposes. Further, Maslow's hierarchy is problematic in its own right. Although this seminal contribution is intuitively satisfying, it resists empirical confirmation. Moreover, the final step in the hierarchy, i.e., self-actualization, is impossibly vague. For some, it simply confirms the fact that some outgrow their need for external rewards; for others, it points to a latent need to build or to create; and, for still others, it suggests a willingness among some to subordinate their own concerns to a larger purpose of one kind or another. Further, there is considerable evidence that it is not at all uncommon for individuals to subordinate their own interests at each of the five stages of Maslow's hierarchy. Self-sacrifice is not unknown among those who sojourn through life at each of these levels.

Our second overarching criticism is related to the first. It pertains more specifically to the purpose of work, however. Each of our several managerial language games is grounded, in fact, on a particular understanding of work: it should be oriented instrumentally to ends established by the organization. These ends have been variously defined as profit, efficiency, a stipulated policy goal, effectiveness, results, the optimal use of resources, the maximization of shareholder wealth, and conformance to specifications. We can all too easily think of these ends as value-neutral, but they are not. Lacking grounding in any larger moral framework, they often serve themselves as guiding values. We can all too easily think of them as impersonal as well, but they are not. These various ends, purposes, and objectives can have profound impacts on people inside the organization and on people external to it as well.

In fact, little purchase is provided in these several language games for foregrounding or pursuing other ends or other purposes, including moral claims of one kind or another, i.e., our understanding of ourselves and our understanding of and behavior toward others. Little purchase is provided, too, for social justice. As a result, the disparate treatment of communities, e.g., mortgage redlining, food deserts, underfunded schools in communities of color, etc.; collateral damage, e.g., second-hand smoke, the mass marketing of opioids, gun violence, etc.; and societal externalities, e.g., global warming, are—more often than not—ignored by many of today's organizations. Again, moral claims seem to have no place in the boardroom or the management suite or on the shop floor. They have no place in the language games practiced in many of today's organizations.

Donald A. Schön, the author of *The Reflective Practitioner: How Professionals Think in Action* (1983), pointed to the internal and external barriers that inhibit these broader kinds of conversations. "Managers do reflect-in-action, but they seldom reflect on their reflection-in-action. Hence this crucially important dimension of their art tends to remain private and inaccessible to others. Moreover, because awareness of one's intuitive thinking usually grows out of practice in articulating it to others, managers often have little access to their own reflection-in-action . . . Since he cannot describe his reflection-in-action, he cannot teach others to do it. If they acquire the capacity for it, they do so by contagion."[22] The fact that workers *can* imagine larger purposes for their efforts on the job—as we noted at the end of chapter 1—is not to say that they can do so easily or naturally.

Further, even if a manger reflects on her day-to-day work and then reflects on her reflection, and even if these reflections include concerns of a moral nature, it can be difficult, indeed, to raise them in the boardroom or the management suite or on the shop floor. These kinds of concerns have little place in the language games sanctioned in most of today's private sector, public sector, and nonprofit organizations.

Further, if these kinds of concerns were to be accepted as legitimate and if they could somehow be introduced into conversations in the boardroom or the management suite or on the shop floor, no magic formula exists for balancing them against the instrumental ends sanctioned by most organizations. To further complicate matters, the rational

22. Schön, *The Reflective Practitioner*, 243.

pursuit of instrumental ends is not a "bad thing" in and of itself. Claims of this kind, too, can acquire a degree of moral legitimacy. While a rising tide may not raise all boats, it can certainly raise some. Distribution problems notwithstanding, a rationally organized society tends to produce more goods and services in the aggregate than a failed state or a failed economy. And organizations enveloped in the kinds of managerial language games addressed in this chapter have certainly produced more goods and services over time.

How then do we balance moral concerns and concerns about justice, i.e., the way in which a society's benefits and burdens are distributed, against the circumscribed instrumentality of today's organizations? This is precisely the question that nags at some Christians who hold managerial positions, the kind of question, in fact, that can engender considerable dissonance, given the messages they hear from the pulpit every Sunday: "Tend to the needs of the *anawim*," i.e., those who live on the margins. "Love your enemies." "Do good to those who hate you." And "let the little ones come to me."

How do we reconcile these kinds of imperatives and our work in the secular world? How do we reconcile our commitments to moral behavior and to justice on the one hand and our work inside the closed language games of today's private sector firms and public and nonprofit organizations on the other? To answer these questions, we need to look beyond the language games now dominant in the worlds of business and government and nonprofit and civic organizations, too.

Chapter 3

Servant Leadership
and the Search for Meaning

Again, a central thesis of this text is advanced in four stages in part I. In the preceding chapter, the potential value of the several management theories and models now available to us was acknowledged. Nevertheless, they were found to be deficient in two respects: first, the understandings of human motivation embodied in each of these eight managerial language games are thin; and, second, they are oriented exclusively to narrow organizational purposes. A complementary argument is advanced in this chapter: the servant-leader model proposed by Robert Greenleaf addresses these twin deficiencies, but its claims in this regard are poorly rooted and hence weak. In chapter 4, the perennial need for virtue as a foundation for true leadership in all kinds of organizations will be established, and in chapter 5, we will expand our focus to the public square. Analogues to the several management theories and models examined in chapter 2 will be found to be deficient in this domain as well.

The servant-leader paradigm can be considered a language game in its own right, of course, but it differs from the other language games celebrated in management theory and practice in important ways. As we shall see, it alludes to a richer understanding of human motivation than do those other language games. Additionally, the servant-leader model can potentially encompass a broader array of organizational purposes and can, as a result, accommodate moral discernment in a way that the other language games cannot.

The servant-leader model is associated with Robert Greenleaf. His explication of it is developed most fully in *Servant Leadership* (1977), a remarkably influential text. Indeed, Greenleaf's influence can be detected in the work of an entire generation of thinkers, including, most notably, perhaps, Peter Block, Stephen Covey, Ken Blanchard, Parker Palmer, and Peter Senge. A practitioner, Greenleaf worked for the American Telephone and Telegraph Company for forty years and later founded what would eventually become the Greenleaf Center for Servant Leadership.

As influential as Greenleaf has been, his work can be maddening, nonetheless, for academics and practitioners alike. Scholars decry his imprecise use of such key terms as "service" and "meaning." Further, the depth of Greenleaf's analysis with respect to these and other key concepts is thin in places. Still further, Greenleaf migrated all too easily between and among the several normative and descriptive claims he made. Finally, Greenleaf made little effort to support any of his claims empirically. He drew largely from his considerable personal experience, his personal reflections on those experiences, and his personal faith commitments, too.

Practitioners also struggle with Greenleaf's work. Like Peter Drucker, he viewed leadership as an art rather than a science and argued that management challenges demand responses that are—for the most part—situational in nature. Given this, practitioners who look long and hard in Greenleaf's work for concrete principles, clear-cut strategies, and crisply detailed techniques will be disappointed. Further, they will find little guidance with respect to conflicting priorities and competing claims on the leader's time and attention.

There is no denying the impact of Greenleaf's work, however. To use the language of the New Testament, Greenleaf's understanding of servant leadership gives us "ears to hear and eyes to see." This is the value of conceptual models, of course; they give us new ways of imagining the circumstances in which we find ourselves, in Greenleaf's case, a new way of imagining the management challenges we encounter in all kinds of organizations. There is broad consensus that Greenleaf's critique is an important one. There is a growing consensus, too, that Greenleaf's servant-leader model taps into a potentially valuable stream of wisdom, a stream of wisdom that had been rather cavalierly dismissed by scholars and practitioners alike through much of the twentieth century.

A brief summary of Greenleaf's work follows. The analytic elements used in the preceding chapter will again be employed. We will examine the servant-leader model's focus or "unit of analysis," its most important goals and objectives, its signature methods and techniques, and its notable strengths and enduring value. As we shall see, the servant-leader model's strengths pertain specifically to the two overarching deficiencies associated with the management theories and models addressed in the preceding chapter. These strengths undergird, as well, the sharp distinction drawn in this text between management and leadership. Finally, three shortcomings in Greenleaf's work will be noted.

In terms of focus, Greenleaf was primarily concerned with the servant-leader and how she impacts other people. This represents a dramatic departure from the foci of our several other theories of management and their associated models. Greenleaf was primarily concerned about people—both the leader and those who are affected by the leader—rather than tasks, organizational structure, asset values, or work processes. Moreover, he viewed people as ends rather than as means to ends. Scholars in the human relations movement were concerned about people, too, of course, but only to the extent that the "logic of sentiment" could be manipulated to improve productivity. Peter Drucker was concerned about a particular class of people, i.e., the chief executive officer and other decision-makers, but only to the extent that their decisions could help ensure the ongoing flourishing of the firm. In Greenleaf's view, people in organizations should be viewed as ends in themselves, as stakeholders, in fact, who harbor interests that may have little to do with the organization *per se*, but that, nonetheless, should be of concern to the organization.

Further, Greenleaf argued that one's identity as a servant must precede the exercise of her responsibility as a leader. In this sense, the servant-leader option should not be thought of as but one of several management theories or models that can be chosen *after* one assumes a leadership position. One's identity as a servant-leader cannot be selected "off the rack," as it were. It inheres, first, in one's emerging identity as a servant. "The servant-leader is servant first . . . It begins with a natural feeling that one wants to serve, to serve *first*. Then conscious choice brings one to aspire to lead. The person is sharply different from one who is *leader* first, perhaps because of the need to assuage an unusual power drive or to acquire material possessions."[1] In this sense, servant-leaders cannot be "trained." According to Greenleaf, "they are competent people to begin with, and they can be given a vision and a context of values. Beyond that they need only opportunity and encouragement to grow."[2]

---

1. Greenleaf, *Servant Leadership*, 27.
2. Greenleaf, *Servant Leadership*, 102.

Still further, Greenleaf recognized that leaders serve not just at the tops of organizations but more widely in and among any people gathered for a common purpose or a common enterprise. "*Leadership* going out to show the way—is available to everyone in the institution who has the competence, values, and temperament for it, from the chair to the least skilled individual."[3]

According to Greenleaf, an organization's priorities should include the intrinsic needs of its people. Good pay, benign working conditions, harmony in the workplace, and the "logic of sentiment" are not enough. He advocated, instead, for something more akin to the Greek concept of *eudemonia* or human flourishing. "The best test, and difficult to administer, is this: Do those served grow as persons? Do they, *while being served*, become healthier, wiser, freer, more autonomous, more likely themselves to become servants? *And*, what is the effect on the least privileged in society? Will they benefit or at least not be further deprived?"[4] (Greenleaf does not provide a rationale for the latter two questions, but this concern corresponds, as we shall see, to the Catholic social justice tradition's "preferential option for the poor.")

Human flourishing is a vague concept, however, and hence difficult to translate into concrete action. Clearly, though, the idea of human flourishing does not do justice to Greenleaf's work if it is construed solely in material terms. Elsewhere, Greenleaf attested to the experience of meaning and, in doing so, exhibited a passing understanding of existential literature, most notably the works of Hermann Hesse (1877–1962) and Albert Camus (1913–60). As we shall see, Greenleaf's failure to fully develop this idea is a notable weakness in his work.

Greenleaf's primary concern was people. Indeed, he viewed organizations as important, but only to the extent that they serve people. Indeed, "an institution is a gathering of persons who have accepted a common purpose, and a common discipline to guide the pursuit of that purpose, to the end that each involved person reaches higher fulfillment as a person, through *serving and being served* by the common venture, than would be achieved alone or in a less committed relationship."[5] Greenleaf used the term "care" when referring to the responsibilities of "trustees," i.e., those who exercise authority in organizations. Trustees are

3. Greenleaf, *Servant Leadership*, 109.

4. Greenleaf, *Servant Leadership*, 27.

5. Greenleaf, *Servant Leadership*, 250.

called to serve people, that is, to care for them. Further, the term "people" is broadly construed by Greenleaf. "The most important qualification for trustees should be that they care for the institution, which means that they care for *all of the people the institution touches*, and they are determined to make their caring count."[6]

Before moving on to the kinds of methods and techniques associated with servant leadership, we would do well to pause for a moment in order to appreciate the sheer breadth of Greenleaf's vision and the radical nature of his assessment of the challenges so many of today's organizations are facing: "The disease is more fundamental; the whole institutional arrangement of our society is flawed, and no aspirin-like treatment will deal with it. Nothing short of a comprehensive rebuilding, according to a deep yearning for a true and warm humanity, will do it."[7]

The servant-leader model also stakes out new ground in terms of its signature methods and techniques. Five are particularly noteworthy: deep listening; persuasion in place of coercion[8]; a *primus inter pares*, i.e., first among equals, leadership style[9] in which the servant-leader functions more as a facilitator or coach than a judge or wisdom figure; a tolerance for imperfection; and love grounded in one's sense of "unlimited liability" for the other.[10] Of these, deep listening may be the key to Greenleaf's thought because it speaks to the profound respect that should be accorded to all people. "*Listening*, as I use it here, is not just keeping still, or even remembering what is said. Listening is an attitude, an attitude toward other people and what they are trying to express. It begins with a genuine interest that is manifest in close attention, and it goes on to understanding in depth—whence comes wisdom. It is openness to communication—openness within the widest possible frame of reference—openness to hear the prophetic voices that are trying to speak to us all the time."[11]

Greenleaf did not dismiss out of hand the many other methods and techniques associated with the several language games examined in the preceding chapter. He acknowledged the value of organizational goals

6. Greenleaf, *Servant Leadership*, 68.

7. Greenleaf, *Servant Leadership*, 255.

8. Greenleaf, *Servant Leadership*, 44.

9. Greenleaf, *Servant Leadership*, 74.

10. Greenleaf, *Servant Leadership*, 52.

11. Greenleaf, *Servant Leadership*, 313.

and strategies and the need to rationally implement policies and initiatives, too.[12] He argued, however, that these other methods and techniques will be more effective and their effects longer lasting if they are grounded in deep listening, persuasion, the collegial exercise of authority, a tolerance for imperfection, and love.

> The first order of business is to build a group of people who, under the influence of the institution, grow taller and become healthier, stronger, more autonomous. Some institutions achieve distinction for a short time by the intelligent use of people, but it is not a happy achievement, and eminence, so derived does not last long. Others aspire to distinction (or the reduction of problems) by embracing gimmicks: profit plans, paternalism, motivational management. There is nothing wrong with these in a people-building institution. But in a people-using institution they are like aspirin—sometimes stimulating and pain relieving, and they may procure an immediate measurable improvement of sorts. But these are the means whereby an institution moves from people-using to people-building.[13]

Again, evocative language of this sort is not typically associated with the kinds of theories and models most familiar to practitioners. It can be disorienting and potentially disruptive. It may be more helpful, therefore, to think of servant leadership as a disciplined discernment process.

The illustration employed in chapter 1 can be helpful in this regard. Again, it was suggestive rather than exhaustive. Consider two of the management challenges noted in chapter 1, this time through the lens of servant leadership. In the first, a potential scandal involving an allegation of sexual harassment was detailed. Again, the chair of the board had recently learned of a credible accusation of sexual harassment lodged by a low-ranking employee against the executive director of a nonprofit organization. The executive director is highly regarded and is himself a prominent figure in the community. He is also a longtime friend of the board chair. The clients served by the nonprofit organization are themselves vulnerable individuals, and the organization is heavily dependent on the financial support of the community.

It would not be uncommon in an instance of this kind for a board chair to privately "counsel" the executive director. In other instances, she might speak to the human resources director or to the organization's

---

12. Greenleaf, *Servant Leadership*, 71.

13. Greenleaf, *Servant Leadership*, 53.

attorney. There is every likelihood, in fact, that an "accommodation" of some sort would be reached and that a non-disclosure agreement would be signed by all parties. More often than not, every effort would be made to avoid the taint of scandal.

As detailed in figure 2, the discernment process implied in the servant-leader model would proceed differently.

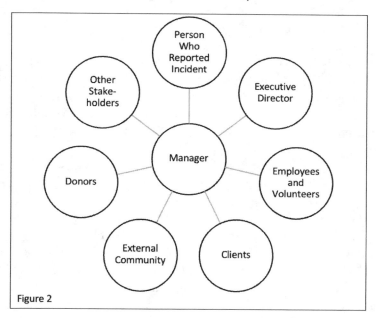

Figure 2

Again, "the best test, and difficult to administer, is this: Do those served grow as persons? Do they, *while being served*, become healthier, wiser, freer, more autonomous, more likely themselves to become servants? *And*, what is the effect on the least privileged in society? Will they benefit or at least not be further deprived?"[14] Following these principles, the board chair might assess the potential impacts of the accusation on all of the individuals who are significantly touched by the organization, paying particular attention, all the while, to those who are the most vulnerable or least powerful with respect to the matter at hand. The board chair might then make every effort throughout the ensuing process to view each of these individuals as persons rather than as "characters" played in an unfolding drama, i.e., friend, accuser or victim, accused or perpetrator, colleague, client, fellow employee, or donor.

14. Greenleaf, *Servant Leadership*, 27.

It is unlikely that this kind of discernment process would dictate any particular outcome. It is not designed to function as an algorithm, hence our use of the term "discernment." Moreover, Greenleaf resisted every effort to formulate hard and fast decision rules. Again, he viewed leadership as an art and managerial challenges as situational in nature. The use of a discernment process of this kind would impose, however, a certain discipline in the board chair's exercise of her responsibilities with respect to this situation.

In a second management challenge outlined in chapter 1, a chief executive officer had concluded that a certain product had reached the end of its life cycle and that it would soon need to be abandoned or significantly reengineered. The kind of discernment process suggested by Greenleaf could lead to the identification of a broad array of individuals who could potentially be affected by this decision, including the firm's employees, their family members, the firm's long-term suppliers, its retail partners, and its shareholders, too. Again, every effort should be made to ascertain any significant impacts that might accrue with respect to each of these stakeholders as people.

We cannot know in advance if the outcome would be different in this instance if another decision rule was employed, for instance, the maximization of shareholder wealth rubric. Nevertheless, the discipline imposed in the discernment process implied in the servant-leader model would likely change the kinds of conversations that ensued among all of the affected parties, and it could suggest possibilities for some that might not otherwise have been considered.

It should be readily apparent why the servant-leader model appeals to Christians and to other people of faith who hope to better integrate their beliefs and their core values into their lives in the secular world. Indeed, Greenleaf explicitly appealed to the "wisdom literature" associated with the world's great religions.

Beyond this, the servant-leader model can be viewed as an antidote to the two overarching deficiencies found in the eight sets of management theories and models examined in chapter 2: first, that the understandings of human motivation undergirding each of these approaches are thin; and, second, that they are oriented almost exclusively to instrumental ends. Each of these deficiencies will be addressed in turn.

As noted in the preceding chapter, administrative management theory and management science essentially ignore the concept of human motivation in work settings. As positivists, behavioralists focus on behavior and hence have little to say about human motivation. Scientific management and those who promote the maximization of shareholder wealth perspective understand human motivation to be exclusively economic in nature. The same is true for MBO and other productivity and incentive schemes. Some interest in the intrinsic "meaning" of work is hinted at in the quality literature, but this line of thinking is woefully underdeveloped in this body of work. The dominant language games in management theory and practice simply do not address human motivation in any substantial way.

As noted above, Greenleaf demonstrated a passing acquaintance with existential thought, most notably, the literary works of Hermann Hesse and Albert Camus, but much less so the critical and systematic thought of certain non-religious philosophers, including Martin Heidegger (1889–1976) and Jean-Paul Sartre (1905–80), or the insights of religious existential thinkers beginning with Søren Kierkegaard (1813–55). Brent M. Keith, a former chief executive officer of the Greenleaf Center, drew more explicitly on Viktor Frankl, an existential psychologist, in promoting servant leadership.[15] Again, however, the centrality of "meaning" experienced in work and in life, more generally, is not fully developed by Keith or by other proponents of the servant-leader model.

Meaning—in the existential sense—goes well beyond the final step in Maslow's hierarchy of needs. In fact, self-actualization is a vague concept that may simply acknowledge the fact that the need for external rewards is sated in some and that others are moved at one point or another by a latent desire to build or to create. Even this latter understanding can be relatively shallow in nature, however, if it refers to nothing more than the all too common desire to "make a name for oneself" or "leave a mark."

An existential understanding of meaning as a powerful and universal motivator goes deeper. Meaning can be understood as a personal sense of unity and purpose distinct from the satisfaction of any physical or psychological need. Although he resists identification as an existential thinker, Alasdair MacIntyre affirmed this view. According to MacIntyre, life can be understood as a narrative "quest"[16] in which we craft our own unique stories, stories that are invariably oriented to the experience of meaning. "I am the subject of a history that is my own and no one

---

15. Keith, *The Case for Servant Leadership*, 61–62.
16. MacIntyre, *After Virtue*, 175.

else's, that has its own peculiar meaning. When someone complains—as do some of those who attempt to commit suicide—that his or her life is meaningless, he or she is often and perhaps characteristically complaining that the narrative of their life has become unintelligible to them, that it lacks any point, any movement toward a climax or a telos."[17] Servais Pinckaers (1925–2008) concurred using language that is explicitly Christian: "The problem of life's meaning and goal is primordial . . . Since the question of life's goal or ultimate end is so important, we might define Christian ethics as the science that teaches us the meaning of life. It shows us the supreme end toward which all our actions should be directed, the end that gives them meaning, value, and wholeness."[18]

In the view of existential philosophers and theologians, the "drive for meaning" is prompted by five realities that together define the human condition. One, the prospect of suffering and death and the nagging sense of life's absurdity prompt a degree of dread or *angst* in reflective human beings. Two, the creation or discovery of meaning is fundamental to who we are as persons. It is universal in nature. The felt need for a sense of meaning demands satisfaction. Clifford Geertz thus argued that "the drive to make sense out of experience, to give it form and order, is evidently as real and as pressing as the more familiar biological needs."[19] Meaning cannot be achieved in the satisfaction of an ephemeral disposition or need. Three, meaning entails the whole person, not just a particular aspect or dimension of a life, e.g., work life, a personal affiliation, a defining relationship, or identity as a member of a particular community. Meaning cannot be compartmentalized. It must be experienced as a natural unity. Four, meaning must be appropriated at the personal level; it cannot be imposed from outside. Five, meaning is oriented to the future. This explains why it is experienced as a purposeful drive.

Frankl's thought is helpful in this regard. In *Man's Search for Meaning* (1946), Frankl drew on his experiences in two Nazi concentration camps in defining human beings as meaning-seeking beings. He further explained that meaning can be experienced in one or more of three ways: first, in work and in the execution of other kinds of creative tasks; second, in relationships that are central to our lives; and, third, in the attitude one assumes in the face of an unavoidable circumstance. "Life can be

17. MacIntyre, *After Virtue*, 217.

18. Pinckaers, *Sources*, 23.

19. Geertz, *The Interpretation of Cultures*, 140.

meaningful in a three-fold way: one, through *what we give* to life (in terms of our creative acts); two, by *what we take* from the world (in terms of our experiencing values); and three, through *the stand we take* toward a fate we no longer can change."[20]

Others have explored these dimensions of meaning from a religious or spiritual perspective. Paul Tillich, a Lutheran, focused on the individual's need to "create" meaning: "Man's being includes his relation to meanings."[21] Further, "spiritual self-affirmation occurs in every moment in which man lives creatively in the various spheres of meaning. 'Creative,' in this context, has the sense, not of original creativity as performed by the genius, but of living spontaneously in action and reaction."[22] Martin Buber (1878–1965) drew on his roots in Hasidic Judaism in affirming authentic relationships with people and with God as precursors to the existential experience of meaning: "The basic word 'I-You' can only be spoken with one's whole being. The basic word 'I-It' can never be spoken with one's whole being . . . 'You' has no borders."[23] Miguel De Unamuno (1864–1936), a Catholic, joined Frankl in linking his understanding of meaning to the stance one takes against an unwanted future over which one has little or no control. In doing so, he invoked the tragicomic hero of Miguel de Cervantes's novel *Don Quixote*: "This personal and affective starting point for all philosophy and all religion is the tragic sense of life."[24] Further, "this tragic sense is the spring of heroic achievements."[25]

Consider, too, the substantial legacy of Karl Rahner, a Jesuit who studied under Martin Heidegger for a time. Rahner would go on to have a significant influence on the work of the Second Vatican Council (1962–65). Rahner did not believe that our understanding of human purpose is predetermined. It must be selected or developed from among an available set of options. "There are no ultimate basic attitudes, no absolute standards of value or systems of co-ordinates for determining the meaning of existence."[26] Freedom thus served as the root of Rahner's existential analysis. His understanding of freedom differed, however, from

20. Frankl, *Psychotherapy and Existentialism*, 115.

21. Tillich, *The Courage to Be*, 50.

22. Tillich, *The Courage to Be*, 46.

23. Buber, *I and Thou*, 54–55.

24. De Unamuno, *Tragic Sense of Life*, 37.

25. De Unamuno, *Tragic Sense of Life*, 125.

26. Rahner, "Intellectual Honesty," 262.

the anemic notions with which most of us are familiar. In Rahner's view, freedom touches on the very meaning of human existence. "Freedom is first of all 'freedom of being.' It is not merely a quality of an act and capacity exercised at some time, but a transcendental mark of human existence itself."[27] Indeed, human beings "determine,"[28] "realize,"[29] or "form"[30] themselves. In Rahner's view, a human being can be understood as a "mystery,"[31] indeed, as a "question" with no self-evident "answer."[32]

Like other existential thinkers, Rahner believed that human beings define themselves in the context of an uncertain future. "Man is *par excellence* the being which is *in fieri*, the being which in virtue of its very nature (in virtue of nature and grace alike) is bound to keep itself open to an ever-greater future."[33] Life is thus experienced as "a venturing, planning, devising anticipation of the future."[34] Indeed, the past is constantly reworked in the light of an emerging future.[35]

This goes well beyond the typical fare of today's management literature, of course. Nevertheless, an existential conception of meaning lies at the heart of Greenleaf's work. This brief excursus into what is certainly unfamiliar territory for some can thus be helpful. Most importantly, it reveals the remarkable depth and breadth of the belief system into which Greenleaf consciously or unconsciously tapped.

Further, it reminds us why we care so much about our work. In our best moments, work satisfies our felt need to define and develop ourselves in our creative acts, hence the appeal of enriched jobs and empowered teams and hence the lure of leadership positions, too, positions that often draw upon a rich pallet of opportunity. At its best, our work also engages us in meaningful relationships, a phenomenon developed to great effect by scholars in the human relations movement. Great frustration and failure can be experienced in our work lives as well. Frankl's threefold understanding of meaning thus rings true as it pertains to work and to leadership opportunities, in particular.

27. Rahner, "Theology of Freedom," 287.

28. Rahner, "The Experiment with Man," 212.

29. Rahner, "Theology of Freedom," 195.

30. Rahner, "On Christian Dying," 287.

31. Rahner, "Proving Oneself," 278.

32. Rahner, "Thoughts," 14.

33. Rahner, "Being Open," 27.

34. Rahner, "The Dignity and Freedom," 237.

35. Rahner, "The Sin of Adam," 253.

Still further, a full appreciation of the roles the search for meaning and the experience of meaning play in our lives can reveal others we encounter as autonomous individuals who are seeking meaning in their own lives. Frankl believed that healthy individuals living in healthy environments are compelled to ascribe to others the very same dignity they claim for themselves. Heidegger agreed in holding that authentic living can contribute to the development of an ethic that esteems the other not for his or her "handiness" but for the intrinsic value of the other's own unique journey toward authentic living.[36] Jean-Paul Sartre concurred, and, in doing so, revealed the bankruptcy of certain assumptions embedded in the kinds of unhealthy environments and systems in which far too many of us live and work:

> I can choose myself as looking at the Other's look and can build my subjectivity upon the collapse of the subjectivity of the Other. It is this attitude which we shall call *indifference toward others*. Then we are dealing with a kind of *blindness* with respect to others . . . I practice then a sort of factual solipsism; others are those forms which pass by in the street, those magic objects which are capable of acting at a distance and upon which I can act by means of determined conduct. I scarcely notice them; I act as if I were alone in the world. I brush against "people" as I brush against a wall; I avoid them as I avoid obstacles. Their freedom-as-object is for me only their "coefficient of adversity." I do not even imagine that they *look at* me. Of course, they have some knowledge of me, but this knowledge does not touch me . . . Those "people" are functions: the ticket-collector is only the function of collecting tickets; the café waiter is nothing but the function of serving the patrons. In this capacity they will be most useful if I know their *keys* and those "master words" which can release their mechanisms.[37]

We are again confronted by the sheer breadth and radical nature of Greenleaf's vision: "The unrelenting demand is that each of us confront the exacting terms of our own existence."[38] The implications for organizations may be even more profound. According to Greenleaf: "The new ethic, simply but quite completely stated, will be: *The work exists for the person as much as the person exists for the work*. Put another way, the

36. Heidegger, *Being and Time*, 274.

37. Sartre, *Being and Nothingness*, 495.

38. Greenleaf, *Servant Leadership*, 25.

business exists as much to provide meaningful work to the person as it exists to provide a product or service to the customer . . . Speaking to those in business who presume to manage, it is important that this principle be embraced as an ethic and not simply as a 'device' to achieve harmony or increase productivity or reduce turnover."[39] Moreover, the ethic to which Greenleaf subscribed pertains not just to the worker's employment relationship but to her "life goals,"[40] too. The servant-leader model can thus serve as a powerful counterweight to the anemic understandings of human motivation espoused in the language games of management theory and practice examined in chapter 2.

Greenleaf was not alone in this regard, however. As we shall see, his focus on human flourishing is mirrored in Thomist personalism, a "movement" in twentieth-century philosophy and theology that seems to have been unknown to Greenleaf.

The second overarching criticism detailed in the preceding chapter pertains to the narrow ends or objectives articulated in the dominant language games of management theory and practice, which have been variously identified as profit, efficiency, a policy goal of one kind or another, effectiveness, results, the optimal use of resources, the maximization of shareholder wealth, and conformance to specifications. With the possible exception of Peter Drucker, scant purchase is provided in any of these language games for foregrounding moral claims of one kind or another or for the consideration of any social justice claims. As a result, any disparate treatment of communities, collateral damage, or societal externalities that could result are all too easily ignored. Again, little oxygen is available in the boardroom or the management suite or on the shop floor for claims pertaining to moral behavior or matters of justice beyond that which may or may not be legal. These kinds of concerns simply have no standing in the language games practiced in most of today's organizations.

In contrast, Greenleaf's understanding of service pertains to people, and not just to people who are formally associated with the firm or the organization. His use of the term "service" applies to "all who are touched by the institution or its work" in the expectation that they, too, will "become, because of that influence, healthier, wiser, freer, more autonomous,

39. Greenleaf, *Servant Leadership*, 154–55.
40. Greenleaf, *Servant Leadership*, 169.

more likely themselves to become servants."[41] Further, "any institution that does not strive with all its resources, human and material, to achieve the reasonable and the possible in these dimensions is not being adequately cared for by its trustees."[42] Indeed, a standard of care reflecting "unlimited liability"[43] is endorsed by Greenleaf with respect to "all who are touched" by the institution.

Again, the boldness of Greenleaf's diagnosis and his prescription, too, is breathtaking. Greenleaf's concept of servant leadership goes well beyond the thinking of those who were associated with the dominant language games of management theory and practice in the twentieth century.

We are now in a position to further clarify the distinction drawn in this text between management and leadership. Whereas management can be understood as the responsibility for and performance of any one or more of several organizational or societal functions, e.g., planning, organizing, staffing, directing, coordinating, reporting, and budgeting, in a manner oriented to ends external to the manager, leadership can be defined as the balanced exercise of these same responsibilities in service to a broader array of stakeholders in a manner constrained by the leader's internalized virtues and informed by values and intellectual commitments drawn from a larger belief system, but oriented, nonetheless, to ends sanctioned by the organization or by society. Authentic leadership can thus be distinguished from management in four ways: first, it is oriented to service; second, the scope of its concern extends to a broad array of stakeholders; third, the exercise of its responsibilities is constrained by virtues internal to the leader; and fourth, the exercise of its responsibilities is informed by values and intellectual commitments drawn from a larger belief system.

Again, this distinction is somewhat arbitrary. Some associate leadership almost exclusively with visioning and planning. Greenleaf did not eschew either function. In fact, he described "the failure (or refusal) of a leader to foresee as an *ethical* failure."[44] Further, visioning and planning are specifically cited in the above definitions for both management and leadership. At the same time, the four elements unique to the definition

41. Greenleaf, *Servant Leadership,* 27.

42. Greenleaf, *Servant Leadership,* 143.

43. Greenleaf, *Servant Leadership,* 52.

44. Greenleaf, *Servant Leadership,* 39.

of leadership proposed here celebrate Greenleaf's seminal contributions to the management literature. The servant-leader is oriented to service, more specifically to the service of people. Further, the servant-leader attends not just to the material needs of people but to their personal development, too, and not just to the personal development of people contractually associated with the firm or the organization. The servant-leader attends to the development of all who are "touched" by the firm or the organization in one way or another. Still further, the servant-leader is constrained by virtues she has internalized. Finally, the servant-leader's exercise of her responsibilities is informed, not just by the firm's objective measures of performance, e.g., efficiency, financial objectives, the accomplishment of a policy goal, market share, etc., but by values and intellectual commitments associated with a larger belief system as well, a larger belief system that—more likely than not—will have been embraced prior to the servant-leader's engagement with the firm or the organization she serves.

As valuable as Greenleaf's contributions have been, three criticism are in order. First, despite his obvious appeal to the "wisdom literature" associated with the world's great religions, Greenleaf's argument is crafted in teleological terms. He certainly edged up to a deontological claim on behalf of servant leadership, but backed off at the very last moment, arguing, instead, that servant leadership works better than other management theories and models. This is surprising given the compelling case Greenleaf made for servant leadership. In the end, committed Christians and other believers are looking not so much for a more effective way to manage as for a way to express their Christian identities more authentically in the workplace, indeed, a way to more fully integrate their faith commitments into their roles as managers and as leaders.

Second, Greenleaf is eloquent in arguing for the human development of an array of stakeholders, but he does not provide a precise formula for balancing competing demands and different time horizons. This is to be expected, perhaps, given his assumption that leadership is an art. Something more needs to be said in this regard, however. In another era, Greenleaf might have appealed to the virtue of prudence or to other traditional virtues, but he was largely silent with respect to this possibility.

Third, Greenleaf's prescription for developing servant-leaders is incomplete. He dismissed training as the answer. He also decried the decline of liberal education and the waning influence of churches, but offered no curriculum, as such, in this regard and certainly no program of formation. Greenleaf referred, instead, to a "natural feeling"[45] acquired "through a long arduous discipline of learning to listen, a discipline sufficiently sustained that the automatic response to any problem is to listen first."[46] Clearly drawing on his association with the Religious Society of Friends, Greenleaf also pointed to our "*inner conscience—our inward moral sense of what is right and what is wrong.*"[47] Indeed, "if a flaw in the world is to be remedied, to the servant, the process of change starts *in here*, in the servant, not *out there*. This is a difficult concept for that busybody, modern man."[48] As appealing as this good counsel might be, it is entirely too vague a prescription given the nature of the leadership challenge now apparent in so many organizations and in society, too. Again, Greenleaf might have appealed in another era to the need for virtue, a topic we will turn to in the next chapter.

Collectively, the several management language games examined in chapter 2 and Robert Greenleaf's servant-leader model represent the wisdom of the world as it pertains to management and leadership in organizations. A table comparing these several language games is provided in appendix 1.

45. Greenleaf, *Servant Leadership*, 27.

46. Greenleaf, *Servant Leadership*, 31.

47. Covey, "Foreword," 4.

48. Greenleaf, *Servant Leadership*, 57.

Chapter 4

The Case for Moral Virtue

TWO OF OUR FOUR preliminary arguments have now been advanced. In chapter 2, the several management theories and models now available to us were revealed as useful, but deficient in two important respects: first, they harbor severely circumscribed understandings of human motivation; and second, they are oriented to instrumental ends variously disclosed as profit, efficiency, one or more particular policy goals, effectiveness, results, the optimal use of resources, the maximization of shareholder wealth, and conformance to specifications. In chapter 3, the servant-leader model attributed to Robert Greenleaf was introduced as an alternative, but it was revealed, nonetheless, as poorly rooted and hence weak. As we shall see, the two missing elements in the servant-leader model are, first, virtue and, second, values and intellectual commitment anchored outside the organization. And so our third argument: virtue and externally grounded values and intellectual commitments are needed in the exercise of authentic leadership in all kinds of organizations.

Our brief excursus into the existential concept of meaning was acknowledged as "unfamiliar territory." This is no less so in the case of virtue. As we have seen, the principal management theories and models of the last century have had little to say about virtue. At best, virtue is viewed in these language games as a private matter that has no place in the boardroom or the management suite or on the shop floor.

Virtue is unfamiliar territory in the broader culture, too, and this is so for reasons that pertain both to religion and the intellectual history of the West. *Sola gratia*, i.e., by grace alone, was adopted as a rallying cry in the sixteenth century in both the Lutheran tradition and the Reformed tradition. In embracing this principle, the Protestant Reformers rejected the view that human beings can in any sense earn or merit salvation. The very idea that human beings can play any role in developing or forming virtue was dismissed out of hand. Virtue is entirely God's work, the Reformers argued. What we perceive to be virtues are gifts that cannot be earned or merited. The Reformed tradition's understanding of "sanctification," in particular, holds that any apparent growth in "godliness" is entirely attributable to the store of grace accumulated by Jesus in his death and resurrection. John Calvin even argued that virtues are gifted out of this store of grace to those who are predestined to damnation in order to ensure the right ordering of society. Virtue lies entirely beyond the influence or control of any human being.

This explains, perhaps, Robert Greenleaf's reluctance to assert the need for formation in the virtues in the ongoing exercise of servant leadership. Greenleaf identified Christianity as but one of several "wisdom traditions" in order to broaden the appeal of the servant-leader model, of course, but he located the innate desire to serve in one's "inner conscience," i.e., an inward moral sense of what is right and what is wrong[1] as well, and described the innate desire to serve as "natural." Both views are consistent with a Protestant theology of grace.

Remarkably, Roman Catholicism also pivoted away from virtue ethics in the wake of the Reformation. A two-tiered understanding of discipleship developed in the post-Tridentine church: on the one hand, a path pursued in a rigorous formation experience designed exclusively for priests and for members of religious communities; on the other, a nominal Christianity oriented more explicitly to the Ten Commandments than to Matthew's version of the Beatitudes. Virtue was thus deemed supererogatory, i.e., as something "good," but certainly not expected of secular Christians. According to Servais Pinckaers, "we thus find Protestant thought in agreement with post-Tridentine Catholic tradition, at least on this point: the relegation of the Sermon on the Mount to a marginal position with respect to [our] central teachings. The Decalogue now claimed first position with respect to [Catholic] moral teaching and in Protestant morality."[2]

This new moral regime was embraced in short order. According to Charles Taylor, "it was perhaps more than understandable that,

---

1. Covey, "Foreword," 4.
2. Pinckaers, *Sources*, 139.

after the terrible struggles around deep theological issues to do with grace, free will, and predestination, many people should hunger for a less theologically elaborate faith which would guide them toward holy living . . . What is significant is that the plea for a holy life came to be reductively seen as a call to center on morality, and morality, in turn, as a matter of conduct . . . Religion is narrowed to moralism."[3] This tendency was prominently featured in the Catholic Jansenism of seventeenth- and eighteenth-century France and in the Reformed tradition as well.

This turn away from a more traditional understanding of virtue was further accelerated during the Enlightenment, a new, wholly secular way of thinking that celebrated reason and the scientific method. Any conception of virtue grounded in a religious belief system was dismissed as an outdated form of obscurantism by those on the cutting edge of seventeenth- and eighteenth-century philosophy and science.

According to Taylor, Reformers and Roman Catholics who sensed the need for something more suffered from these developments, which deprived succeeding generations of Christians of a robust understanding of virtue ethics, a tradition refined, in fact, over the first 1,600 years of the church's existence. As Taylor has argued, the abandonment of this traditional wisdom may be the source of much of our discontent, most notably in the world of work and in our politics, too: "There may be—and I want to argue, frequently is—a lack of fit between what people believe, as it were, officially and consciously believe, even pride themselves on believing on the one hand, and what they need to make sense of some of their moral reactions on the other."[4]

Fortunately, virtue ethics has made something of a comeback over the course of the last forty years. Led by Alasdair MacIntyre, Philippa Foot (1920–2010), Deirdre N. McCloskey (b. 1942), and others, virtue ethics is experiencing a revival of sorts. As we shall see, Thomistic personalism has played a significant role in this regard as well. Still, the resurgence of virtue ethics is facing formidable opposition in the academy. Postmodernists are skeptical of virtue ethics, and few scholars show any interest in the wearisome "grace versus merit" debates of the sixteenth and seventeenth centuries.

The Second Vatican Council's affirmation that "all are called to holiness" and its reimagining of the church as a pilgrim people may provide

3. Taylor, *A Secular Age*, 225.
4. Taylor, *Sources of the Self*, 9.

an opportunity, however, an opportunity in which we might reclaim the role virtues have historically played in the spiritual lives of Christians. This ongoing re-conception of discipleship should enable us to side-step any concerns we might still harbor concerning the precise nature of the role we play in the development of virtue. Whether our progression in holiness is attributable to supernatural gifts, to formation, or to some combination of the two should make no practical difference as we plumb the unrealized potential of a Christian conception of virtue. For our purposes, growth in the virtues can be understood *either* as a life of responsible discipleship *or* as an irresistible response to God's grace. We can leave it to theologians on both sides of the Protestant/Catholic divide to work out their respective positions in this regard.

This rather lengthy introduction is intended to orient readers to a topic rarely addressed in the management literature. Having dipped our toe into these unfamiliar waters, we can now proceed a bit more methodically. We will begin with a brief primer on virtue, a primer that will include both a conceptual overview and a high-level historical analysis. Because the term "virtue" is used in so many different ways in our culture, both should prove helpful. We will then introduce the first iteration of an existential model pertaining to moral virtue. Finally, we will make the case for moral virtue in management theory and practice.

A virtue can be understood as a human excellence or *arete*. Following Aristotle, but with a Christian gloss, we traditionally categorize individual virtues as theological, intellectual, or moral in nature. The theological virtues include faith, hope, and charity. One cannot be trained in the theological virtues as such, nor are they developed by habit. The theological virtues are celebrated as "infused" gifts. The intellectual virtues include wisdom, science, and understanding,[5] all three of which can be developed through explicit instruction and the disciplined application of certain decision rules or through the affirmation of certain intellectual commitments. In contrast, the moral virtues can only be developed by habit or sustained practice. Our primary concern here is the moral virtues.

Although there are competing taxonomies, four moral virtues, i.e., prudence, justice, temperance, and fortitude or courage, in particular, are traditionally thought of as all-encompassing in nature and hence as cardinal or "hinge" virtues. Deirdre N. McCloskey thus argues that prudence

---

5. Pegis, *Introduction to St. Thomas*, 568–77.

encompasses "know-how, foresight, *phronesis*, self-interest, and contextual rationality." Justice implies both "social balance and honesty." Temperance requires "individual balance and restraint, chastity, sobriety, and humility." And "autonomy, daring, endurance, and steadfastness" are part and parcel of the cardinal virtue of fortitude or courage.[6] Aquinas attributed this understanding of the cardinal virtues, not just to Aristotle, but to two of the early church fathers, too: Ambrose (338–97) and Gregory the Great (539–604). McCloskey argues persuasively that structuring any discussion of the virtues around the three theological virtues and the four cardinal or hinge virtues is advisable because these taxonomies enable us to tap into the West's rich patrimony of moral thinking.[7]

As a practical matter, prudence or right judgment is often thought of as the most useful of the cardinal virtues. As noted by Paul J. Wadell, "prudence connects the everyday with the ultimate."[8] In turn, "justice is doing what needs to be done in the way it needs to be done"; and temperance and fortitude or courage "both pertain . . . to impediments to action. Their focus is the emotions, particularly when they make doing good more difficult instead of facilitating the doing of good."[9]

Further, moral virtues are located in particular individuals rather than in particular acts. Reflecting this view, McCloskey orients moral virtue to "being" rather than to "doing": "A virtue is a habit of the heart, a stable disposition, a settled state of character, a durable, educated characteristic of someone to exercise *her will to be* good."[10] She follows Aquinas in advancing this claim: "Virtue disposes to that which is best and the best is the end."[11] Prudence can thus be described as a predisposition to discern wisely, justice as a latent ability to apply the law rightly,[12] and temperance and fortitude as personal orientations to a larger good. Indeed, Aquinas described virtue as an inclination or a power rather than an act, a decision, or a behavior as such. As explained by Pinckaers, "virtue is not a habitual way of acting . . . It is a personal capacity for action, the

6. McCloskey, *The Bourgeois Virtues*, 66.

7. McCloskey, *The Bourgeois Virtues*, 361.

8. Wadell, "Virtue," 1005.

9. Wadell, "Virtue," 1005–06.

10. McCloskey, *The Bourgeois Virtues*, 64. Emphasis added.

11. Pegis, *Introduction to St. Thomas*, 567.

12. MacIntyre, *After Virtue*, 152.

fruit of a series of fine actions, a power for progress and perfection. In the tradition of Aristotle, it is deemed a *habitus*."[13]

Still further, a moral virtue is properly ordered or oriented to a particular end. Moral virtues are traditionally thought of as habits oriented to the good. Conversely, a vice can be described as a habit oriented to that which is evil or to that which could impede our realization of the good. The good, in turn, can be understood as something that speaks to a larger human purpose or *telos*. It concerns more than a particular good or an ephemeral experience of one kind or another.

Over much of the last 2,300 years, philosophers in the West have tended to follow Aristotle in defining this overarching *telos* as *eudaemonia*, a term that refers not to happiness *pe se*, but to the concept of human flourishing. According Wadell, "a virtue is a characteristic way of behavior which makes both actions and persons good and which also enables one to fulfill the *purpose of life*."[14] Further, "when anyone both possesses and exercises the virtues, that person is brought to the wholeness proper to human nature; conversely, a lack of virtue constitutes a depraved nature and a diminished self."[15] Recall from chapter 3 that some have further defined human flourishing as the individual experience of meaning. This is consistent, in fact, with Wadell's orientation of virtue to the larger "purpose of a life."

Finally, the moral virtues are expressed in action that is positively informed by certain values and intellectual commitments. As noted in chapter 1, Christians have traditionally grounded these values and intellectual commitments in the Old Testament prophets's condemnation of idolatry and the indifference exhibited by Israel's leaders to the plight of those who lived on the margins of life, i.e., the *anawim*, in the Beatitudes delineated in chapter 5 of Matthew's Gospel, in the parable of the sheep and the goats in chapter 25 of Matthew's Gospel, and in the commandment to love one another in chapter 13 of John's Gospel.

As helpful as this conceptual analysis might be, our primer in the moral virtues would be incomplete without an accompanying historical overview. Although we now tend to think of virtue as a Christian concept, virtues were also prized in the pre-Christian world, most notably with respect to the twin poles of honor and shame that so circumscribed

---

13. Pinckaers, *Sources*, 364.

14. Wadell, "Virtue," 998. Emphasis added.

15. Wadell, "Virtue," 998.

life in the ancient world. According to MacIntyre, "in many pre-modern societies, a man's honor is what is due him and his kin and his household by reason of their having their due place in the social order. To dishonor someone is to fail to acknowledge what is thus due."[16] Like all moral virtues, this sense of honor and shame pertains more to identity or "being" than to "doing" *per se*.

The ancient Greeks thought a great deal about virtue. Socrates (468– 399 BCE) equated virtue and knowledge; Plato (427–346 BCE) located the virtues in the habitual and loyal performance of one's predetermined role in society; and, as detailed above, Aristotle (383–321 BCE) oriented the virtues to *eudaemonia* or human flourishing. Most importantly, the ancient Greeks distinguished between and among three types of knowledge: *episteme*, i.e., intellectual knowledge; *phronesis*, i.e., practical or moral knowledge; and *techne*, i.e., skill in application. In an Aristotelian moral framework, virtues, i.e., habits oriented to human flourishing, are honed and perfected through intellectual training or *episteme*, to be sure, but they require practice as well.

The ancient Romans were also concerned about virtue. The leading lights of Rome borrowed extensively from the philosophers of ancient Greece, most productively, perhaps, from the Greek stoics and their understanding of moral behavior. In fact, Roman stoicism competed toe-to-toe with Christianity for hearts and minds in the earliest days of Christianity. Eschewing Plato's understanding of forms, the stoics celebrated virtue as a disciplined adherence to the moral law of the universe. According to Rome's stoics, "men as rational beings can become conscious of the laws to which they necessarily conform, and that virtue consists of conscious assent to, vice in dissent from, the inevitable order of things."[17] The stoics's understanding of life was not moderated by any concept of grace and could be unremittingly dour as a result. "Desire, hope, and fear, pleasure, and pain are against reason and nature," they argued; "one should cultivate a passionless absence of desire and disregard of pleasure and pain. They called this principled stance *apathy*."[18]

Christianity absorbed much of this thought in reimagining the role the virtues play in our lives. We see vestiges of Greek and Roman thought, for instance, in the wisdom of the early church fathers pertaining to the

16. MacIntyre, *After Virtue*, 116.

17. MacIntyre, *After Virtue*, 105.

18. MacIntyre, *After Virtue*, 106.

virtues. Although platonic categories tended to be favored during the church's first millennium, Aristotle's ethics were influential as well. And in the thirteenth century, Thomas Aquinas (1225–74) embraced Aristotle's ethical framework altogether. To this day, it remains a privileged framework from within which to understand virtue in the Catholic Church.

As noted above, this disciplined and very traditional way of thinking about our moral obligations was largely abandoned in the wake of the sectarian rivalries of the sixteenth and seventeenth centuries and, then, during the time of the Enlightenment. This does not mean, however, that Enlightenment philosophers did not recognize the need for standards pertaining to behavior. David Hume (1711–76), anchored his moral thinking in the complex emotional lives of human beings; Immanuel Kant (1724–1804) turned to natural reason as an alternative to virtue; Jeremy Bentham (1748–1832) calculated "utiles"; and Geoge Wilhelm Frederich Hegel (1770–1831) defined moral behavior expansively as that which is in accord with the "world spirit" or *zeitgeist*.

Because of its singular importance in European history, most notably its association with the United Nations's Universal Declaration of Human Rights (1948), we would do well to linger a bit over Kant's understanding of virtue. Kant's ethical framework demonstrates the challenge of living in a world that has abandoned God and, as a result, any traditional conception of moral virtue. In place of prudence, Kant promoted "categorical imperatives," binding principles derived through the individual's exercise of her reason. According to Kant, we should "act only on that maxim through which you can at the same time will that it should be a universal law."[19] Following this logic, a moral person would not lie because she would not want to be lied to. Kant grounded his assumption of human dignity in the fact that human beings reason and hence are capable of crafting categorical imperatives on their own. (Why a belief in human dignity should follow from our ability to reason is not explained, however.)

Although Kant's scheme is generally recognized as a noble effort to underwrite a non-theological but nonetheless universal morality, it fails in three ways. First, Kant's concept of the categorical imperative is better categorized as an intellectual virtue than a moral virtue *per se*. He did little more than proffer a method for articulating decision rules. Habit and formation play no role in Kant's ethics. Second, Kant's ethics are

19. Kant, *Groundwork*, 88.

rigid. He goes to great lengths—tortuous lengths, in fact—in prescribing how a man should respond to an ax-murderer demanding to know the whereabouts of the poor man's son! The problem with categorial impera-tives is that they are just that: categorical. They demand a "yes" or "no" response. Disciplined judgment or *phronesis* plays no role in a binary moral framework of this kind. This is a far cry from the Rule of Benedict of Nursia, for instance, a governing document oriented to the virtues that resembles more a procedure for the prudent granting of dispensations or exceptions than a rigid set of categorical decrees. Third, Kant was raised as a Pietist and was clearly imbued with a deep religious sensibility.[20] In-deed, he has been rightly criticized for appropriating religious virtues and values in order to stave off the prospects of a world that Thomas Hobbes (1588–1679) more forthrightly acknowledged to be "solitary, poor, nasty, brutish, and short,"[21] given the perceived absence of any metaphysical or ontological warrants for moral behavior and social control.

More recent developments in secular philosophy have drifted even further away from a traditional understanding of virtue. Perversely, Friedrich Nietzsche (1844–1900) located morality in a hypothesized "will to power." And contemporary postmodernists go even further; they re-ject the very idea of virtue—including the will to power—as a technique employed by those in control to exploit those who lack power. Prominent postmodernists thus promote the "deconstruction" of traditional virtues and values in order to liberate those who have long been oppressed. Hav-ing removed God from the moral equation, we have now journeyed far from the ethics of Aristotle and Aquinas.

It is enough for our purposes to know that each of these several "post-Christian" moral frameworks has adherents in our contemporary world. Again, however, this text is intended for committed Christians who experience dissonance, discomfort, or conflict in their secular lives. Our key concern thus remains: Can a traditional Christian conception of moral virtue enable committed Christians who are fully engaged in the world to integrate their faith into their employment and into other key commitments in their secular lives? Our more particular interest in this regard pertains to those who exercise managerial and leadership respon-sibilities in private sector, public sector, and nonprofit organizations.

---

20. MacIntyre, *After Virtue*, 44.

21. Hobbes, *Leviathan*.

A final historical development must be considered. The "rediscovery" of an Aristotelian understanding of virtue that runs first through Thomas Aquinas and then through Alasdair MacIntyre and others has been bolstered by the "rediscovery" of Thomist personalism. This "movement" in both philosophy and theology is quite broad. It can best be understood as a protest against the totalitarian extremes of collectivism and the fascist "will to power." As affirmed by Thomas D. Williams, Karol Wojtyla, later Pope John Paul II, embraced Thomist personalism in response to "his experience of Hegelian totalitarianism in his native Poland, both the Nietzchean (National Socialism) and Marxist (Leninist Communism) stamp."[22] Thomist personalism is associated with Jacques Maritain, Etienne Gilson, and others as well.

Proponents of Thomist personalism celebrate the human person as the central focus of all philosophical discourse. Wojtyla, for example, pointed to the documents of the Second Vatican Council "in which Christ is presented as a revealer of the full mystery of man and of human dignity . . . The dignity proper to man, the dignity that is held out to him both as a gift and as something to be striven for, is inextricably bound up with the truth. Truthful thinking and truthful living are the indispensable and essential components of that dignity."[23]

Today's proponents of Thomist personalism address certain concerns and employ language that would have been unfamiliar to Thomas Aquinas. Nevertheless, Aquinas's reorientation of Aristotle's moral framework to Christian values and to Christian intellectual commitments underwrites today's Thomist personalism. Citing Genesis 1:26, Aquinas insisted on the inviolability of human dignity: "Let us make man in our own image and likeness." He insisted, too, on the universal destination of all goods in God. These twin foci explain why human flourishing is privileged over property rights or the claims of the state in Thomist thought. We can also see a clear but philosophically untethered version of this same personalist orientation in Robert Greenleaf's servant-leader model.

Together, our conceptual overview of virtue and our historical framing of virtue ethics have narrowed our focus in four important ways. First, we have affirmed that virtue pertains not to what we do, but to who we are. Second, we have narrowed our field of concern to the moral virtues, including, most importantly, the four cardinal virtues,

22. Williams, "What is Thomistic Personalism," 172.
23. Wojtyla, *Sign of Contradiction*, 118–19.

i.e., prudence, justice, temperance, and fortitude or courage. Third, we have identified prudence acquired through formation or *phronesis*, i.e., practiced living, as key to the proper exercise of the other moral virtues. (According to MacIntyre, prudence can also be thought of as an intellectual virtue, indeed, as an intellectual virtue "without which none of the virtues of character can be exercised."[24]) Finally, we have affirmed that the virtues understood as habitual inclinations or dispositions are typically oriented to certain values and intellectual commitments, two topics that will be more fully developed in chapters 8 and 10.

We are now in a position to propose a normative model for virtue-based behavior and decision-making in the workplace. In the several managerial language games examined in chapter 2, behavior and managerial decision-making were oriented to objectives determined exclusively by the organization. Three factors have now been added to this all too common conception of organizational life.

Most importantly, the unique human drive to experience meaning is identified in figure 3 as the motive force animating the whole model.

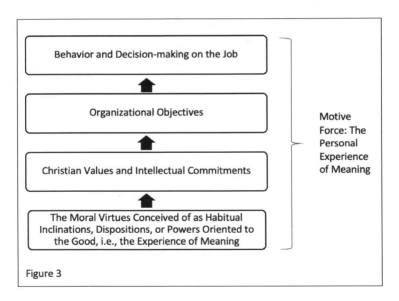

Figure 3

Maslow's hierarchy of needs and other instrumental conceptions of motivation—no matter how benevolent they may seem—are thus abandoned in favor of a motive force that is more fundamental to our identity as

24. MacIntyre, *After Virtue*, 154.

beings who are challenged continuously to develop and "tell our stories," to use MacIntyre's turn of phrase. (It is important to keep in mind, of course, that work is not the only domain in which the experience of meaning can be pursued. Recall from chapter 3 that Frankl posited three such domains: work and other kinds of creative acts, key relationships, and the stance we take against circumstances over which we have little or no control. Managerial work performed in organizations provides a particular focus for this inquiry, however.)

A foundation based on an Aristotelian conception of the moral virtues as habitual inclinations, disposition, or "powers" has been added as well. And the third addition pertains to Christian values and intellectual commitments. The virtues must be oriented to some purpose or end. This is the sense in which Aquinas insisted that "man's virtue perfects him *in relation to good.*"[25]

Whereas the "quest" to develop and tell our stories to ourselves and to others, i.e., the pursuit and experience of meaning, is viewed as universal and the need for moral virtue is recognized as universal, too, there can be no such expectations in this regard with respect to Christian values or Christian intellectual commitments. This place in our model could be occupied by Jewish or Islamic values or intellectual commitments or even by humanist values. In this sense, this element in the model is bounded by time and place and can even be considered cultural or sectarian rather than anthropological or ontological in nature. Moreover, in the case of Christians, "intellectual commitments" can have at least three possible meanings. They can refer to articles of faith that are intellectually affirmed; they can be described in personal or "emotivist" terms, again borrowing a term from MacIntyre; or they can refer to an existential "leap of faith." Indeed, different denominational traditions within the larger Christian tradition could interpret this element in the proposed model differently. This aspect of the model will be further articulated in this regard in chapters 8 and 10.

The addition of these three elements can serve two purposes. Most importantly, they can awaken us to the fact that every aspect of our lives can potentially contribute to the existential experience of meaning. Again drawing on MacIntyre, a manager is more than a "character" in a drama scripted, produced, cast, and directed by the organization for which she labors. At its best, work provides a vehicle through which we can satisfy

---

25. Pegis, *Introduction to St. Thomas*, 600. Emphasis added.

not just one or more of the five levels of physiological and psychological need hypothesized by Maslow or some other ephemeral need, but something much deeper, too. Second, moral virtues conceived of as habitual inclinations, dispositions, or "powers" oriented to a faithfully articulated set of Christian values or to the intellectual commitments one subscribes to as a Christian can provide a check on instrumental behaviors that could conflict with an individual's more fundamental identity as a disciple of Jesus.

So why, then, is moral virtue needed in life generally, and, more particularly for our purposes, in the exercise of our managerial and leadership responsibilities? Is it just a matter of personal dissonance, discomfort, or conflict, or is something more sometimes at stake? The larger problem, of course, is moral failure, including the kinds of serious and destructive dysfunction that can be difficult to fathom once it is revealed. In chapter 3, we described several such scandals that came to light during the heyday of the "maximization of shareholder wealth" perspective.

We tend to make two mistakes, however, when we focus too intently on a select set of highly sensationalized scandals. First, we fail to recognize that moral failure comes in all shapes and sizes. The taint of scandal is attached to other times and other places, too, and scandal is by no means limited to the private sector. Further, the "slippery slope" is real. One small failure tends to lead to another and then to another and then to still more. A seemingly innocent lie is followed by another and then another, and soon the individual who told the initial lie takes on the identity of a liar. This is the nature of vice honed by habit. As noted by Wadell, "the most basic reason why human beings need the virtues is that they can through the choices and decisions they make become something other than human; they can end up with a life they ultimately regret."[26]

A second mistake pertains to our tendency to explain inexplicable moral failures away. Trying to make sense of these troubling events, we can all too easily attribute moral failure to evil. The perpetrator is thus reconceived as a sociopath, a fiend, or a beast. This kind of corruption certainly exists. As Karl Rahner affirmed, however, corruption can take one of two forms: the kind of venal corruption or evil that is often attached to scandal, and a subtler version as well. According to Rahner, we can be "seized by a creaturely influence" and so "defect from [our] own

---

26. Wadell, "Virtue," 999.

nature."[27] We can devote ourselves to "money, or success, or science, or social progress, or [our] children, or carnal lust, or any other of the idols which [we] set up upon the altar of [our] heart[s]."[28] In the end, we can hide in our skepticism and lose ourselves in the "wretchedness of everyday life."[29] According to Rahner, our failure to respond to the existential freedom gifted to us in ways that are truly meaningful in the threefold sense explored in chapter 3, i.e., through our work and in our creative acts, in relationships that are dear to us, and in the stance we take against circumstances over which we have little or no control, can be deemed "immoral."[30]

Even this fails to explain moral failure entirely, however, especially the kind of moral failure perpetrated in the names of organizations in the private sector, the public sector, and the nonprofit sector, too. Two other explanations should be considered, as well, both of which can be attributed to the two overarching deficiencies associated with the eight sets of theories and models that have dominated management thinking over the course of the last century: their severely constrained understandings of human motivation and their exclusive orientation to instrumental ends.

The first of these explanations pertains to the enclosed worldviews in which decision-makers are enveloped in organizations given over entirely to one or more of the dominant language games of management theory and practice. We can think of this as a kind of managerial myopia or tunnel vision. Three well-documented examples, one from the public sector and two involving private sector firms, will be examined in this regard.

The Tuskegee syphilis study[31] was launched by the United States Public Health Service in 1932. It only ended in 1972. It remains the longest running such study in American history. Researchers were hoping to learn about the unique progression of syphilis in African American males. The study was designed to complement a Norwegian study, but there was a substantial difference between the designs of these two investigations. The Norwegian study employed a retrospective design in which the medical records of men who had died of syphilis or from

27. Rahner, "The Dignity and Freedom," 242.

28. Rahner, "The Scandal of Death," 142.

29. Rahner, "Thoughts," 8.

30. Rahner, "On Christian Dying," 290.

31. Fourtner, "Bad Blood."

complications related to the disease were examined after the men had
died. In the Tuskegee study, a control group of 399 African American
sharecroppers—all of whom had been diagnosed with a latent form of
syphilis—were matched against an experimental group of 201 of their
peers. The two groups of men were then tracked prospectively. They
were never told the true purpose of the study. When symptoms of the
disease emerged, men in the control group were "treated" with placebos.
Remarkably, they were even deprived of penicillin, a certain cure, after it
had been adopted as the standard treatment for syphilis in 1947.

The Tuskegee syphilis study was continued over the course of several administrative regimes at the United States Public Health Service
and later at the Centers for Disease Control, with the full cooperation of
Tuskegee Institute, later Tuskegee University, an historically black college
located in Alabama. Numerous physicians and nurses played significant
roles in the study over the course of its four-decade run, including a number of African American healthcare professionals. Peter Buxtun, a Public
Health Service employee, began to question the study on ethical grounds
in 1966. His protests were rebuffed by his superiors, who continued to
insist that knowledge gained through the study would "benefit mankind."
Buxtun finally went to the press in 1972, and the study was discontinued
shortly thereafter.

The consequences of the Tuskegee syphilis study were devastating
on several levels. Of the 399 men included in the control group, only
seventy-four were still living in 1972. Some 128 of the men had died from
syphilis or from complications associated with the disease. Forty of their
wives had been infected, too, and nineteen of their children had been
born with congenital syphilis. Because of the public scandal that ensued,
some $10 million in damages were paid over time, and President Bill
Clinton issued a public apology in 1997 to those who had been impacted
by the study. To this day, persistent concerns in the African American
community pertaining to vaccinations and other medical procedures is
attributable to the way in which African American subjects were abused
in the Tuskegee syphilis study.

What is clear in this horrific incident is that the instrumental logic
of the study itself and its ostensibly altruistic objectives created a kind of
hermetic bubble in which all other possible considerations were screened
out. Remarkably, this proved true for several generations of researchers,
research aides, and administrators, and, even more remarkably, it proved
true both for White professionals and for African American professionals

involved in the study. There is no question that racism played a role, of course, but racial animus cannot entirely explain what occurred in this long-running tragedy. Managerial myopia of an egregious nature played a role as well.

Is it reasonable to think that moral virtues oriented to Christian values and intellectual commitments might have made a difference in this instance? We have certainly witnessed our fair share of scandals—big and small—in recent decades, but we are not unacquainted with the exercise of virtue as well. Prudence, justice, temperance, and fortitude are not unknown to us. Why, then, did so many fail in the Tuskegee syphilis study to step outside of the instrumental bubble that had enveloped them?

To answer this question, consider a reframing of the Tuskegee syphilis study using the illustration first introduced in chapter 1 and then employed again in chapter 3. See figure 4.

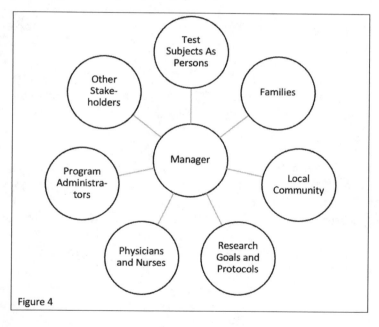

Figure 4

A personalist analysis by anyone associated with the study over the course of so many years would have centered not on the study's research goals and protocols but on the individuals who were involved; and, if those involved had adopted Robert Greenleaf's prescriptions in this regard, this analysis would have begun with those who were least in a position to control the circumstances of their involvement. This would have reflected, as well, a Christian concern for those who live on the margins of society, i.e., the *anawim*.

This is why the development of moral virtues cannot happen in a value-free vacuum, but must be oriented instead to an external set of values and intellectual commitments. It is difficult to believe that the Tuskegee syphilis study would have lasted for even a minute following a formal analysis of this kind. A significant caveat is in order, however. Even a personalist analysis would likely have been compromised to the extent that racism—rather than managerial myopia or tunnel vision *per se*—may have corrupted the perceptions of those in positions of authority with respect to the study. Racism can all too easily underwrite the sinful and profoundly un-Christian rationalization that racial minorities are something less than full persons.

What would it have taken for someone in authority—a leader, in fact—to have stepped outside the narrow confines of the Tuskegee syphilis study's established goals and protocols in order to ameliorate the damage done? Why did it take forty years for a whistleblower to secure an audience? Aquinas would likely have answered this question by pointing to the need for virtue honed by long practice, virtue fully oriented to Christian values and intellectual commitments. "The appetitive power is inclined variously, and to many things, while the reason judges, in a single act, what should be willed in the light of various conditions and circumstances. Therefore, the appetitive power is not thereby entirely overcome, so as to be inclined naturally to the same thing in the majority of cases; which inclination belongs to the habit of virtue. Therefore, a habit of virtue cannot be caused by one act, but only by many."[32] Lacking deeply ingrained virtues and practice oriented by long habit to that which is good, managers and administrators are susceptible to the decision-making frameworks imposed on them by the organizations for which they labor.

A similar case of managerial myopia or tunnel vision unfolded in north-central Indiana following a tragic accident on August 10, 1978. Two young sisters and their cousin were burned to death after the gas tank in their 1973 Ford Pinto burst into flames when they were struck by a van.[33] As first revealed in a 1977 article in *Mother Jones*,[34] Ford Mo-

---

32. Pegis, *Introduction to St. Thomas*, 552–53.

33. Cocoş, "Case Study."

34. Dowie, "Pinto Madness."

tor Company had long been aware of a design flaw in the positioning of the Pinto's gas tank. Indeed, it had been flagged in pre-production safety tests, and the company subsequently acknowledged that it had tracked accidents involving the Pinto for some time. In fact, some five hundred to nine hundred deaths have since been associated with rear-end collisions involving the Pinto. Further, the company knew what was needed to correct the defect: an $11 part. Still further, by the time of the accident, Ford had been involved in a multi-year lobbying effort to delay a federal motor vehicle standard that would have required the after-market installation of the inexpensive part.

The most telling aspect of this story was exposed in discovery, however: a cost-benefit analysis, one of the privileged tools of management science, a legacy, in fact, of Robert McNamara's time with Ford. An analysis prepared by the director of automotive safety at Ford was acknowledged in court as having proven decisive with respect to the firm's disposition of its dilemma pertaining to the Pinto's design flaw. Assuming 180 burn deaths at $200,000 per death, 180 burn injuries at $67,000 per injury, and 2,100 lost and damaged vehicles at an average cost of $700 per vehicle, the analysis estimated the firm's potential liability to be $49.5 million. Assuming a total production run of 12.5 million vehicles with the defect and a cost of $11 per part if all of these vehicles were recalled, the report estimated the total cost of a recall to be $137 million. Since this cost exceeded the cost of damages the firm expected to incur if the vehicles were not recalled, the decision was made to do nothing about the design flaw.

The logic is unassailable, of course, *unless* one steps outside the entirely instrumental reasoning that was employed. Nevertheless, this is not as easy a case to analyze as one might think. First, the $200,000 valuation of a lost life had been established by the federal government, albeit under intense lobbying from the auto industry. Further, this kind of financial analysis has long been employed in the adjudication of workers compensation claims and in private insurance calculations of damages. Still further, cost-benefit analyses have their place. Few would argue that the potential loss of a single life should forestall any kind of social change. If that were so, no roads would ever be built.

Still, there is something profoundly disturbing about this case, including, especially, the "loud cheer" from Ford Motor Company's board of directors that was reported by the *New York Times* when the firm was found not guilty of criminal homicide in the case of the two sisters and their cousin.[35]

Again, is it reasonable to think that moral virtues oriented to Christian values and intellectual commitments could have made a difference in the case of the Ford Pinto? The problem in this instance is that a financial analysis alone proved controlling. A personalist analysis would have called attention to the needs of others—other persons, in fact—who were impacted. In the Christian view, they were ididual human beings endowed with an inviolable dignity. Most importantly, a personalist analysis of this kind would have called attention to those who were least in a position to control the circumstances in which they had unknowingly become embroiled, including, most notably, the two sisters and their cousin who died in that fiery crash in north-central Indiana on August 10, 1978.

The complicating factors in this story call attention, as well, to the essential role that prudence plays in moral thinking. Again, "prudence connects the everyday with the ultimate."[36] Lacking prudence, moral analyses can all too easily break down either to a hard and fast decision rule, e.g., a motor vehicle safety standard, or to a teleological calculation using metrics of one kind of another, e.g., a cost-benefit analysis.

Our third example of managerial tunnel vision involves Nestlé, a Swiss firm that has manufactured and marketed baby formula across the globe for decades. (This example is the subject of a well-known Harvard Business School case study[37] with which generations of business students have wrestled.) The hermetic bubble in this instance is embedded in a particular policy pertaining to the company's marketing decisions. As such, it demonstrates the managerial myopia inherent in an exclusive reliance on the administrative policy language game described in chapter 2.

The moral dilemma in this case was prompted in the late 1970s by the marketing of powdered infant formula in less-developed countries. Infant formula had long been a profitable staple in Nestlé's portfolio of food products, but market growth for infant formula in the developed world had slowed by the early 1970s due to market saturation and lower birth rates. In contrast, sales growth for the product was skyrocketing in less-developed countries. Indeed, annual sales growth of 19 percent was

---

35. Cocoş, "Case Study."

36. Wadell, "Virtue," 1005.

37. Harrison, *Nestlé Alimentana S. A.*

projected in these emerging markets for the years 1977 through 1979. Nestlé faced stiff competition in these less-developed countries in the mid-seventies, but still enjoyed a commanding market share of approximately 35 percent.

At the same time, a number of disturbing news reports were beginning to draw widespread attention. Because powdered infant formula has to be mixed with water and because bottles and nipples need to be sterilized, the risk to babies's health caused by waterborne infections was substantially increased by the use of this product in areas where clean water is often unavailable. Further, the immunological benefits of breast-feeding were lost when new mothers in these countries opted for infant formula over breastfeeding. Studies began to show an undeniable correlation between declines in breastfeeding in these markets and infant deaths caused by measles, diarrhea, bronchitis, pneumonia, and other respiratory infections, all of which can be obviated, at least to some extent, by the sharing of a mother's antibodies with her baby via sustained breastfeeding.

Given the obvious vulnerabilities of those involved in this long-running incident, we might think that a personalist analysis oriented to Christian values and intellectual commitments would have been undertaken. This does not seem to have been the case, however; and, even if Nestlé had authorized an analysis of this kind, several complicating factors would have undoubtedly "muddied the waters," again demonstrating the need for prudent judgment. The most vexing complication had to do with the firm's distributed marketing strategy. Its corporate office in Vevey, Switzerland, prescribed in great detail how marketing plans should be developed in each of the countries in which Nestlé then had a presence, but it left the drafting of individual country-level plans to the firm's "country managers." In a number of Nestlé's markets, these country managers were known to use hyper-aggressive marketing strategies that minimized the risks to babies incurred as mothers abandoned breast-feeding. These country-specific strategies included the widespread use of mass media, the distribution of pamphlets that omitted or downplayed the benefits of breastfeeding, the distribution of free samples, financial incentives offered to health care providers, and the employment of "milk-craft nurses" or "mother-craft nurses," uniformed and hence authoritative contractors, in fact, who promoted the use of infant formula to new mothers.

Despite this, it was a matter of policy for Nestlé's corporate office to defer to the firm's country managers on all such matters. It could be easily rationalized, in fact, that these country managers "knew best" when it came to their home countries. This hands-off approach was further incentivized by the growth in profits promised in these emerging markets. The need for anything resembling a personalist analysis could thus be brushed aside with relative ease on the basis of longstanding corporate policy. The managerial myopia in this instance was certainly due to the value-neutral way in which business had long been conducted at Nestlé.

Nevertheless, it would be reasonable for a reflective practitioner to think that alarming reports of increasing infant mortality rates in several of the lesser developed countries in which Nestlé had a presence should have set off an alarm. Indeed, a personalist analysis that would have privileged the interests of poor mothers and their vulnerable children could have contributed to the development of proactive interventions or alternative marketing strategies. In fact, Nestlé only responded to this concern when a boycott was launched in the United States in the 1970s, a boycott that migrated to Europe in the early 1980s, a boycott, in fact, that has persisted intermittently over the last several decades.

In addition to the forms of corruption described above and the enclosed worldviews that can sometimes blind decision-makers to their moral commitments, a third moral hazard must be examined. This additional risk can be attributed not to myopia or tunnel vision but to stress. The insights of Irving L. Janis and Leon Mann can be helpful in this regard. In their 1977 text *Decision Making: A Psychological Analysis of Conflict, Choice, and Commitment*, the two scholars advanced a novel theory of decision-making. Janis and Mann developed a sequence of four questions to predict dysfunction in situations in which stress is being experienced. One, will the risks be serious if no change is made in the previously decided-upon course of action? If "no," the decision-maker will procrastinate; if "yes," she will likely proceed to the next question. Two, will the risks be serious if a change is made? If "no," the decision-maker will simply make the change; if "yes," she will proceed to the third question in the sequence. Three, is it realistic to think that a better solution can be found? If, "yes," the decision-maker will proceed to the final question; if "no," she will likely be susceptible to one or more forms of "defensive avoidance," i.e., the abandonment of a vigilant search, selective inattention, selective forgetting, the distortion of warning messages, the construction of wishful rationalizations, and the minimization of negative consequences. Four, assuming that a better solution may still be available, is there sufficient time to search and to deliberate? If "yes," the decision-maker will continue searching; if "no," a hypervigilant and likely dysfunctional search will ensue.

Unless a decision-maker is steeled against stress, according to Janis and Mann, there is a high probability that dysfunction will ensue in its wake. We will examine two such instances while noting that well-honed virtues oriented to Christian values and to other Christian intellectual commitments can serve this "steeling" function in the case of authentic leaders.

The first instance involves the tragic loss of the space shuttle *Challenger* on January 28, 1986, together with its crew of seven astronauts, including Christa McAuliffe, NASA's first "teacher in space." As so many former school children who were watching that day recall, the shuttle exploded in spectacular fashion seventy-three seconds into its flight.

In their final report dated June 6, 1986, William P. Rogers and other members of the special commission appointed by President Reagan to investigate the disaster attributed it to the failure of a single "O-ring," i.e., a type of gasket, in one of the two 116-foot long solid rocket boosters used to lift the shuttle into orbit.[38] Morton-Thiokol, a private sector firm, had long held a sole-source contract for designing, building, and assembling the solid rocket boosters used in all shuttle flights. The Rogers Commission determined that near-freezing temperatures had degraded the resilience of an O-ring and that the subsequent blowby of hot gases had ignited the two propellants stored in the shuttle's large external fuel tank.

Although technically accurate, this account does not tell the whole story. Hearings before the House of Representatives later in June 1986 revealed a severely compromised decision-making process.[39] The day before the launch, fourteen engineers from Morton-Thiokol had met to discuss the low temperatures anticipated for the next day's launch. They were concerned because some blowby of hot gases had been detected on O-rings recovered from prior launches. A hastily arranged conference call then followed with NASA officials from the Kennedy Space Flight Center at Cape Canaveral and the Marshall Space Flight Center in Huntsville, Alabama. In this call, the fourteen engineers recommended against

38. Presidential Commission, "Report to the President."

39. Hearing before the Subcommittee on Science, Technology, and Space, "Investigation of the *Challenger* Accident."

any launches at temperatures below fifty-three degrees. A verbal confron-
tation erupted, with one NASA official exclaiming: "My God, Thiokol,
when do you want me to launch, April?" Another NASA administrator
joined in, saying that he was "appalled" by the engineers's recommendation. In a second conference call, the fourteen engineers refused to budge
from their position. One of the two Morton-Thiokol vice presidents who
participated in the call then turned to the other and said: "We have to
make a management decision. [It's time to] take off [our] engineering
hats and put on [our] management hats." Although they were still on the
line, the fourteen engineers later reported that they had been frozen out
of the conversation from that point forward. When asked at the end of
the conference call if anyone on the line had any further comments, no
one spoke up.

The temperature at the time of the space shuttle *Challenger*'s launch
was thirty-six degrees, fifteen degrees colder than any previous launch.
Confirming the validity of the concerns voiced by Morton-Thiokol's
fourteen engineers, an O-ring in one of the shuttle's solid rocket boosters
failed and the mission and the entire crew were lost as a result.

In applying the conflict theory model to this incident, we must first
establish the presence of stress in the moments leading up to the launch
decision. In fact, there is considerable evidence to this effect. By 1986,
NASA was a full five years behind in its launch schedule, and the launch
slated for January 28, 1986, had already been delayed eight times. As
a result, NASA was losing commercial contracts to its European com-
petitor, and it had become something of a laughingstock in some media
circles as well. Further, Morton-Thiokol had just been advised that the
contract it had long held with NASA would soon be put out for bid. Still
further, a paragraph touting the triumph of the space shuttle *Challenger*
and celebrating Christa McAuliffe's presence in orbit had been inserted
in the next night's State of the Union Address. This opportunity would
have been lost had the launch been delayed. The prerequisite of stress was
certainly present when the fateful decision to launch the space shuttle
Challenger was made.

We can now follow the sequence of questions proposed by Janis and
Mann. First, would the risks have been serious if the launch were permitted to proceed as planned? Yes, the Morton-Thiokol engineers predicted
the potential loss of the mission and the crew. Second, would the risks
have been serious if the engineers and administrators involved in the decision had accepted the engineers's recommendation? Yes, because winter

THE CASE FOR MORAL VIRTUE

temperatures in Florida often fall below fifty-three degrees, a decision to postpone the launch would have crippled NASA's launch schedule and its competitive position *vis-à-vis* the European consortium then launching rockets from a base in South America. Additionally, NASA would have had to forego the highly coveted nod in President Reagan's State of the Union Address. A third question follows: Was it realistic to think that a "better solution" could have been found? No, the only other option available to the decision-makers, had they accepted the engineers's recommendation, would have been a lengthy and very costly redesign of the entire shuttle system.

Under these circumstances, Janis and Mann predict a pattern of defensive avoidance, and this, of course, is precisely what ensued. Most critically, NASA's traditional "framing" for launch decisions was turned on its head. A NASA official later reported that they had moved at some point in their conversation from "needing to prove this bird can fly" to "needing to prove that this particular flight will end in disaster." We see evidence of buck passing, too. Although no sign-off was required, NASA directed Morton-Thiokol's representatives to put the firm's final launch recommendation in writing. Still further, we see considerable evidence of what Janis and Mann refer to as "bolstering," including the distortion or misinterpretation of key facts, uncritical analysis, and wishful thinking. Most importantly in this regard, the multiple O-ring design was reimagined at some point in the conversation as a redundant system, even though it was clearly not designed as such.

Could moral virtues oriented to Christian values and to well-articulated Christian intellectual commitments have made a difference in this instance? The missing virtue, it seems, was fortitude or courage. Lacking the virtue of fortitude, it can be difficult to resist the dysfunction that can sometimes attend to questions that are both consequential and conflicted. It is possible, too, that a personalist analysis might have awakened the NASA officials involved in this decision to their agency's long-cherished concern for its astronauts and mission specialists and for their families as well. See figure 5.

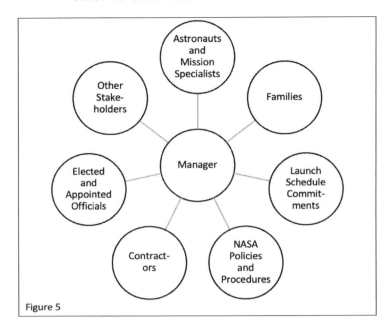

Figure 5

There is a very high likelihood, of course, that anyone who would have endorsed a decision to postpone the launch of Mission 51-L would have paid a very high price professionally for having done so, but not nearly as high as the price paid by the shuttle's seven-member crew.

A similar analysis can be undertaken with respect to a particular aspect of the clergy sexual abuse scandal that has so plagued the Roman Catholic Church in the United States and around the world in recent years. This singular aspect pertains to the individual decisions made by far too many bishops over the course of several decades to transfer priests credibly accused of having sexually abused children from one parish to another, from one diocese to another in the United States, and to other countries, too.

Since the 1980s, several waves of news reports pertaining to the sexual abuse of minors by Catholic clergy have fueled outrage across the globe. In fact, the full dimensions of this scandal may not be known yet. The release in August 2018 of a devastating report of clergy sexual abuse in Pennsylvania and the still emerging revelations concerning Theodore McCarrick, the former archbishop of Washington, DC, have continued to stoke anger concerning the church's failings in this regard.

The overall dimensions of the scandal can now be discerned, however. In June 2004, the John Jay College of Criminal Justice submitted a report to the United States Conference of Catholic Bishops (USCCB) entitled *The Nature and Scope of Sexual Abuse of Minors by Catholic Priests and Deacons in the United States, 1950–2000*.[40] The researchers determined that some 10,667 individuals had lodged credible allegations of child sexual abuse against some 4,392 priests in the United States between the years 1950 and 2002. Just over 50 percent of the victims were between the ages of eleven and fourteen when they had been abused. More than 80 percent of the victims were male. The majority of the priests accused of abuse had been ordained between 1950 and 1979. The abuse reportedly peaked in the 1970s. Although the majority of the priests accused of abuse were alleged to have victimized just one child, some 149 of the accused had abused more than ten children, thereby accounting for some 26 percent of all of the incidents reported over the fifty-two-year time period for which data was gathered.

The initial response of the church can best be described as defensive. For instance, some complained that the problem had been exaggerated or sensationalized by the press. Others argued that the number of priests implicated was always small, approximately 4 percent of the presbyterate by some counts, and comparable, at any rate, to clergy in other denominations and to other professions as well. Some in the church were also keen to defend the discipline of celibacy, its male-dominated ecclesiology, and its asserted independence *vis-à-vis* civil authorities.

This defensive posture has been substantially abandoned in recent years as more and more instances of abuse have surfaced, albeit not to everyone's satisfaction. The USCCB's commissioning of a study by John Jay College represented a major step forward in this regard. Further, the USCCB's adoption of a "zero tolerance" policy in 2002 and its promulgation of a "Charter for the Protection of Children and Young People"[41] have been welcomed, so, too, the Vatican's belated acknowledgement of the sprawling dimensions of the scandal across the globe.

The costs of the scandal have been incalculable, including, most tragically, the harm inflicted on those who had abused and the sense of diminishment caused when their credible allegations were denied,

40. John Jay College of Criminal Justice, "The Nature and Scope of Sexual Abuse of Minors."

41. United States Conference of Catholic Bishops, "Charter for the Protection of Children and Young People."

minimized, or hushed up. Applying regression analysis to data gathered as part of the Pew Forum's Religious Landscape Survey and the General Social Survey, Daniel M. Hungerman has estimated that as many as two million American Catholics have left the Church since 2002 as a direct result of the scandal. Contributions to Catholic parishes have fallen by some $3 billion for the same reason.[42] These impacts are confirmed in other studies, too. Among respondents to the Pew Forum's 2009 survey, 27 percent of former Catholics who now describe themselves as "unaffiliated" cited the clergy abuse scandal as having played a significant role in their decisions to leave the Church. Similarly, 21 percent of former Catholics who now self-identify as Protestants attributed their changes in affiliation—at least in part—to the scandal.[43] Legal settlements to date are estimated to have exceeded $3 billion in the United States, and a number of dioceses have had to declare bankruptcy.

Our interest here is a narrow one, however: How could some bishops have allowed this scandal to develop as it did? In applying the conflict theory model, we must first establish the presence of unremitting stress. This is easy to do. The word "shame" is included in virtually every official statement issued by the Church on this topic. Some now acknowledge that sexual abuse by clergy was always something of an unacknowledged "elephant in the middle of the room," unacknowledged because of the deep shame that was felt by anyone who had anything to do with these incidents. If it was spoken of at all, it was by bishops among bishops because they were responsible for dealing with the fallout emanating from these egregious violations of trust.

Having established the presence of stress, we can now consider the four questions posed by Janis and Mann. First, were the risks serious if the reality of sexual abuse by clergy continued to be ignored? Yes, it was certainly reasonable in decades past to assume that the abuse would continue. According to the John Jay study, some 44 percent of the priests credibly accused of abuse between 1950 and 2002 had victimized more than one young person. Additionally, some bishops—it seems—were greatly concerned about growing shortages of priests in their dioceses. Second, were the risks serious if the bishops had elected to publicly acknowledge the full scope of the problem to the extent they understood it? Yes, as the consequences detailed above make clear, the prospect of

42. Hungerman, "Substitution and Stigma."

43. Pew Forum on Religion & Public Life, "Faith in Flux."

an enormous public scandal posed a significant threat to the Church. A third question then follows: Was it realistic to think that a better solution could be found? No, sweeping the problem under the rug and going public must have both seemed unacceptable to some bishops. Like all such problems, this one has a "between a rock and a hard place" feel to it.

Under these circumstances, Janis and Mann predict a pattern of defensive avoidance. Again, this is precisely what happened. We have already called attention to the full-throated defenses still mounted by some. More critically, however, it is clear that the nature of the problem was reframed or re-imagined over and over again by some bishops. At first, the sexual abuse of children by clergy was defined as a spiritual problem that individual perpetrators could "pray away," aided, perhaps, by astute spiritual directors. In the 1960s, it was redefined as a psychological problem amenable to treatment. In fact, the John Jay study notes that some 32 percent of all priests credibly accused of abusing young people between 1950 and 2002 were "recognized as having other behavioral and psychological problems," and 37 percent had been referred to treatment programs. Then in the 1980s, something inexplicable happened. The problem was reframed as a legal challenge. Lawyers were engaged to defend dioceses across the country in order to protect both assets and reputations. In retrospect, it seems clear that some bishops had "outsourced" their pastoral responsibilities pertaining to this concern to their attorneys.

The conflict theory model suggests that this outcome could have been predicted. It can be understood as a logical consequence of unremitting stress. That being said, we cannot let the offending bishops off the hook with respect to this unconscionable scandal. The dramatic rethinking of the bishop's fundamental identity represents one of the Second Vatican Council's greatest accomplishments. The Council Fathers abandoned their long-established identity as priest-administrators in favor of an identity celebrated in the earliest days of the church; the Council fathers recognized bishops, first and foremost, as pastors. Pastors are counseled to attend to their sheep, of course, especially to those among the flock who are lost or most vulnerable. A pastoral approach—rather than a spiritual, psychological, or legal one—should have been the first option for bishops confronting incidences of this kind, even in the 1960s, the 1970s, and the 1980s. In keeping with their recently reclaimed identity as pastors, bishops should have conducted the kind of personalist analysis recommended in this text. Had they done so, at least some of the victims's stories might have been privileged over the reputations of clergy and the Church's finances.

There is a second reason why we cannot let the offending bishops off the hook. More than most, they should have been formed along the way in the virtues prized in the still-evolving moral tradition of Aristotle and Aquinas. More than most, they had access to the resources of biblical and apostolic teaching and the rich intellectual patrimony of the church. Again, how could this have happened? The answer lies, perhaps, in an astute observation concerning arrogance shared by Robert Greenleaf: "A critical disability that goes with expanding competence is the inability (or unwillingness) to examine the assumptions by which one operates."[44] One is reminded, of course, of Robert McNamara and countless other men and women whose tenures as managers and administrators have been marred by disappointment and failure, but Greenleaf's insight in this regard might be especially applicable to some in the class of men who are regarded as successors to the apostles.

These several tragedies need not have occurred. Nevertheless, even those who labor in organizations that espouse the most noble of virtues, including—as we have seen—both NASA and the church, are suscep-tible to shameful decision-making when the distortions caused by great stress are ignored. The antidote is virtue honed by long practice and fully oriented to Christian values and Christian intellectual commitments. Greenleaf makes this same point, employing language that may be more accessible to our ears than Aquinas's good counsel in this regard: "The opening of awareness stocks both the conscious and unconscious minds with a richness of resources for future need. But it does more than that: it is value-building and value-clarifying, and it *armors* one to meet the stress of life by helping build serenity in the face of stress and uncertainty."[45]

The role that deeply engrained moral virtues—that is, ways of per-ceiving and thinking and ways of being in the world that are oriented to the good and that have been honed by habit—can play in helping us overcome our sinful tendencies, in breaking through the conceptual bubbles that envelop us in organizations, and in enabling us to resist the distortions in thinking that can be caused by great stress can be displayed graphically. See figure 6. This initial rendering will be expanded upon as we proceed.

44. Greenleaf, *Servant Leadership*, 118.

45. Greenleaf, *Servant Leadership*, 41. Emphasis added.

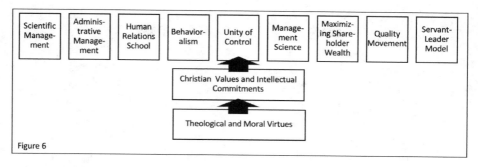

Figure 6

Properly understood, virtues oriented to Christian values and Christian intellectual commitments stand prior to and entirely outside of the decision-making frameworks sanctioned in the nine language games of management theory and practice examined in chapters 2 and 3. We could anticipate that a Thomist or classical understanding of the virtues fully oriented to Christian values and Christian intellectual commitments would be more amenable to the servant-leader model, of course, and much less so to the maximization of shareholder wealth perspective, but we cannot exclude—even in the latter instance—the possibility that a virtuous decision-maker, i.e., a leader, laboring in any of these nine language games might be pulled up short before compromising her deepest spiritual commitments. We cannot exclude, as well, the possibility that situations of this kind could serve as "teachable moments" in which the virtuous decision-maker could give his or her colleagues "ears to hear and eyes to see." According to Alasdair MacIntyre, "the essential function of the virtues is clear. Without them, without justice, courage, truthfulness, practices could not resist the corrupting power of institutions."[46]

It must be noted that this can—at times—require great sacrifice, a not uncommon consequence of faithful discipleship that was fully acknowledged by Charles Taylor: "The call to renounce doesn't negate the value of flourishing; it is rather a call to center everything on God, even if it be at the cost of forgoing this unsubstitutable good; and the fruit of this foregoing is that it becomes on one level the source of flourishing to others, and on another level, a collaboration with the restoration of a fuller flourishing by God. It is a mode of healing wounds and 'repairing the world' (I am here borrowing the Hebrew phrase *tikkun olam*)."[47] We

---

46. MacIntyre, *After Virtue*, 194.

47. Taylor, *A Secular Age*, 17.

will not always be in a position to serve as prophets. At times, the only roles open to us may be that of witness or martyr.

Three arguments have now been advanced. One, the management theories and models now available to us are useful, but deficient nonetheless, in at least two respects. They are undergirded by narrow understandings of human motivation, and they are exclusively oriented to instrumental ends. Two, the servant-leader model proposed by Robert Greenleaf addresses these deficiencies in a compelling way, but its claims in this regard are poorly rooted and hence weak. Greenleaf failed to tap into a traditional understanding of virtue as an essential prerequisite to the effective and sustained exercise of servant leadership. Three, these challenges point to the need for virtue and externally anchored values and intellectual commitments—most notably, for our purposes, Christian values and Christian intellectual commitments—as a foundation for the exercise of authentic leadership in organizations.

It should be clear now that living a life of virtue in a contemporary organization can be challenging. To this point, we have yet to lay out a path one can follow in order to develop or embrace a life of virtue oriented to Christian values and Christian intellectual commitments. This will be the subject of part II of this text in which we will explore a privileged interpretation of Matthew's version of the Beatitudes.

Before moving on to this important topic, however, a detour is in order. We will now explore the implications of the foregoing analysis for our shared life not in today's private, public, and nonprofit organizations but in the civic arena. In the next chapter, we will examine the daunting challenge now facing leaders in the public square. In taking this detour, we are following Alasdair MacIntyre and Robert Greenleaf, both of whom recognized that the leadership challenge we face in our civic life and in our politics mirrors those we face in so many of our contemporary organizations.

Chapter 5

The Public Square

ALASDAIR MACINTYRE'S CRITIQUE AND Robert Greenleaf's, too, address the public square as well as organizations of all kinds. This should not be surprising since management and leadership are required in the public square just as they are in private, public, and nonprofit organizations. Resources are marshaled by managers and leaders to accomplish certain ends. The various ways in which this can be accomplished in the public square thus tend to mirror ways in which they are accomplished in today's organizations.

There are significant differences, too. Most importantly, the ends to be accomplished in the public square tend to be contested more vigorously. Rarely do we see the kind of unanimity that the United States experienced during World War II with respect to the goal to be accomplished: the defeat of fascism in all of its various forms. Further, political discourse tends to appeal to certain ideals in ways that are quite foreign to most organizations. Unfortunately, this appeal is often more conventional than deeply rooted and more feigned than heartfelt in our now-broken politics. The alternative, however, is the bald exercise of power. To this point in our history, our rhetoric continues to provide a buffer of sorts—albeit an imperfect one—against excesses in the way power is wielded in the public square. Still further, management and leadership functions in the public square tend to be diffuse. Checks and balances provide another imperfect buffer against the raw exercise of power.

There are several additional reasons for following both MacIntyre and Greenleaf in extending our critique to the public square as well. First, the various language games of management theory and practice have analogues in the several political philosophies that vie for supremacy in our current politics. Second, the philosophical "roots" of our contemporary politics are weak. They, too, espouse a less-than-fulsome understanding of human nature. Third, the committed disciple of Jesus faces the same problem of a dual identity in the public square that she faces in contemporary organizations. In the public square, the committed Christian is torn between her identity as a disciple of Jesus and her identity as a citizen. Finally, as we shall see, there is a need for virtue in the public square just as there is a need for virtue in today's private, public, and nonprofit organizations.

We will begin with a diagnosis of the philosophical challenge we face in our public discourse. We will then examine four language games now employed in our politics: rules-based constructs of various kinds, utilitarianism, libertarianism, and pragmatism. Having established the nature of the problem and the foundational weaknesses of these several political philosophies, we will consider virtue oriented to an existential understanding of the good, the moral, and the just as a possible foundation for a more life-sustaining form of political discourse. Finally, we will propose a normative model in this regard.

In the West, moral systems have historically assumed an articulated form. See figure 7.

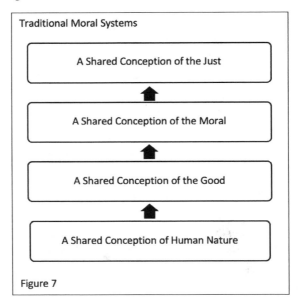

Figure 7

Based on a particular human anthropology or ontology, a conception of the good is postulated. Think, for instance, of Aristotle's concept of *eudemonia* or human flourishing. From this conception of the good, an understanding of the moral, i.e., how we think about and treat ourselves and others as persons, is devised; and from the moral, a conception of justice, i.e., how life's benefits and burdens should be shared among individuals recognized as persons and communities comprised of persons, is articulated.

Recall that our thinking about moral systems faced something of a crisis in the West during the time of the Enlightenment. Having gradually dislodged a belief in God from any role in moral thinking, it became more and more difficult for philosophers to link their conceptions of human nature and the good on the one hand to their conceptions of the moral and the just on the other. As explained by Charles Taylor, the links between and among these four elements in our moral thinking have become increasingly attenuated by deism, utilitarianism, romanticism, and other modern philosophies.[1] In effect, our human anthropologies and ontologies and our understandings of the good, too, have been delinked from our understandings of moral behavior and justice. See figure 8.

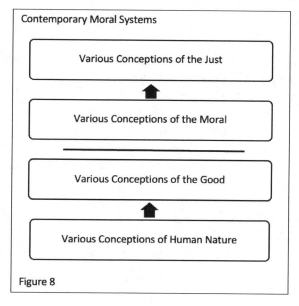

Contemporary Moral Systems

Various Conceptions of the Just

Various Conceptions of the Moral

Various Conceptions of the Good

Various Conceptions of Human Nature

Figure 8

1. Taylor, *Sources of the Self*, 306–20.

As MacIntyre puts it, the political philosophies now available to us are "emotivist" in nature. They are not grounded in any meaningful way in a common understanding of human nature or to a clear conception of the good. They are little more than preferences or opinions. According to MacIntyre, the anthropological roots and the stipulations of the good in these political philosophies are little more than emotional preferences. As a result, we have been left with a tepid form of "civil religion," which is unreflectively accepted by some but, nonetheless, suspect.

Is this a problem? Some moral philosophers, including Alasdair MacIntyre, think it is. Charles Taylor expressed this concern in the form of two questions: "Are [we] living beyond our moral means in continuing allegiance to our standards of justice and benevolence? Do we have ways of seeing good which are still credible to us, which are powerful enough to sustain these standards?" Clearly, he thought the answer to the first question was "yes" and the answer to the second "no."[2] Some others, such as Deirdre N. McCloskey, are more sanguine in this regard.[3] Nevertheless, it seems more than likely that we will pay a steep price at some point in time as certain core beliefs and values that have long undergirded Western civilization are hollowed out. To think otherwise is to conclude that these core beliefs and values were non-essential to begin with.

The state of our politics in the United States underwrites this conclusion as well. The respective views of the right and the left are now virtually incomprehensible to each other. There is a growing tendency to vilify our political opponents. Indeed, overt efforts to demean "others," e.g., immigrants, people of color, etc., and to suppress the vote are now openly endorsed. These several developments suggest that the civil religion that has provided us with a modicum of social cohesion over the course of the last two centuries is now frayed. This does not mean, of course, that Humpty Dumpty can be reassembled. There is no returning to Christendom, an overtly Christian worldview that had once fully encompassed—theoretically, at least—the body politic. This concern may, nonetheless, justify our continuing search for something better.

We will now examine four competing political philosophies: rules-based constructs, utilitarianism, libertarianism, and pragmatism. Wisdom can be found in each of these political philosophies, just as wisdom could be found in each of the several sets of management theories and

2. Taylor, *Sources of the Self*, 515.

3. McCloskey, *The Bourgeois Virtues*, 23, 28–29.

models examined in chapter 2. As we shall see, they are insufficient, nonetheless, in and of themselves.

Two caveats are in order before we begin, however. Michael J. Sandel (b. 1953), for one, has identified "virtue"—most notably, the particular understanding of moral virtue espoused by Immanuel Kant—as an alternative of sorts to rules-based constructs, utilitarianism, and libertarianism.[4] His analysis is compelling, but problematic nonetheless, to the extent that moral virtue—properly understood—is grounded in the decision-maker herself. In contrast, rules-based constructs, utilitarianism, and libertarianism are all anchored in a principle or an idea. Further, considerable formation is required in the case of a moral virtue. A moral virtue is more about who a person is than what she believes *per se* or does. As we have seen, Kant's categorical imperative is better classified as an intellectual virtue or decision rule. All that is required in the case of a categorical imperative is intellectual affirmation and the will to conform one's actions in a certain way. Given this, Kant's categorical imperative should not be classified as a particular manifestation of virtue ethics. It is addressed below, instead, as one of several competing rules-based constructs.

Our second caveat pertains to pragmatism, a quintessentially American political philosophy. Some classify pragmatism as a natural evolution in utilitarian thought. It eschews the goal of optimization, however, the standard or goal promoted by Jeremy Bentham, the father of utilitarianism. Just as it proved helpful to distinguish between behavioralism and the concept of "satisficing" on the one hand and the several optimizing theories and models that preceded and followed Herbert A. Simon's theory of administrative behavior on the other, so, too, it is helpful to distinguish between pragmatism and utilitarianism. The literature pertaining to pragmatism is quite distinct and worthy of consideration in its own right.

RULES-BASED MORAL CONSTRUCTS

Rules-based moral constructs emerged in the West after our shared understanding of Christianity was undermined by the Protestant Reformation and the Enlightenment. As Thomas Hobbes asserted, lacking a common framework for political discourse, society is all too likely to

4. Sandel, *Justice*.

devolve into a state of war of all against all. Life, then, can be expected to become increasingly "solitary, poor, nasty, brutish, and short."[5]

How, then, to ensure something better, something more stable, and something more sustainable? Three types of rules-based moral possibilities are examined here: written or implied social contracts, such as those proposed during the period of the Enlightenment by Thomas Hobbes, John Locke (1632–1704), and Jean-Jacque Rousseau (1712–78); Kant's categorical imperative; and a theory of justice proposed by John Rawls (1921–2002). The analogue to rules-based moral thinking among our several management theories and models is administrative management theory. The constraint in both instances is a binding rule or policy of some kind.

Hobbes, Locke, and Rousseau all proposed forms of government and social order to replace regimes previously legitimized on the basis of a supposed divine right of monarchs. They promoted the use of written or implied constitutions codifying the rules by which any given people should govern themselves.

The starting points for their analyses, i.e., their respective understandings of human nature, differed considerably, however. As noted above, Hobbes's view was pessimistic in this regard. John Locke was somewhat less dour than Hobbes, and Jean-Jacques Rousseau was downright giddy concerning our potential for cooperation with each other. Further, whereas Hobbes understood the purpose of government to be law and order, Locke hoped to protect the people who are governed from those who govern; and, ever the optimist, Rousseau promoted a framework through which the collective aspirations of the people, i.e., the "general will," might be realized.

In the United States, we have benefited greatly from our written Constitution, of course. We owe a great debt to John Locke, in particular, for its inspiration. The body of this seminal document and the Bill of Rights provide a framework for collective decision-making and a bulwark against oppression. Nevertheless, written and implied social contracts are not unproblematic. By definition, constitutional protections are limited to citizens. There is no conception in our Constitution of a universal brotherhood or sisterhood based on a shared relationship with God. This limitation is playing out today, in fact, in our ongoing debate about undocumented immigrants. Viewed as sisters and brothers

---

5. Hobbes, *Leviathan.*

in Christ, undocumented immigrants have certain rights, and committed Christians have certain obligations with respect to them as fellow sons and daughters of God the Father. Our religious views are not controlling in this instance, however. Undocumented immigrants are not citizens, and few legal rights in the United States extend to them.

Further, the precise meaning of the phrase "the common consent of the governed" is unclear. No one alive today was present when the Constitution was signed. Our consent is implied. It is increasingly clear in our politics, however, that some among us do not feel fully embraced as fellow citizens who are entitled to equal protection under the law. This is why we experience incidents of domestic terrorism; and this is why movements such as Black Lives Matter and Occupy Wall Street find support, particularly among the young, many of whom are clearly disillusioned by our national politics.

Finally, written and implied social contracts tend to be defensive in nature and hence minimalist in their aspirations. The rights articulated in our Bill of Rights, for instance, focus on prohibited governmental actions. Positive rights, e.g., the right to health care, the right to affordable housing, the right to an education, etc., fall outside the scope of our enumerated rights. In short, rights, privileges, and obligations articulated in written and implied social contracts tend to be formal and procedural. They do not speak to human flourishing as such.

Immanuel Kant devised a very different approach. An idealist, Kant believed that we can reason our way to certain rules that can ensure civil order. In chapter 4, his *Groundwork for the Metaphysic of Morals* was cited as one of the most influential texts of all time. Kant contended that we do not need God, as such, to reveal the universal laws by which all of us should abide. According to Kant, we can reason our way to certain constraints on human behavior. To this end, he postulated three rules: one, any maxim can acquire the status of a universal law to the extent that it promotes or circumscribes an activity or action in a manner to which we could all be expected to agree; two, people should not be treated as means, but as ends in and of themselves; and three, we should categorically honor any ethical principle that we think should apply to everyone. The word "categorical" is important here. It means that outcomes do not matter. A categorical imperative should be followed regardless of any particular outcome that could follow from its adoption.

A remarkable intellectual achievement, Kant's version of a rules-based politics is problematic, nonetheless. Lacking an ontological foundation, Kant's assertion of an innate human dignity is just that, an assertion, hence MacIntyre's dismissal of Kantian ethics as emotivist in nature. In chapter 4, we noted, too, that categorical imperatives, by their very nature, are unyielding. They do not provide conceptual space for the kind of exceptions that those who promote the virtue of prudence deem essential in moral reasoning. And again, Kant's critics contend that he disingenuously introduced Christian values into the moral framework he promoted as a post-Christian moral philosophy.

Our third example of a rules-based moral construct comes from John Rawls, whose *Theory of Justice* (1971) has drawn considerable attention from moral philosophers over the course of recent decades. Indeed, Rawls rehabilitated the idea of the social contact in our own time in much the same way that Alasdair MacIntyre restored the intellectual legitimacy of moral virtue. Moving beyond Kant, Rawls threw off all vestiges of Christian morality. Instead of reasoning his way to an understanding of social justice that mimics the ends of Christian moral and ethical thinking, Rawls promoted self-interest as a starting point for the development of a theory of justice that was entirely secular in nature.

Rawls began with a thought experiment. Imagine your "original position," he suggested. Imagine your original position before you knew when and where you would be born, before you knew your gender, before you knew your religion or the culture into which you would be born. Imagine your original position before you knew if you would be born into a slave family or a free family or a poor family or a wealthy family. Assume that a "veil of ignorance" has been draped over you, a veil of ignorance through which you cannot see or even imagine the various contingencies that make you who you are. Then, once you have fully embraced this original position, ask yourself the following question: "Into what kind of society would I choose to be born?"

Rawls assumed that most of us would adopt a risk averse position. We would hope to avoid being born into abject poverty in an unfree community that might discriminate against our gender, our religion, or our perceived abilities or lack thereof. Given this, we would opt for certain protections that would ensure a minimal level of security—a minimal level of justice, in fact—for all. Rawls then proposed three rules that should inform our political decision-making: one, each person should enjoy an equal right to the most extensive basic liberty compatible with a similar liberty for all others; two, political decisions should be rendered in such a way that the economic and social circumstances of the least-advantaged among us are improved in some minimal way, at least, as each public policy decision is rendered, i.e., Rawls's "difference principle"; and three, all "offices and positions" should be open to everyone under conditions of fair equality of opportunity. Considered as a whole, Rawls's theory of justice argues for a society that respects individual rights, a society that ensures that its least advantaged members benefit in some way—even if only minimally so—from public policies and social practices adopted over time, and a society that distributes positions of authority on the basis of competence rather than rank or privilege.

The problem with Rawls's theory of justice is that it is entirely theoretical. Its critics charge that no one can truly imagine anything like an "original position." Further, risk aversion as a universal disposition is assumed. In this sense, Rawls's theory of justice, too, can be viewed as an emotivist construct. It envisions a society that John Rawls very much longed for, it seems.

UTILITARIANISM

Utilitarianism holds that a judgment about the justice of any particular political or social policy should be based solely on the consequences resulting from that policy. Utilitarianism is but one of several consequentialist moral systems, and pragmatism is another. (Pragmatism is addressed separately below in recognition of its unique standing in our political imagination.) These kinds of moral systems are also described as "teleological," a term derived from the Greek word *telos*, which means end, purpose, or goal.

Note the adverb "solely" in the above definition. Only the consequences of an action matter. In a utilitarian moral system, nothing is right or wrong *per se*. There is no rule to check against. According to utilitarianism, only one principle should be employed in deciding if a particular decision is just or unjust: the results it produces, both positive and negative, *vis-à-vis* any alternative that might be proposed.

Utilitarianism plays an important role in the development of public policy today. The use of cost-benefit analyses, for instance, reflects utilitarian thinking. Moreover, the several sets of management theories and models examined in chapter 2 that promote optimization, including, most notably, management science, can be viewed as organizational analogues to utilitarian thought, which is examined here as a distinct political philosophy.

Two Englishmen are generally identified as the architects of utilitarian thought. Jeremy Bentham was a thoroughgoing materialist. He did not believe in God, in heaven or hell, or in sin or virtue. This does not mean that Bentham was a wanton sop, however. In fact, he accomplished much over the course of his lifetime that is considered praiseworthy. Bentham contributed significantly to the development of public education in Great Britain and to prison reform, for instance.

John Stuart Mill (1806–73), the son of one of Bentham's friends and the author of *On Liberty* (1859), attempted to rescue utilitarian thinking from some of its more obvious flaws. Most importantly, Mill maintained that the state has no right to interfere in the private lives of individuals. Like Bentham, Mill was a social reformer. He was, for instance, an early advocate for the right of women to vote.

Always the hedonist, Bentham argued that all public and social policy should be oriented to happiness, which he narrowly defined as the experience of pleasure and the avoidance of pain. "Nature has placed mankind under the governance of two sovereign masters, pain and pleasure. They alone point out what we ought to do and determine what we shall do; the standard of right and wrong, and the chain of causes and effects, are both fastened to their throne. They govern us in all we do, all we say, all we think; every effort we can make to throw off our subjection to pain and pleasure will only serve to demonstrate and confirm it. A man may claim to reject their rule, but in reality he will remain subject to it."[6] Bentham's approach was truly hedonistic in this sense; nothing can be considered intrinsically good or bad in his view. As physical beings, we cannot know good or bad *per se*; we can only know pleasure and pain. Further, all pleasures and pains can be quantified as positive or negative "utiles," a term coined by Bentham. And once the values of these pleasures and pains have been calculated for any particular pair of public policy or social alternatives, decision-makers should simply choose the one that maximizes the overall happiness of those whose interests are being considered.

There are obvious problems with utilitarianism. Most importantly, it is difficult to balance pleasure and pain in a simple equation. How should the funding of a community orchestra, for instance, be balanced

---

6. Bentham, *An Introduction to the Principles of Morals and Legislation.*

against street repairs? It is sometimes suggested that money serves this function, but money can be a rather crude way to decide how we should allocate life's benefits and burdens, the primary purpose of any system of justice. Further, how should the intensity of any particular pleasure or pain be weighed? How should we proceed if three people are mildly opposed to a policy proposal, but a fourth thinks it is the greatest thing since sliced bread? There is no way to distinguish "extreme support" from "mild support" or "extreme opposition" from "mild opposition" in most voting systems. Still further, how should we go about ascertaining the perspectives of everyone who might possibly be affected by a proposed policy change?

Timeframe can be a problem as well. Consider global warming. Fossil fuels are cheap now, but their continued use is heating up the planet, thus spawning an array of public policy challenges. Further, global warming may not be reversible. Given this, how should we balance pleasures and pains that have yet to fully manifest themselves against the pleasures and pains of the moment? Hedonistic utilitarianism does not account for the problem of sustainability.

Hedonistic utilitarianism's cavalier approach to minority rights is generally recognized as its most serious flaw, however. Utilitarianism provides no conceptual space for human rights. Among the four political philosophies examined here, the very idea of human rights only makes sense, in fact, in a rules-based moral system. Utilitarianism is only concerned about happiness, which it defines in terms that are exclusively materialistic. Utilitarianism strives to produce the greatest quantity of happiness possible for the greatest number of people. The interests of racial minorities, religious minorities, the LGBTQ community, the mentally ill, etc., can be discounted all too easily in the calculation of utiles associated with any public or social policy of interest to any of these communities.

Finally, hedonistic utilitarianism does not account for personal loyalties. Everyone's utiles are just as good as everyone else's. We know, however, that people hold particular allegiances in real life, affinities that inform their judgments about who should get what and who should bear what. There is no room for this kind of thinking in utilitarianism. There is no room, for instance, for patriotism, a particular kind of affinity, in a utilitarian moral framework.

Again, John Stuart Mill recognized some of these flaws in Bentham's conception of utilitarianism. He was stung, for instance, by the criticism that there is no distinction in Bentham's moral philosophy between lower pleasures and higher pleasures. Given this, Mill opined that higher pleasures should count for more than lower pleasures in the calculation of utiles. How would you know if a particular pleasure is higher or lower? Mill recommended that we ask those who have experienced both. Surely, they would know. Some, of course, view this remedy as a sure prelude to cultural elitism.

Contemporary utilitarians have generally avoided the kind of specificity that can sometimes lead to unacceptable outcomes in utilitarian thinking. Preference utilitarians, for instance, argue that we should calculate utiles associated with broad preferences rather than singular acts. To protect minority rights, rule utilitarians hypothesize that we would all want to live in a society in which minority perspectives and lifestyles are protected. Following this logic, they recommend that we apply the concept of utiles to the development of certain rules rather than to particular decisions or to particular public policies. To avoid the sustainability problem, other consequentialists suggest that we replace the utilitarian commitment to the "maximization" of utility with a lesser standard, "optimization," perhaps, or Simon's concept of "satisficing."

LIBERTARIANISM

Broadly speaking, libertarianism affirms the rights of individuals to acquire, hold, and exchange their own property with minimal interference from the state. From the libertarian point of view, the individual rather than any conception of the community or the state is the moral actor of concern.

We have already been introduced to a particular version of libertarian thought. In chapter 2, we examined the maximization of shareholder wealth perspective, which is closely associated with Milton Friedman. The line drawn from libertarianism as a management theory to the public square is a direct one. Indeed, libertarianism can be understood as an economic and political philosophy as well as a management philosophy. Although John Locke is sometimes identified as the father of libertarianism, F. A. Hayek (1899–1992) and Friedman, together with other economists associated with the Chicago school of economics, are generally credited with breathing life into this contemporary manifestation of classical liberalism. These scholars opposed the interventionist fiscal policies promoted by John Maynard Keynes (1883–1946) and advocated instead for the restrained use of monetary policy, governmental deregulation, and the privatization of certain public services.

In the latter half of the twentieth century, Ayn Rand (1905–82) also fired the libertarian imagination with two best-selling novels, *The Fountainhead* (1943) and *Atlas Shrugged* (1957). The father-and-son team of Ron and Rand Paul are associated with today's political expression of the libertarian impulse in the United States. And Robert Nozick (1938–2002) is often credited with having made the case for libertarianism as a political philosophy. In his 1974 text *Anarchy, State, and Utopia* (1974), Nozick reasoned that nothing more than a minimal state "limited to the narrow functions of protection against force, theft, fraud, enforcement of contracts, and so on" can be justified without violating people's rights.[7]

In fact, two very different language games fall under the rubric of libertarianism. Ayn Rand and Robert Nozick are associated with the deontological version of this resurgent political philosophy. They view property rights as sacrosanct and argue that taxation should be understood as a kind of forced labor or slavery. Self-ownership is a key principle in this strain of libertarian thought.

In contrast, Milton Friedman and other economists associated with the Chicago school contend that the private sector simply produces better results, i.e., more wealth and better societal outcomes, when left to its own devices. Their claims are teleological in nature and hence subject to verification. As we have seen, Friedman's predictions in this regard concerning private sector firms and the overall economy, too, were often overstated. The several waves of governmental deregulation and tax reduction implemented in the United States since the 1980s have not produced the manifold benefits promised by those who have advocated on behalf of "free market reforms."

Like the rules-based and utilitarian political philosophies examined above, libertarianism is not without its problems. First, libertarians generally espouse a negative conception of rights. This is clearly evident in the first ten amendments to the United States Constitution, which is based, to a significant degree, on the political philosophy of John Locke. The Bill of Rights affirms, for instance, that a citizen's speech cannot be abridged, that her home cannot be searched, and that she cannot be jailed without formal charges being filed. These are "freedoms from." "Freedoms to" or

---

7. Nozick, *Anarchy, State, and Utopia*, xix.

"freedom for" are anathema to most libertarians. They are hard-pressed to acknowledge a right to an education, a right to medical care, or a right to adequate housing.

Second, the concept of "self-ownership," which is asserted in no uncertain terms in the deontological version of libertarianism, is anything but self-evident. Libertarianism can thus be dismissed as but one of several language games or emotivist political philosophies, to use MacIntyre's terminology, all of which are essentially unmoored in any anthropological or ontological sense.

Third, libertarians struggle to explain why inherited wealth should be excluded from taxation. This is particularly so in the case of wealth originally acquired through the exploitation of workers or the "unjust" confiscation, at some point in time, of another individual's property. Robert Nozick devised three rules pertaining to private holdings to address this concern: first, a person who initially acquires a holding in accordance with the principle of justice is entitled to that holding; second, a person to whom a holding is transferred in accordance with the principle of justice is entitled to that holding; and third, no one, including the state, is entitled to a holding except by the repeated applications of rules one and two.[8] Nozick then described the circumstances under which the original acquisition and the subsequent transfer of an acquisition can be considered just. Although his reasoning is logical enough, critics contend that the practical application of Nozick's theory of distributive justice in the real world would be unwieldy to the point of impossibility. The insistence that reparations for slavery should be paid is often suggested as a test case in this regard. Where to begin? And where to end?

Fourth, there is an implicit assumption in the teleological version of libertarianism that everyone has the capacity and the wherewithal to pull themselves up by their own bootstraps. This is not necessarily so in the case of deeply impoverished communities, that is, in communities with few financial, social, or cultural resources with which to work.

PRAGMATISM

Pragmatism is often celebrated as a uniquely American philosophy. It features a practical perspective, an ethic of individualism, confidence in the scientific method, and optimism, four ideas sometimes associated with

8. Nozick, *Anarchy, State, and Utopia*, 3.

the American character. Pragmatism's first generation of theorists included Charles Sanders Peirce (1839–1914), William James (1842–1910), and John Dewey (1859–1952). As a political philosophy, it was held in esteem from the turn of the prior century through the 1940s, but was then eclipsed to a considerable extent by other views. This changed in the 1970s with the work of two philosophers, Jürgen Habermas (b. 1929) and Richard Rorty (1931–2007), both of whom have acknowledged a substantial debt to John Dewey.

Several elements in the thinking of pragmatism's first generation of scholars persist in the work of today's pragmatists. One, the community should be approached through the individual, rather than vice-versa. The value of autonomous choice recurs as a priority in their work. Two, the world should be understood in natural terms. There is no appeal in pragmatism to spiritual or ideal beliefs. Three, the experimental attitude is embraced. This is evident in today's pragmatists in their consistent appeal to the need for discursive engagement. Four, many of today's pragmatists share the optimistic outlook for which Peirce, James, and Dewey were celebrated.

Jürgen Habermas is one of today's most frequently cited pragmatists. Our interest here is his theory of communicative action, which he outlined in *The Theory of Communicative Action: Reason and the Rationalization of Society* (1984). Habermas argues that social norms have been reduced to the status of mere conventions. He then focuses on four distinct kinds of "action": teleological or strategic action, normatively-regulated action, dramaturgical action, and communicative action.[9] Further, the "demythologization" of worldviews has severely reduced the salience of normatively regulated action.[10] Because of this, shared belief systems are no longer available to guide behavior. Still further, instrumental rationality is filling a void created by the reduced authority of norms. Finally, instrumental rationality is rapidly "colonizing the lifeworld."[11] Reification, i.e., the sense of oneself as a thing among other things rather than as a person, thus follows from our growing tendency to view ourselves and others not as ends but as means to ends defined by our consumer society and the bureaucratic systems in which we live.

9. Habermas, *The Theory*, 85.

10. Habermas, *The Theory*, 48, 70, 162.

11. Habermas, *The Theory*, 10.

Habermas promotes communicative action as an antidote to this deteriorating situation. According to Habermas, communicative action can be pursued in five distinct kinds of discourse, each of which should be evaluated on its own terms. Theoretical discourse addresses the truth of propositions and the efficacy of teleological action. Practical discourse is used to assess the "rightness" of an action. Aesthetic criticism pertains to the adequacy of evaluation standards. Therapeutic critique refers to the truthfulness or sincerity of expressions. Finally, explicative discourse focuses on the comprehensibility of symbolic constructs.[12]

Habermas devotes considerable attention to what he calls the "ideal speech situation," a set of standards, in fact, that details the circumstances that make communicative action possible. These standards include knowledge pertaining to the question at hand, a modicum of communications skills, the complete absence of constraints, and self-consciousness.[13] With respect to practical discourse, Habermas draws a sharp distinction between the good and the moral. He does not believe that a common conception of the good can be recovered. Habermas thus acquiesces to the now widely accepted separation of any human anthropology or ontology and our understanding of the good on the one hand from the moral and the just on the other.

Habermas's theory of communicative action can be criticized on at least two grounds. First, he may be premature in discounting the possibility of achieving common ground with respect to our conception of the good. Habermas's concept of the lifeworld is so culturally oriented, in fact, that it obscures the possibility of any ontological perspective that might be considered universal.

Second, Habermas's theory of communicative action represents a procedural rather than a substantive approach to justice. It thus postpones the adjudication of particular claims. Communicative action may involve parties in a conversation who were previously excluded. It may even contribute to a less confrontational form of discourse. These are praiseworthy goals, to be sure. Lacking a standard against which claims can be assessed, however, one or more parties to a dispute could simply refuse to redistribute the community's benefits and burdens in any substantial way. They may be willing to explain their refusal, and they may even do so in a civil fashion. Nevertheless, given their different

12. Habermas, *The Theory*, 18.
13. Habermas, *The Theory*, 119.

conceptions of the good, agreement might not be achievable. Because it defines justice procedurally rather than substantively, communicative action lacks a rhetorical lever that can be used in a consistent manner to promote the equitable resolution of certain claims.

Richard Rorty contributed even more to the resurrection of pragmatism at the close of the twentieth century than Habermas. This is due, it seems, to the consistency with which he thought through the implications of pragmatism's epistemological assumptions. Rorty followed Peirce, James, and Dewey in holding that there is no difference between that which is true and that which works. His uncompromising stance in this regard distinguishes Rorty from other pragmatists, including Habermas.

According to Rorty, there are no external standards against which any idea, fact, or claim can be assessed. There is no foundation, as such, on which to build either an epistemology or an ethical system. In fact, "there is nothing to people except what has been socialized into them— their ability to use language, and thereby to exchange beliefs and desires with other people."[14] There is "no deep down there."[15] Indeed, Rorty defined pragmatism as "anti-essentialism applied to notions like 'truth,' 'knowledge,' 'language,' 'morality,' and similar objects of philosophical theorizing."[16] According to Rorty, the only standards we have access to are those that we arrive at discursively.

Rorty thus dismissed Rawls's theory of justice as futile. The need for discursive engagement cannot be avoided through the use of a mythical "veil of ignorance." He chastised Habermas, too, for failing to live up to the logic of his project. According to Rorty, Habermas's "ideal speech situation" is nothing more than a thinly disguised "transcendental" standard against which institutions and society as a whole can be evaluated.[17]

Rorty believed that human nature is malleable or contingent. Further, we engage in "sentence uttering" in order to cope with our environment and nothing more.[18] We "muddle through."[19] Rorty was not interested in pursuing the question of human motivation any more

14. Rorty, *Contingency, Irony, and Solidarity*, 177.

15. Rorty, *Consequences of Pragmatism*, xxxviii.

16. Rorty, *Consequences of Pragmatism*, 162.

17. Rorty, *Consequences of Pragmatism*, 173.

18. Rorty, *Philosophy and the Mirror*, 11.

19. Rorty, *Philosophy and the Mirror*, 11.

deeply than this. As a thoroughgoing materialist,[20] he was indifferent to Freudian analysis, existential angst, and all other theories of human motivation.

The understanding of the good that follows from Rorty's critique is less clear, however. At one point, he identified the good as success, thereby echoing Dewey's circular argument on behalf of growth: the goal of success is simply continued success.[21] At another point, Rorty extolled freedom as an important value, but pointedly backed away from any suggestion that liberty might be a preeminent good. Contra deontological libertarians, liberty is but one value among many others for pragmatists.[22]

Rorty had little to say about moral behavior, since he did not believe that there are any standards, as such, against which human interactions can be assessed. According to Rorty, there is simply no getting around the fact that all human interactions require discursive engagement.

Rorty had more to say about justice, however. His understanding of justice was culture-bound; indeed, he restricted the parties with whom we can expect to engage productively in meaningful discourse to the industrialized West.[23] Rorty thus joined John Rawls in discounting our ability to overcome the formidable barriers of geography, culture, and religion in our pursuit of justice.

The Achilles's heel of Rorty's thesis lies in his expectation that individuals will respond positively to the abandonment of any and all external standards of judgment. The following passage is quoted at length because the claim advanced in it is central to Rorty's work. It also reveals the source of Rorty's optimism. Indeed, it explains why he did not share the anxiety that compelled Rawls to develop his theory of justice and Habermas to advance his theory of communicative action.

> I prefer to [characterize] pragmatism [in this way] because it seems to me to focus on a fundamental choice which confronts the reflective mind: that between accepting the contingent character of starting points and attempting to evade this contingency. To accept the contingency of starting points is to accept our inheritance from, and our conversation with, our fellow humans as our only source of guidance. To attempt to evade this contingency is to hope to become a properly-programmed machine.

20. Rorty, *Philosophy and the Mirror*, 37.

21. Rorty, *Consequences of Pragmatism*, 172.

22. Rorty, *Contingency, Irony, and Solidarity*, 50, 53.

23. Rorty, *Consequences of Pragmatism*, 173.

This was the hope which Plato thought might be fulfilled at the top of the divided line, when we passed beyond hypotheses. Christians have hoped it might be attained by becoming attuned to the voice of God in the heart, and Cartesians that it might be fulfilled by emptying the mind and seeking the indubitable. Since Kant, philosophers have hoped that it might be fulfilled by finding that *a priori* structure of any possible inquiry, or language, or form of social life. If we give up this hope, we shall lose what Nietzsche called "metaphysical comfort," but we may gain renewed sense of community. Our identification with our community—our society, our political tradition, our intellectual heritage—is heightened when we see this community as *ours* rather than *nature's*, *shaped* rather than *found*, one among many which men have made.[24]

The claim that an individual will be more interested in, more committed to, or more loyal to a community because she is no longer weighed down by culturally transmitted ideas of the good, the moral, and the just is suspect to say the least. It reflects a blind belief in progress that seems out of place given the history of the twentieth century.

Absent an underlying belief in progress, however, Rorty's optimism is problematic. He derided Habermas because "he is more afraid of the sort of 'romantic' overthrow of established institutions, personified by Hitler and Mao, than of the suffocating effects of what Dewey called the 'crust of convention.'"[25] The desire to find shelter that is more secure than that which Rorty offers makes a great deal more sense after the flimsy foundation of his optimism is exposed, however. Habermas's ongoing search for an Archimedean lever seems more than justified. In the end, Rorty's "easygoing liberalism"[26] amounts to little more than whistling in the dark. Of course, the felt need for ontological shelter does not mean that it exists. It may, however, justify a continuing search.

The separation of a common conception of human nature, together with a shared understanding of the good, from a common conception of moral behavior, i.e., how we think about and treat ourselves and others as persons, and justice, i.e., how life's benefits and burdens should be shared

24. Rorty, *Consequences of Pragmatism*, 166.
25. Rorty, *Contingency, Irony, and Solidarity*, 66.
26. Klingwell, *A Civil Tongue*, 37.

among individuals recognized as persons and communities comprised
of persons, has been very costly, indeed. The various understandings of
the human person that undergird the moral systems developed since the
Enlightenment are undeniably anemic. This is particularly so in the case
of the various rules-based constructs examined above and utilitarianism, which views human beings as little more than pleasure-seeking and
pain-minimizing animals. Libertarianism assumes an agnostic position
on this question, and pragmatists tend to view human beings as culture-
bound and culturally determined. Anything deeper or more respectful
of the human person is simply beyond the reach of these several political
philosophies. The secular moral systems developed over the course of
the last three centuries claim to fill a gap left by the abandonment of a
Christian worldview, but they do so poorly.

Further, these various alternatives to a Christian worldview promise little beyond law and order, i.e., contract theory; the maximization
of pleasure and the minimization of pain, i.e., utilitarianism; a jealous
regard for privacy and property, i.e., libertarianism; and more and more
conversation, i.e., pragmatism. Lacking a more complex understanding
of human nature and a shared conception of the good, none of them can
offer much in terms of decision-making that is truly moral or a conception of justice, for that matter, that holds the promise of meaningful
change in the way life's benefits and burdens are shared.

Still further, the motive for pursuing change from within any of
these several moral systems is off-putting, to say the least. A fear of chaos
and risk aversion are assumed in the case of the three rules-based constructs examined above. Motivation is explained exclusively in terms of
pleasure and pain in the case of utilitarianism. Antipathy to interference
serves this same purpose for libertarians. And communicative competence and cultural affinity are assumed, respectively by Habermas and
Rorty, to be entirely sufficient to satisfy our felt need for norms and a
measure of social stability.

Is this enough: fear, the promise of pleasure, the forestalling of
pain, and value-free competence? Assessing the situation from within
the Aristotelian-Thomist tradition, Alasdair MacIntyre believes the answer is "no." To participate in civic discourse as an authentic leader, one
must first be formed in moral virtue, e.g., prudence, justice, temperance,
and fortitude or courage, understood, again, as an inclination or disposition oriented to moral and just behavior. Further, to attain salience,
this inclination, disposition, or "power" must be filtered through a set

of values or intellectual commitments that stand outside of or prior to the philosophical framework, i.e., a rules-based construct, utilitarianism, libertarianism, or pragmatism, deemed applicable to any particular question or concern about which the community might choose to deliberate.

This assumes, of course, that the genie can be put back in the bottle. It assumes, as well, that rules-based constructs, utilitarianism, libertarianism, and pragmatism will continue to be employed as frameworks for collective decision-making in our pluralistic society for some time to come. Which of these moral frameworks is most appropriate with respect to any given question or concern can be disputed, of course. Still, a leader who is steeped in virtue and whose judgments are informed by clearly articulated values and intellectual commitments, all of which lie outside of or prior to the formal decision-making process employed in addressing any given question or concern, should be in a position to suggest the most appropriate decision-making framework in each instance. Further, she should be better prepared to anticipate and then ameliorate, to some extent at least, any unintended consequences or unjust outcomes that could accrue from any given decision.

In chapter 4, Christian values and Christian intellectual commitments were recommended. This was entirely appropriate in the case of a committed disciple of Jesus who is discerning her role in the organization she serves and how she should respond to any given question. The public square is a more complex arena, however. In the public square, the key question goes beyond: "What should *I* think and what should *I* do?" It is instead: "What should *we* think and what should *we* do?" In the public square, one can no longer revert exclusively to Christian values and to Christian intellectual commitments. They can be introduced into the conversation and they can be asserted, but we cannot expect that they will automatically trump any other decision frame.

How, then, should we proceed? What mix of external values and intellectual commitments can a virtuous leader reliably employ as a check on decision-making being channeled through the secular decision frame adopted in the case of any given question or concern? The four political philosophies examined above have despaired of this possibility. Again, our conceptions of human nature and hence our conceptions of the good have been delinked from our understandings of moral behavior and justice. Is it reasonable to think, then, that we can construct an articulated moral framework that can secure broad acceptance in our pluralistic society on the basis of something other than a Christian worldview and, at the same time, promise results that are compatible with Christian moral thinking and a Christian conception of social justice?

Perhaps. In chapter 3, we noted that Robert Greenleaf appears to have had some exposure to existential thinking. Further, we observed that there is broad consensus that human beings can be understood as meaning-seeking beings. In this view, we all face a common question: "How should I pursue meaning in my life?" This question may provide a "backdoor" of sorts to a universal understanding of the human person, indeed, a backdoor into a kind of human anthropology. It may represent, in effect, a Socratic formulation of a universal conception of human nature that may be acceptable to many, even in our increasingly pluralistic society. To the extent this may be so, is it possible that this most meager of conceptual starting points might, nonetheless, provide a viable foundation for the development of a moral system that is both robust *and* fully compatible with Christian beliefs?

The analysis that follows explores this possibility. Again, existential thinkers understand all of us to be meaning-seeking beings. Given this, the good can be understood as the experience of meaning. As useful as this idea of the good might be, however, we will not have advanced very far unless it can be linked to viable conceptions of the moral and the just. If one experience of meaning is the moral equivalent of all other such experiences, our hope to provide a foundation for an articulated moral framework would be short-circuited. Fortunately, the Socratic formulation of the existential question extends a conceptual link to robust conceptions of both the moral and the just.

The concept of the moral, i.e., how we think about and treat ourselves and others as persons, that corresponds to this understanding of the good as the experience of meaning is respect for others based on their inherent dignity. In fact, the framing of the moral as dignity enjoys widespread support among moral philosophers, Friedrich Nietzsche notwithstanding. Some cite Descartes and Kant, both of whom believed that dignity, as a basis for moral action, follows from a recognition of the other as a rational being.[27] Kant, in particular, believed dignity to be superior to benevolence as a moral principle because it is based on reason rather than sentiment.[28] Bruce Ackerman relies on the liberal assertion of equality: "I am a person with a conception of the good. Simply by virtue

27. Taylor, *Sources of the Self*, 152, 315, 364.
28. Kant, *Groundwork*, 36.

of being such a person, I'm at least as good as you are."[29] He also relies on doubt, however, and asks: "Have you *so* transcended your doubts that you can look with disdain upon those who are struggling for knowledge of the kind you think you already possess? All people ought to model themselves on Socrates . . . It would be transparently silly to deprive people of power when all you can say is that you know what's good better than they do—for this way of presenting yourself is the very opposite of Socratic virtue."[30] Rawls acknowledged that one's sense of self-respect as a being who reasons demands a measure of reciprocity in her dealings with others.[31] Habermas uses the same argument in advancing the "notion of [an] ego identity that centers around the ability to realize *oneself* under conditions of *communicatively shared intersubjectivity*."[32] Rawls also cited self-interest,[33] as did John Dewey,[34] and a natural sympathy that is a product of evolution,[35] an explanation which also enjoys broad acceptance. The point is that a predisposition towards the recognition of an inherent dignity in others is widely accepted, even within the several very different language games explored in this chapter.

What then of justice? Whereas the moral pertains to the ways in which we understand and treat ourselves and others as persons, justice pertains to the distribution of society's benefits and burdens. The opportunity to fully explore one's life project can be defined as justice. This definition follows from an existential ontology, the concept of the good as the experience of meaning, and respect for the inherent dignity of others as a foundation for moral action. An individual requires certain enabling capacities—only some of which are material in nature—in order to pursue the experience of meaning in her life. The six "spheres" of an individual's life David Held describes in his theory of cosmopolitan governance provide a useful framework for conceptualizing the kind of substantive concerns that a system of justice based on opportunity might address. These spheres or domains include the body, social welfare, culture or cultural life, civic associations, the economy, and the organization of violence and

---

29. Ackerman, *Social Justice*, 66–67.

30. Ackerman, *Social Justice*, 367.

31. Rawls, *A Theory of Justice*, 179, 337, 396.

32. McCarthy, "Translator's Introduction," in Habermas, *The Theory*, xxiii.

33. Rawls, *A Theory of Justice*, 338.

34. Festenstein, *Pragmatism & Political Theory*, 60.

35. Rawls, *A Theory of Justice*, 460, 503, 522.

coercive relations.[36] Uniquely, however, our definition of the good as the individual experience of meaning provides a focus for Held's theory that it otherwise lacks. Substantive decisions in each of these six spheres could thus be based on the extent to which any given decision could be expected to contribute to the individual's potential to experience meaning in her life and the extent to which it could inhibit anyone else's potential to do likewise. Indeed, justice understood as opportunity could prompt an ongoing conversation about those enabling capacities that promise to contribute most to the experience of life as meaningful.

Although justice understood as opportunity could underwrite a substantial redistribution of society's benefits and burdens, it would not provide the kind of formulaic resolution of rival claims for which some moral philosophers have long hoped. Nevertheless, it could garner considerable support as a framework for conversations to this end. Even Deirdre McCloskey, a scholar who is profoundly suspicious of any kind of governmental intervention in the economy, supports this conception of opportunity in principle: "I agree with my favorite Marxist economist, Nancy Folbre, that education should be financed from the center, that maternity care and early child care should be expanded and be state financed, that inheritance taxes should be steep, that corporate welfare should be eliminated, that military expenditures should be cut to a tiny fraction of their present levels, that a modest minimum income should be given to every American, that tax laws should 'encourage both men and women to combine paid work with family and community work . . .' The existing governmental programs to help the poor are too small to do their alleged job, for the excellent reason that the relatively rich arrange this to be done."[37]

In place of a neat calculus, the framework for ongoing conversation would rely on dialogue, discursive engagement, and prudent judgment. Conversations of this sort would be grounded, however, on a common understanding of human nature. The world would not be accepted as entirely contingent as Richard Rorty would have us believe. In this sense, meaning as the good, respect for others based on their inherent dignity

36. Held, *Democracy*, 176–85.

37. McCloskey, *The Bourgeois Virtues*, 43–44.

as a basis for moral action, and opportunity reimagined as justice could serve as powerful "regulative ideas"[38] or "benchmarks."[39] See figure 9.

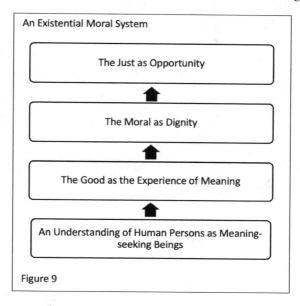

An Existential Moral System

The Just as Opportunity

The Moral as Dignity

The Good as the Experience of Meaning

An Understanding of Human Persons as Meaning-seeking Beings

Figure 9

In Bruce Ackerman's view, "there is a way that you and I can talk about power without claiming the right to judge the merit of each other's conception of the good. While we may disagree about the meaning of a good life, each of us is prepared to say that our own image of self-fulfillment has *some* value . . . And once we are prepared to affirm the value of fulfilling our own life plan, we may use this initial affirmation as the foundation of a public dialogue of right."[40] A theory of justice oriented to opportunity thus holds considerable potential to advance our conversations about the allocation of life's benefits and burdens.

The alternatives to something of this nature are threefold. First, our moral reasoning in the public square could be abandoned to the secular moral frameworks that would otherwise be employed in any particular instance: a rules-based construct of one kind or another, utilitarianism, libertarianism, or pragmatism. Second, contending parties could engage in value-free contests of wills based on their own self-interest. Third, we could continue to hope that our increasingly frayed, always tepid, and

38. Bernstein, *Beyond Objectivism and Relativism,* 163.

39. Held, *Democracy,* 209.

40. Ackerman, *Social Justice,* 57.

largely mythic "civil religion" continues to restrain our more egregious displays of power politics.

We are now in position to propose an analogue to the normative model recommended in chapter 4 for leaders in organizations. See figure 10.

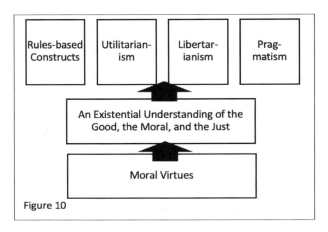

| Rules-based Constructs | Utilitarian-ism | Libertar-ianism | Prag-matism |

An Existential Understanding of the Good, the Moral, and the Just

Moral Virtues

Figure 10

In place of the nine sets of management theories included in our organizational model, this model features the four secular political philosophies that now constitute a conceptual menu of sorts for discourse in the public square. In keeping with our definition of leadership as the balanced exercise of a broad range of management responsibilities in service to a broad array of stakeholders in a manner constrained by the leader's internalized virtues and fully informed by values and intellectual commitments drawn from a larger belief system, but oriented, nonetheless, to ends sanctioned by the organization or by society, virtue is again posited as an essential precondition for the exercise of true leadership. Because we live in a pluralistic society, however, an articulated moral framework that is based on an existential understanding of human persons as meaning-seeking beings, an understanding of the good as the experience of meaning, an understanding of the moral as the full recognition of the inherent dignity that attaches to all persons, and an understanding of justice as opportunity, is substituted for the Christian values and the Christian intellectual commitments featured in the prior model.

Although not explicitly Christian in origin, this articulated moral framework certainly reflects the broader wisdom literature cited by

Robert Greenleaf and other proponents of the servant-leader model. More to the point, meaning, dignity, and opportunity are Christian values, too.

PART II

The Wisdom of the Beatitudes

When he saw the crowds, he went up the mountains, and after he had sat down, his disciples came to him. He began to teach them, saying:

"Blessed are the poor in spirit,
for theirs is the kingdom of heaven.
Blessed are they who mourn,
for they will be comforted.
Blessed are the meek,
for they will inherit the land.
Blessed are they who hunger and thirst for righteousness,
for they will be satisfied.
Blessed are the merciful,
for they will be shown mercy.
Blessed are the clean of heart,
for they will see God.
Blessed are the peacemakers,
for they will be called children of God.
Blessed are they who are persecuted for the sake of righteousness,
for theirs is the kingdom of heaven.
Blessed are you when they insult you and persecute you and utter every kind of evil against you [falsely] because of me. Rejoice and be glad, for your reward will be great in heaven. Thus they persecuted the prophets who were before you" (MATT 5:1–12).

FOUR ARGUMENTS WERE ADVANCED in part I: one, the management theories and models available to us are useful, but deficient in two respects; two, the servant-leader model proposed by Robert Greenleaf addresses these twin concerns, but its claims in this regard are poorly rooted and hence weak; three, these challenges point to the need for virtue and externally anchored values and intellectual commitments as prerequisites for authentic leadership in all kinds of organizations; and four, analogues to the management theories and models now available to us pertain more broadly to the public square as well. They too, however, are deficient.

Together, these four arguments underwrite the sharp distinction drawn in this text between our understanding of "management" on the one hand and the concept of "leadership" on the other. Whereas management can be understood as the responsibility for and performance of any one or more of several organizational or societal functions, e.g., planning, organizing, staffing, directing, coordinating, reporting, and budgeting, in a manner oriented to ends external to the manager, authentic leadership requires the balanced exercise of these same responsibilities in service to a broader array of stakeholders in a manner constrained by the leader's internalized virtues and informed by values and intellectual commitments drawn from a larger belief system, but oriented, nonetheless, to ends sanctioned by the organization or by society. Again, leadership has been distinguished from management in four ways: first, it is oriented to service; second, leadership it oriented to an array of stakeholders; third, its exercise is constrained by virtues internal to the leader; and fourth, its exercise is informed by values and intellectual commitments drawn from a larger belief system. The Aristotelian/Thomist tradition's understanding of moral virtue and Christian values and intellectual commitments were recommended to those who seek to better integrate their commitments as disciples of Jesus and their responsibilities on the job. In effect, a definition of leadership consistent with Robert Greenleaf's understanding of servant leadership—a definition that is fully compatible, as well, with our understanding of Christian discipleship—has been proposed.

This text is not aimed at those who are seeking to accommodate their faith to the world, nor is it intended as a way to proselytize those who do not believe or those who live casually or comfortably with their faith commitments. It is intended, instead, for managers and nominal leaders who are discomfited by the conflicting demands of faith on the one hand and their obligations on the job and in society more broadly on the other.

Everything shared to this point has been conceptual or theoretical, however. One may accept the need for moral virtue oriented to Christian values and Christian intellectual commitments, but still not know how to proceed. This felt need for clearer direction will provide a focus as we turn to the second portion of this text. The resources of the Christian tradition with respect to this concern are very rich, indeed. In the earliest days of the church, the individual Beatitudes detailed in chapter 5 of Matthew's Gospel, in particular, were understood as a depiction of the ideal progression in the life of virtue recommended to Jesus' disciples. The early church fathers, most notably John Chrysostom and Augustine, endorsed this understanding of Matthew's version of the Beatitudes, an understanding that was embraced by Thomas Aquinas in the twelfth century, too: "The sermon contains the whole process of forming the life of a Christian. Therein man's interior movements are ordered. Because after declaring that his end is Beatitude; and after commending the authority of the apostles, through whom the teaching of the gospel was to be promulgated, he orders man's interior movements, first in regard to man himself, secondly in regard to his neighbor."[1]

We will explore this ancient conception of the Beatitudes as a path forward for those who are discomfited by the demands of their faith *vis-à-vis* competing demands encountered in the roles they play as managers and as nominal leaders in all kinds of organizations and in the public square, too. To this end, we will first locate the Beatitudes in the context of Matthew's Gospel and the New Testament as a whole. We will then introduce an interpretive framework endorsed by the early church fathers. This will be followed by a short reflection on certain conceptional concerns pertaining to the New Testament's use of such terms as "virtue," "gift," and "fruit." Further, we will address a vexing denominational dispute involving Matthew's version of the Beatitudes. Finally, we will examine four insights pertaining to the Beatitudes articulated by the early church fathers, insights that establish the Beatitudes as a privileged path forward for disciples of Jesus who struggle in balancing their faith commitments and their lives in the world.

It is generally believed that Matthew's Gospel was written between the years 85 and 90, perhaps in Antioch. Further, given the lengths to

---

1. Aquinas, "Things that Are Contained."

which the evangelist goes in portraying Jesus as the embodied fulfillment
of the Jewish scriptures, it was likely written for a Christian community
made up largely of ethnic Jews, a community that probably included a
small but growing number of gentile converts as well.[2]

Contemporary biblical scholarship provides us with several strategies for use in analyzing Matthew's Gospel. We will briefly consider two
of them: source criticism and genre criticism.[3] Source criticism is a historical-critical or diachronic method that searches for and then examines
the "original sources" that undergird or lie behind a biblical text. This
method is of particular relevance to this inquiry because we have two
versions of the Beatitudes, a shorter version in Luke's Gospel comprised
of four Beatitudes, and, depending on how you count them, seven, eight,
or even nine Beatitudes in Matthew's Gospel.

A key question arises as a result: Which version came first? This is an
example of what Scripture scholars refer to as the "synoptic problem," the
recognition that Matthew, Mark, and Luke share a great deal of information, but differ in substantial ways as well. Matthew and Luke appear to
draw on Mark, but also on another common "source," the hypothesized
"Q" or *Quelle* source,[4] which seems to have consisted of various sayings
attributed to Jesus. They rely, as well, on their own unique materials.
Scripture scholars believe that Luke's version of the Beatitudes and the
core of Matthew's version, too, are largely drawn from "Q," and that the
additional Beatitudes contained in Matthew's version are drawn from a
tradition unique to Matthew's community. According to John P. Meier, a
highly regarded Scripture scholar, "Beatitudes 1 (poor), 2 (mourners), 4
(hungry) and 9 (long one on persecution) come from Q, while Beatitudes
3 (meek), 5 (merciful), 6 (pure of heart), 7 (peacemakers), and 8 (short
one on persecution) come from either Matthew's special source (M),
Matthew's creative redaction, or a mixture of both."[5]

A second question concerning Matthew's Gospel is addressed by
scholars who employ the historical-critical method: Do the Beatitudes in
Matthew's version go back to Jesus himself or do they reflect the wisdom
of Matthew's community or, perhaps, the wisdom of the early church as
a whole? Relying on criteria often employed in source criticism, Meier

---

2. Harrington, *The Gospel of Matthew*, 21, and Senior, *Matthew*, 2.

3. Pontifical Biblical Commission, "The Interpretation of the Bible," 121–96.

4. Pontifical Biblical Commission, "The Interpretation of the Bible," 136.

5. Meier, *A Marginal Jew*, 319.

has concluded that Matthew's version of the Beatitudes can, indeed, be traced back to Jesus: "One can forge a good argument from [the criterion of] discontinuity for ascribing the core Beatitudes of the Q Sermon to Jesus himself rather than to early Christians. One can also appeal to the criterion of coherence . . . Jesus sums up all eschatological good, all that is to come and to be hoped for, in terms of the kingdom of God. It is not for nothing that 'thy kingdom come' is the key petition of the Lord's Prayer."[6] Reaching the same conclusion, Helen Doohan describes the Beatitudes as "the oldest summary of Jesus' teaching."[7]

Scholars who employ literary-critical methods are less concerned about the primary sources enfolded into Matthew's version of the Beatitudes than the essential meaning of the Beatitudes and the reason this teaching was so prized by Matthew's community. Some have concluded that Matthew's version of the Beatitudes speaks to identity. As noted above, the author of Matthew's Gospel addressed a community perplexed by two questions of existential importance. First, how could its members continue to think of themselves as faithful Jews when so many of their co-religionists had rejected Jesus and his Jewish disciples? And second, could Jesus' mission really pertain to the gentile world, too? Clearly, Matthew's community stood at an inflection point in Christian history.

The author of Matthew's Gospel answered these two questions by portraying Jesus as the definitive fulfillment of the Jewish scriptures. To this end, Matthew drew on Isaiah 2:2–4 and Zechariah 8:20–23 in revealing Jesus as the embodiment and fulfillment of Israel's primary task in the overall economy of salvation history: the reconciliation of all the nations of the world with God. It seems clear that Matthew wrote his Gospel to help his friends and neighbors find their way through the crisis in identity with which they struggled.

Further, Jesus invited those who attended to his voice to internal transformation or conversion. In his many confrontations with the Pharisees, in particular, Matthew's Jesus argued not that the legal requirements derived from the Pentateuch were no longer valid but that the rigorous practices enforced by Jesus' adversaries missed the point. According to Jesus, the Father wants us to love and care for one another. Indeed, Jesus excoriated the kind of unreasoning compliance that impedes a loving response to those in need. This is clearly evident in Jesus' teachings on

6. Meier, *A Marginal Jew*, 330.

7. Doohan, "Beatitude(s)," 78.

the Sabbath and on a number of other issues pertaining to cultic purity. When the Pharisees condemned Jesus' hungry disciples for picking grain on the Sabbath, he responded: "If you knew what this meant, 'I desire mercy, not sacrifice,' you would not have condemned these innocent men" (Matt 12:7). With respect to food and ritual washings, Jesus censured the Pharisees in no uncertain terms: "Hypocrites, well did Isaiah prophesy about you when he said: 'This people honors me with their lips, but their hearts are far from me; in vain do they worship me, teaching as doctrines human precepts.' He summoned the crowd and said to them, 'Hear and understand. It is not what enters one's mouth that defiles that person; but what comes out of the mouth is what defiles one'" (Matt 15:7–11). Jesus oriented the law as it was understood by the Pharisees to a new law of love, a new set of commandments, in fact, which are expressed not just in the Beatitudes but throughout Matthew's Gospel as a whole: "You shall love the Lord, your God, with all your heart, with all your soul, and with all your mind. This is the greatest and the first commandment. The second is like it: You shall love your neighbor as yourself. The whole law and the prophets depend on these two commandments" (Matt 22:37–40).

It is also clear that Matthew's Jesus taught with great authority. This is especially important in the case of the Beatitudes. As all four Gospels make clear, Jesus was not a systematic teacher as such. Indeed, the Beatitudes enumerated in chapter 5 of Matthew's Gospel are the closest we come in any of the Gospels to a systematic program of instruction. Genre criticism, a particular type of literary-criticism, thus calls attention to the setting established by Matthew for the Sermon on the Mount, the colloquy in which the Beatitudes were proclaimed by Jesus. He first ascends a mountain, the typical setting for a theophany or encounter with God. Jesus then sits down, thereby assuming the traditional position of an authoritative teacher in the Judaism of Jesus' day. The seminal importance of the Beatitudes is thus affirmed. As Servais Pinckaers noted: "The Sermon on the Mount is a gospel of prime importance for Christian ethics. This seems to have been St. Matthew's intention in writing this Gospel."[8]

Several contrasts drawn later on in the Sermon on the Mount illustrate this point as well, for instance, "You have heard that it was said to your ancestors, 'You shall not kill; and whoever kills will be liable to judgment.' But I say to you, whoever is angry with his brother will be liable to judgment" (Matt 5:21–22). In Donald Senior's view, Matthew

---

8. Pinckaers, *Sources*, 134.

portrays Jesus as a regal figure with the authority to exercise royal pre-rogatives: "It is not only a matter of the priority of human need over cultic observance . . . but the royal authority of both David and Jesus as David's Son—and in Matthew's eyes—one far greater than David."[9] According to Daniel J. Harrington, Matthew depicts Jesus as a new Moses, most nota-bly in the parallels drawn in chapter 2 of Matthew's Gospel between the circumstances surrounding the births of Moses and Jesus.[10]

Additionally, Matthew positions Jesus as the embodied fulfillment of key passages in the Jewish scriptures, most notably certain passages in the prophetic books, but in the wisdom books and in the psalms, too. This is evident in several "fulfillment passages" dispersed throughout Matthew's Gospel. See, for instance, the circumstances surrounding Jesus' birth (Matt 1:22), the holy family's flight into Egypt (Matt 2:15), the location of Jesus' ministry in Galilee (Matt 4:14), Jesus' concern that word of a healing might be distributed too widely (Matt 12:17), and the circumstances surrounding Jesus' triumphal entry into Jerusalem (Matt 21:4). These passages all have analogues in the Old Testament. Indeed, Matthew goes to great lengths to reinterpret the Jewish scriptures in the light of Jesus' teachings, his ministry, and his passion and death.

It is not surprising, therefore, that Matthew's Jesus declares: "I have come not to abolish but to fulfill. Amen, I say to you, until heaven and earth pass away, not the smallest letter or the smallest part of a letter will pass from the law, until all things have taken place" (Matt 5:21–22). Mat-thew's neighbors thought of themselves as faithful Jews. In a substantial break with the pharisaic Judaism of their day, however, they believed they had been called, nonetheless, to internal conversion, i.e., *shub* in Hebrew or *metanoia* in Greek, the very essence, in fact, of Matthew's version of the Beatitudes.

Contemporary biblical scholarship offers another useful way to approach Matthew's version of the Beatitudes: an interpretive lens that focuses on the various uses to which a particular text has been put over time, i.e., *wirkungsgeschichte*,[11] in this instance, by the fathers of the early church. (As we have seen, the Beatitudes were gradually discounted as pertinent to the life of discipleship beginning in the sixteenth century. To the Reformers, the Beatitudes smacked of "salvation by works," and

9. Senior, *Matthew*, 136.

10. Harrington, *The Gospel of Matthew*, 46.

11. Pontifical Biblical Commission, "The Interpretation of the Bible," 149.

to Catholics, they came to be viewed as supererogatory: certainly praise-worthy, but not essential to salvation *per se*.) It may be helpful, then, to spend a moment introducing them to an audience that might be unfamiliar with these churchmen. In fact, their collective influence on the church we know today cannot be overestimated, and this extends well beyond the Beatitudes, of course. As we shall see, their interpretation of Matthew's version of the Beatitudes, in particular, speaks to their collective wisdom pertaining to the journey of discipleship conceived more broadly.

In fact, a number of the early church fathers served as a bridge between the apostolic era and the four great councils that together codified orthodox belief for the generations of Christians that followed. As noted by the Biblical Pontifical Institute: "The fathers of the church, who had a particular role in the process of the formation of the canon, likewise have a foundational role in relation to the living tradition which unceasingly accompanies and guides the church's reading and interpretation of Scripture."[12] The Nicene Council was called in 325 to confront the Arian controversy, which centered on the pre-incarnate Son's relationship to the Father. The First Council of Constantinople was convened in 381 to address other Christological concerns. It focused, as well, on the Trinity. Although the Trinity had been celebrated at the Nicene Council, a contentious debate quickly ensued concerning the precise nature of the relationships shared by the Father, the Son, and the Holy Spirit. To address these controversies, the First Council of Constantinople added language to the creed first promulgated by the Council of Nicaea. The Council of Ephesus was convened in 431 to repudiate Nestorianism, an adoptionist heresy that rejected Mary's identity as the "Mother of God." (At its heart, this heresy had more to do with Christology than Mary *per se*.) Rejecting all forms of adoptionism, the council declared Mary to be *Theotokos*, i.e., birth-giver to God, God-bearer, and Mother of God, as opposed to *Christokos*, i.e., Christ-bearer. The Council of Ephesus also repudiated Pelagianism, a rigorist heresy that rejected the orthodox view that human beings are irretrievably tainted by original sin and hence unable to resist sin without the aid of grace. And in 451, the Council of Chalcedon repudiated the doctrine of monophysitism, which argued that Jesus' human nature had been overwhelmed by the Second Person of the Trinity. To this end, the council drafted the "Chalcedonian Definition," which

---

12. Pontifical Biblical Commission, "The Interpretation of the Bible," 173.

is sometimes referred to as a creed. It affirms the "hypostatic union" of Jesus' two natures. He was declared to be one person, not two, albeit with two natures, human and divine.

Different beginning and ending dates for the patristic era have been suggested by scholars. Generally, the early church fathers wrote and preached between the second century and the fifth century. Lists of various early church fathers abound.

Various criteria have been suggested for status as an early church father. Most scholars hold, first, that a father's theology must be accepted as orthodox or at least generally so. In effect, the fathers of the early church codified, adhered to, and handed on the apostolic tradition. The fathers must have persevered in communion with the church. (In fact, some of the most influential thinkers in the early church were thought to have lapsed into heresy at one or more points in their lives. Given this, Origen (184–253), who was viewed by some as a proto-Arian, and Tertullian (160–240), who led a Montanist schism in Carthage, are not officially recognized as saints, as are so many of the early church fathers. Even though Origen, Tertullian, and others are left off some lists of the early church fathers, they nonetheless had profound impacts on the development of Christian theology.) Second, a father must be recognized as having led an exemplary life. Third, status as an early church father is generally reserved to those who influenced or were cited by a general church council or by another father.[13]

Again, the early church fathers codified, affirmed, and handed on the apostolic tradition. Indeed, they focused to a considerable extent on the development of doctrine as the church moved out of its original Jewish setting into the larger Greco-Roman world. In the second century, the early church fathers's primary concern was the relationship shared by Christianity and Judaism on the one hand and the relationship shared by Christianity and the Roman Empire on the other. Clement of Rome (35–99), Ignatius of Antioch (35–108), and Polycarp (69–155) are generally viewed as the greatest of these earliest of the early church fathers. Collectively, they are sometimes referred to as the "apostolic fathers." The early church fathers of the third and fourth centuries tended to focus more on the development of doctrine, e.g., Christology, soteriology, pneumatology, etc., often in dialogue with Platonic and neo-Platonic thought, and on the crafting of arguments designed to refute heresies of various kinds.

13. Chapman, "Fathers of the Church."

In their homilies and in their other writings, the early church fathers tended to rely more on intuition than finely crafted logic. Nevertheless, they drew extensively on the books of the Old Testament and on the four Gospels and Paul's Letters in the New Testament. In this sense, their work can be considered canonical.[14] At the same time, the early church fathers exercised considerable freedom in interpreting Scripture, often crafting imaginative allegorical analyses. For instance, they often explored Christological themes using evocative images drawn from the Old Testament. They drew, as well, on liturgical practice and traditional forms of prayer,[15] thus establishing the principle of *lex orandi, lex credendi,* a phrase that can be roughly translated as "we believe what we pray."

A number of the early church fathers embraced Plato's idealism as a philosophical foundation for their work. The changeable and the unchangeable on the one hand and the temporal and the eternal on the other thus emerged as important criteria in the work of the early church fathers. In keeping with this philosophical orientation, the central task of believers, they argued, was to "purify" themselves by ascending, in turn, from a fear of God to piety, to charity, to fortitude, to mercy, to purification of the heart, and finally to wisdom. The spiritual life was thus viewed as a progression in holiness.

In the East, John Chrysostom (347–407) is widely acknowledged as the greatest of the early church fathers. Together with Basil, who drafted an influential monastic rule, and Gregory Nazianzen, Chrysostom is recognized as one of the "three hierarchs." He served as the Archbishop of Constantinople and was highly regarded for his homiletic skills. Chrysostom's extant works include hundreds of homilies on both the Jewish scriptures and the New Testament. Athanasius, who led the fight against the Arian heresy at the First Council of Nicaea, is regarded as one of the great Eastern fathers as well.

In the West, Augustine is generally recognized as the greatest of the early church fathers. Together with Ambrose, Jerome, and Gregory the Great, he is identified as one of the preeminent Latin fathers. In later centuries, only Thomas Aquinas would achieve a comparable status in the Western church. After a youth engaged in dissolute living and an unsatisfying pursuit of learning, Augustine converted to Christianity. In time, he was installed as Bishop of Hippo. A thoroughgoing Platonist,

14. Pontifical Biblical Commission, "The Interpretation of the Bible," 156.
15. Pontifical Biblical Commission, "The Interpretation of the Bible," 174.

Augustine fought against Manichaeism, Arianism, Pelagianism, Dona-
tism, and other heresies. We have over one hundred of Augustine's texts
and sermons. His extended treatises include *On Christian Doctrine*, an
apologetic work; *The Confessions*, the West's first great autobiography;
The City of God, which was written in the traumatic wake of the sack of
Rome by the Visigoths in 410; and *On the Trinity*. Augustine profoundly
influenced the church's understanding of grace, sin, the Trinity, sexual
ethics, just war theory, and a number of other theological topics.

So what can we say about the early church fathers? First and foremost, they are widely recognized as the principal developers of Christian
doctrine. They did not undertake this task in a *de novo* fashion, however.
They adhered to the Scriptures and to the apostolic tradition. When
the fathers of the Second Vatican Council committed themselves to *ressourcement*, i.e., a return to the sources, it was both to Scripture and to the
early church fathers that they turned.

It may be helpful if we clarify a number of key terms before we examine the collective view of the early church fathers regarding Matthew's
version of the Beatitudes. Following Aristotle, they tended to understand
the moral virtues as inclinations or dispositions formed by habit. However, other terms were used for virtue as well, including "blessings," "gifts,"
and "fruits."

The term "blessing" tends to emphasize less the will of the one who
is cultivating a particular virtue than God's action in the disciple's life.
According to Harrington, "a formal 'blessing' is a divine action, sometimes brought about through an intermediary, e.g., a priest, a king, or a
prophet."[16] The blessings to which Matthew refers, for instance, cannot be
earned as such. To illustrate this point, consider the man who discovered
a treasure in a field in Matthew 13:44. The man did nothing, it seems, to
earn his good fortune. He was simply lucky or blessed! The lucky man
responds to this blessing, of course; he sells all that he has in order to
purchase the field. There is no doubt, however, that it is God, rather than
the man himself, who engineered this happy circumstance.

The term "gifts" was also employed by the early church fathers.
Augustine associated the Beatitudes with the gifts of the Holy Spirit as
first enumerated in chapter 11 of Isaiah and, then, distilled over time as
wisdom, understanding, counsel, fortitude, knowledge, piety, and fear of

---

16. Harrington, *The Gospel of Matthew*, 78.

the Lord.[17] According to both Augustine and Aquinas, these gifts draw us to the Beatitudes.[18] As affirmed by Pinckaers, "Augustine was the first to have linked the texts of Matthew and Isaiah, and consequently to have attributed the gifts of the Holy Spirit to the very Christians to whom the Beatitudes were addressed."[19] In effect, these gifts can be understood as the "nudges" or "invitations" we sense as we are drawn ever deeper into the life of discipleship. Paul, too, followed Isaiah in using the language of gifts in 1 Corinthians:

> There are different kinds of spiritual gifts but the same Spirit; there are different forms of service but the same Lord; there are different workings but the same God who produces all of them in everyone. To each individual the manifestation of the Spirit is given for some benefit. To one is given through the Spirit the expression of wisdom; to another the expression of knowledge according to the same Spirit; to another faith by the same Spirit; to another gifts of healing by the one Spirit; to another mighty deeds; to another prophecy; to another discernment of spirits; to another varieties of tongues; to another interpretation of tongues. But one and the same Spirit produces all of these, distributing them individually to each person as he wishes (1 Cor 12:4–11).

Alternately, the term "fruits" is used in Paul's Letter to the Galatians: "The fruit of the Spirit is love, joy, peace, patience, kindness, generosity, faithfulness, gentleness, [and] self-control" (Gal 5:22–23). The point of emphasis, in this instance, is the results realized in the life of the disciple.

We should not make too much of the distinctions drawn here between and among these three seemingly distinct terms and their respective synonyms: "moral virtues," "blessings," and "fruits" or "results." Neither Isaiah nor Paul was writing as a linguist. Both hoped to communicate the Spirit's singular role in the development of a life reoriented to God. In fact, it was only in the thirteenth century that theologians sought to draw a sharp distinction between the related concepts of gifts and fruits.[20]

Further, God's seminal role in this regard does not negate the need for a response from those who receive these invitations or gifts. After all,

17. Augustine, "Our Lord's Sermon," 17,833.
18. Aquinas, "First Part of the Second Part, Question 86."
19. Pinckaers, *Sources*, 151.
20. Ten Klooster, *Thomas Aquinas*, 97.

gifts can go unopened, and gifts have to be nurtured if they are to bear fruit. Our particular interest in this text is our responsibility as disciples of Jesus to respond appropriately and as faithfully as possible to the gifts we have received. This is why the Aristotelian/Thomist tradition's understanding of the moral virtues as inclinations, dispositions, or "powers" nurtured by habit is employed here. We should not lose sight of the fact, however, that the Beatitudes as enumerated in chapter 5 of Matthew's Gospel, in particular, both flow from and are dependent on gifts and that these gifts are given to us so that they can bear fruit in our lives.

It is noteworthy, nonetheless, that the relationship drawn by Augustine between the gifts enumerated, respectively, by Isaiah and Paul on the one hand and Matthew's version of the Beatitudes on the other goes a long way toward resolving the aforementioned dispute concerning the post-Tridentine understanding of charitable works on the one hand and the Reformers's commitment to *sola gratia* on the other. God's utter graciousness does not relieve us of our responsibility to respond to God's grace and to follow the example of Jesus in the way we live our lives. According to Pinckaers, "we should note in passing how easily St. Augustine passed over the chasm later created by Protestant thought between the Sermon on the Mount and the Letter to the Romans. The relation between Beatitudes and gifts unites Matthew and Paul closely through Isaiah."[21]

Still, we cannot simply ignore the sectarian controversies pertaining to the early church fathers that have arisen over the course of the last several centuries. To do so could prove an impediment to the fruitful embrace of the Beatitudes for some. At times, the three principles that so distinguished Martin Luther's critique of Catholicism have proven a formidable barrier in this regard: the principle of *sola gratia*, the idea that believers are saved by grace alone, tends to devalue the efficacy of human effort; the principle of *sola fide,* the idea that we are justified or saved by faith alone, diminishes the value of charitable works to a considerable extent; and the principle of *sola scriptura*, the belief that the Bible is the only legitimate source of authority in the church, tends to relegate the early church fathers and even the great councils of the early church to a lesser status.

It is not surprising, therefore, that Luther could be remarkably dismissive of the early church fathers.

---

21. Ten Klooster, *Thomas Aquinas,* 152.

Behold what great darkness is in the books of the fathers concerning faith; yet if the article of justification be darkened, it
is impossible to smother the grossest errors of mankind. St.
Jerome, indeed, wrote upon Matthew, upon the Epistles to the
Galatians and to Titus; but, alas, very coldly. Ambrose wrote
six books on Genesis, but they are very poor. Augustine wrote
nothing to the purpose concerning faith; for he was first roused
up and made a man by the Pelagians, in striving against them.
I can find no exposition upon the Epistles to the Romans and
Galatians in which anything is taught pure and right. What a
happy time have we now as to the purity of the doctrine; but
alas, we little esteem it. We must read the fathers cautiously, and
lay them in the gold balance, for they often stumbled and went
astray, and introduced into their books many monkish things.
Augustine had more work and labor to wind himself out of the
writings of the fathers, than he had with the heretics . . . The
more I read the books of the fathers, the more I find myself of-
fended; for they were but men, and, to speak the truth with all
their repute and authority, undervalued the books and writings
of the sacred apostles of Christ . . . Augustine was the ablest and
purest of all the doctors, but he could not of himself bring things
back to their original condition, and he often complains that
the bishops, with their traditions and ordinances, trouble the
church more than did the Jews with their laws.[22]

From the outset, the Reformed tradition tended to assume a somewhat mixed view of the early church fathers. In the preface to the fourth
edition of his *Institutes of the Christian Religion* (1581), John Calvin
dealt at some length with their teachings. His tone was highly polemi-
cal, however. Indeed, he accused those promoting the Catholic Counter-
Reformation of selective reading.

It is a calumny to represent us as opposed to the fathers (I mean
the ancient writers of a purer age), as if the fathers were sup-
porters of their impiety. Were the contest to be decided by such
authority (to speak in the most moderate terms), the better
part of the victory would be ours. While there is much that is
admirable and wise in the writings of those fathers, and while
in some things it has fared with them as with ordinary men;
these pious sons, forsooth, with the peculiar acuteness of intellect, and judgment, and soul, which belongs to them, adore only
their slips and errors, while those things which are well said they

22. Luther, "The Creation."

either overlook, or disguise, or corrupt; so that it may be truly said their only care has been to gather dross among gold. Then, with dishonest clamour, they assail us as enemies and despisers of the fathers. So far are we from despising them, that if this were the proper place, it would give us no trouble to support the greater part of the doctrines which we now hold by their suffrages. Still, in studying their writings, we have endeavoured to remember that all things are ours, to serve, not lord it over us, but that we axe Christ's only, and must obey him in all things without exception. He who does not draw this distinction will not have any fixed principles in religion; for those holy men were ignorant of many things, are often opposed to each other, and are sometimes at variance with themselves.[23]

The Reformed tradition's ambivalence concerning the early church fathers continues to this day. As Steven Wedgeworth, a Presbyterian pastor and popular blogger, observed:

The Reformed tradition has of late found some difficulty in understanding and articulating its relationship to the early church tradition and the patristic record. It typically takes one of two approaches. The first, and unfortunately most common, is to dispense with the tradition altogether. This approach takes at least two modes: that of simply rejecting the early church as corrupted and erroneous or that of claiming appreciation of the early church while also "moving beyond it" into the infinite future of possibilities, whether they be consistent with wide-ranging traditional consensus or not. The second approach seeks to move in the opposite direction, pledging fidelity to the early church and thus using it as the primary standard (though often interpreted by non-Reformed or anti-Reformed readings) by which to critique its own dogmatics and exegesis.[24]

The challenge for the Reformers on this and so many other issues is clear: How can one claim continuity with the church founded by Jesus on the foundation of his apostles while, at the same time, rejecting so much of Christian history and theology? Further, when precisely was the church pure and untainted by heresy: through the apostolic age, through the sub-apostolic era, i.e., approximately 100–155, or through the period of the great councils of the fourth and fifth centuries?

23. Calvin, "Prefix."
24. Wedgeworth, "John Calvin and the Tradition."

Despite persistent angst on this and so many other issues, there has been something of a *rapprochement* of late between the Catholic Church and some Protestant denominations with respect to the early church fathers. In fact, the ongoing dialogue involving Lutherans and Catholics has made considerable progress in recent decades. Indeed, the Lutheran World Federation and the Vatican have issued a series of joint declarations since the 1970s highlighting broad areas of agreement; and, on topics in which differences in perspective persist, polemics have been replaced by appreciative inquiry and nuanced dialogue. This is particularly so with respect to the relationship shared by charitable works and grace.

> The Lutheran churches and the Roman Catholic Church have together listened to the good news proclaimed in Holy Scripture. This common listening, together with the theological conversations of recent years, has led to a shared understanding of justification. This encompasses a consensus in the basic truths; the differing explications in particular statements are compatible with it. In faith we together hold the conviction that justification is the work of the triune God. The Father sent his Son into the world to save sinners. The foundation and presupposition of justification is the incarnation, death, and resurrection of Christ. Justification thus means that Christ himself is our righteousness, in which we share through the Holy Spirit in accord with the will of the Father. Together we confess: By grace alone, in faith in Christ's saving work and not because of any merit on our part, we are accepted by God and receive the Holy Spirit, who renews our hearts while equipping and calling us to good works.[25]

This welcomed development is pertinent to our present discussion because it disavows any sense of the Beatitudes as salvation by "works" or presumed "merit." It affirms that the journey of faith can be understood, nonetheless, as a kind of progression in which our hearts are renewed and in which we are equipped for and then sent forth to perform good works of various kinds. For our purposes, the Beatitudes as enumerated in chapter 5 of Matthew's Gospel, in particular, both flow from and are dependent upon gifts. Most importantly for our purposes, this is the interpretation of Matthew's version of the Beatitudes that was embraced by the early church fathers.

25. *Joint Declaration.*

Over the course of the last thirty years, the "paleo-orthodox" theology espoused by Thomas C. Oden, Christopher Alan Hall, and others writing from within a number of Protestant traditions has celebrated a hypothesized "Great Church," which, in its day, produced a faithful consensus embodied, most notably, in the teachings of the great councils of the fourth and fifth centuries. Christopher A. Hall, in particular, has acknowledged the seminal contributions of the early church fathers in crafting a nuanced understanding of discipleship.

> The church fathers' emphasis on *askesis*—a training program—
> if life is to be lived well may initially strike some readers as simply a misguided step into legalism. Aren't they trying to earn salvation? After all, salvation is by grace, not by works. Any sane Christian knows that. The fathers would readily agree, at least regarding the issue of legalism. They might well reply, though, "Who is trying to earn anything from God? Paul himself, the great apostle of grace, also engaged in a training program." And the fathers would be right. Paul specifically employs an athletic metaphor in 1 Corinthians 9:24–27 to describe how he stayed in spiritually good shape . . . Paul's letters and Jesus' teaching are replete with specific examples of practices engaged in on a regular basis.[26]

These positive developments coincide with the "rediscovery" of the early church fathers among Catholics, beginning in the years immediately preceding the Second Vatican Council. The formation of priests had emerged as a key concern following the Council of Trent, which had gathered in twenty-five sessions between the years 1545 and 1563. Thereafter, seminary training had been increasingly oriented to the formation of effective confessors. By the time the dust had settled in the middle of the seventeenth century, Catholic moral theology had shifted away from the Christian virtues to an explicit focus on sin. Like Protestants, but for a very different reason, Catholic moral theologians of the modern era tended to view the Ten Commandments, rather than the Beatitudes, as the primary guide to faithful living for the laity. The Beatitudes were viewed as something optional, as something exceptional, or as something reserved, in effect, for mystics, contemplatives, and professed members of religious communities.

The *nouvelle théologie* or "new theology" of certain Catholic theologians in mid-twentieth century France and Germany promoted

26. Hall, *Living Wisely*, 235.

ressourcement, i.e., a return to the sources, as an antidote to this bifurcated understanding of morality. The sources to which these scholars hoped to return included both the Scriptures and the writings of the early church fathers. *Ressourcement* was subsequently adopted as a key watchword in the Second Vatican Council.

In truth, a renewed appreciation for the early church fathers is apparent both in contemporary Catholicism and in various branches of Protestantism. Most importantly for our purposes, this renewed appreciation pertains not just to the signature doctrines promulgated during the great councils of the early church but to Christian spirituality, too.

It is high time, in fact, to abandon the tiresome "grace versus merit" debates of the sixteenth and seventeenth centuries. As noted in chapter 3, our progression in holiness can be attributed *both* to supernatural gifts *and* to formation requiring disciplined and sustained acts of will. These understandings of God's work in the world are not mutually exclusive. Growth in the virtues can be understood *both* as a life of responsible discipleship *and* as a response to God's call. As expressed by Anton Ten Klooster: "Merit begins with grace, it is moved forward by grace, and is brought to completion by grace."[27]

We are now in a position to examine the teachings of the early church fathers with respect to the version of the Beatitudes included in chapter 5 of Matthew's Gospel. Four lessons, in particular, stand out: first, the Beatitudes are not optional; second, the Beatitudes provide a privileged template for formation in the life of the disciple; third, the Beatitudes are arranged as a progression in the life of the spirit; and fourth, the Beatitudes hold implications for how we live with each other. Each of these lessons will be addressed in turn.

First, according to the early church fathers, the Beatitudes are for all of us. The early church fathers did not view the Beatitudes as optional or supererogatory or for just a few among us. Indeed, the great teachers of the patristic era believed the Beatitudes to be applicable to all Christians. Augustine, John Chrysostom,[28] Leo the Great[29] and other early church fathers certainly affirmed this view.

Again, this perspective was largely abandoned during the Reformation and during the Catholic Counter-Reformation, too. According to

---

27. Ten Klooster, *Thomas Aquinas*, 89.

28. Chrysostom, "On the Epistle to the Hebrews," 27,072–73.

29. Leo the Great, "Sermon XCV, A Homily."

Pinckaers, the two-tiered spirituality embraced by the Catholic Church during the modern era "rests on a distinction between a moral code designed for all Christians, expressed primarily in the Decalogue, and a more spiritual and exacting doctrine reserved for an elite group such as religious, who have freely chosen to strive for evangelical perfection . . . In restricting the Sermon on the Mount to a select group, it opposes the patristic tradition to say nothing of the Evangelist's intentions."[30]

This changed in the 1960s. The rediscovery of the early church fathers's views in this regard was fulsomely endorsed in one of the Second Vatican Council's most important documents, *Lumen Gentium: The Dogmatic Constitution on the Church*, which affirms—in no uncertain terms—that we are all called to holiness. There is only one church, not two. This rich understanding of discipleship pertains not just to mystics, contemplatives, and professed members of religious communities but to all of us. By virtue of our baptisms, we are all called to holiness in all aspects of our lives.

Notable Catholic theologians, including Donald Senior,[31] Matthew J. Harrington, and Servais Pinckaers, now cite the early church fathers in embracing this view as a lens through which to understand the Beatitudes. As affirmed in the Catechism of the Catholic Church, the Beatitudes "express the vocation of the faithful, a vocation that is addressed to each individual personally."[32] According to Helen Doohan, "these Beatitudes are not an ideal but a way of life for believers in Jesus. The attitudes embraced become conditions for salvation, but in their acceptance lies the very energy needed to live the radical teaching of Jesus."[33] More to our purposes, this includes managers in all kinds of organizations and nominal leaders in these organizations and in the public square, too.

Second, the early church fathers recognized the Beatitudes as a privileged template for discipleship. This is where the rubber hits the road, of course. Yes, we may accept that we are gifted and that we are called to discipleship. Indeed, we may accept that we have a responsibility to cultivate the Beatitudes in our lives. We may even believe that this path is not in any way optional. Still, what do the Beatitudes mean in terms of

---

30. Pinckaers, *Sources*, 136.
31. Senior, *Matthew*, 70.
32. *Catechism* 1719.
33. Doohan, "Beatitude(s)," 79.

our day-to-day struggles as family members, as employees, as managers, and as members of particular communities?

According to the early church fathers, the Beatitudes matter a great deal, in fact! Reflecting, perhaps, on his own circuitous journey of faith, Augustine was adamant in this regard:

> If anyone will piously and soberly consider the sermon which our Lord Jesus Christ spoke on the mount, as we read it in the Gospel according to Matthew, I think that he will find in it, so far as regards the highest morals, a perfect standard of the Christian life: and this we do not rashly venture to promise, but gather it from the very words of the Lord himself. For the sermon itself is brought to a close in such a way, that it is clear there are in it all the precepts which go to mould the life. For thus he speaks: Therefore, whosoever hears these words of mine, and does them, I will liken him unto a wise man, which built his house upon a rock: and the rain descended, and the floods came, and the winds blew, and beat upon that house; and it fell not: for it was founded upon a rock. And every one that hears these words of mine, and does them not, I will liken unto a foolish man, which built his house upon the sand: and the rain descended, and the floods came, and the winds blew, and beat upon that house; and it fell: and great was the fall of it. Since, therefore, he has not simply said, Whosoever hears my words, but has made an addition, saying, Whosoever hears these words of mine, he has sufficiently indicated, as I think, that these sayings which he uttered on the mount so perfectly guide the life of those who may be willing to live according to them, that they may justly be compared to one building upon a rock. I have said this merely that it may be clear that the sermon before us is perfect in all the precepts by which the Christian life is moulded.[34]

The Beatitudes constitute a working definition of discipleship. They pertain, in fact, to our common call to holiness. "As I have loved you," Jesus tells the disciples, "so you also should love one another" (John 13:34). The church has interpreted this "new commandment" as a directive that applies to all of us.

But who was Jesus and how did he love? In fact, we can think of Jesus as someone who was poor in spirit, as someone who mourned, as someone who was meek, as someone who hungered and thirsted for righteousness, as someone who was merciful, as someone who was clean

---

34. Knight, "On the Sermon on the Mount."

of heart, as someone who engendered peace, and as someone who suffered greatly. The Beatitudes deconstruct, in fact, the essential holiness that was so clearly evident in the life and ministry of Jesus. According to the Catechism of the Catholic Church, "the Beatitudes depict the countenance of Jesus Christ and portray his charity."[35] This is who Jesus was; this is how he lived; and this is how he loved. The implication, of course, is that we are to emulate Jesus with respect to these attributes. As affirmed by Augustine:

> "Blessed are the poor in spirit"; imitate him, who, whereas "he was rich, was made poor for your sakes." "Blessed are the meek"; imitate him, who said, "Learn of me, for I am meek and lowly of heart." "Blessed are they that mourn"; imitate him, who "wept over" Jerusalem. "Blessed are they, who hunger and thirst after righteousness"; imitate him, who said, "My meat is to do the will of him who sent me." "Blessed are the merciful"; imitate him, who came to the help of him who was wounded by robbers, and who lay in the way half-dead and despaired of. "Blessed are the pure in heart"; imitate him, "who did no sin, neither was guile found in his mouth." "Blessed are the peace-makers"; imitate him, who said on behalf of his persecutors, "Father, forgive them, for they know not what they do." "Blessed are they, who suffer persecution for righteousness sake"; imitate him, who "suffered for you, leaving you an example, that ye follow his steps." These things, whoso imitate, in these they follow the Lamb.[36]

Third, the Beatitudes are arranged to reflect a certain progression in the life of the disciple. Today, we tend to think of the Beatitudes as a series of independent blessings that Matthew arrayed in no particular order. This is not how the early church fathers viewed them. Augustine referred to Matthew's Beatitudes as a series of "stages."[37] Tertullian counseled the need for "patience" in the pursuit of these blessings,[38] and John Chrysostom spoke of the need to move ever deeper into a state of spiritual "sobriety."[39] Augustine, in particular, viewed the Beatitudes as an iterative formation process: "Seven in number, therefore, are the things that bring perfection: for the eighth brings into light and shows what is

---

35. *Catechism* 1717.

36. Augustine, "Of Holy Virginity," 15,148.

37. Augustine, "Our Lord's Sermon," 17,827.

38. Tertullian, "Of Patience," 3,981.

39. Chrysostom, "Homily XXXIII," 26,535.

perfect, so that starting, as it were, from the beginning again, the others are also perfected."[40] Following both Augustine and Aristotle, Aquinas, too, argued that this progression is oriented to the goal, end, or ultimate purpose of human existence: happiness, fulfillment, or *eudemonia*.[41]

Fourth, according to the early church fathers, this understanding of the Beatitudes holds profound implications for how we should interact with others. Again, morality can be understood as how we think about and treat ourselves and how we think about and treat others; and justice pertains to how we share life's benefits and burdens with others. The early church fathers affirmed that Matthew's version of the Beatitudes was profoundly spiritual in nature. They insisted that the Beatitudes require personal transformation, i.e., *shub* or *metanoia*. If this transformation is genuine, however, it will produce fruit in the lives we share with others. In holding this view, the early church fathers affirmed the truth of Scripture and the apostolic tradition: "The way we came to know love was that he laid down his life for us; so we ought to lay down our lives for our brothers. If someone who has worldly means sees a brother in need and refuses him compassion, how can the love of God remain in him? Children, let us love not in word or speech but in deed and truth" (1 John 3:16–18). Love requires concrete action on our part in every aspect of our lives.

How do we love as Jesus loved in thought, word, *and* deed? Drawing on the teachings of the early church fathers, the celebrated German theologian Gerhard Lohfink argues that Jesus' disciples are challenged to do exactly as he did: Jesus proclaimed the reign of God; he healed; and he confronted evil when and where he could.[42] We see this threefold dynamic at work most clearly in Luke's Gospel. In chapter 9, Jesus sends his closest associates out ahead of him. "He summoned the Twelve and gave them power and authority over all demons and to cure diseases, and he sent them to proclaim the kingdom of God and to heal [the sick]" (Luke 9:1–2). Jesus then extends this same threefold mission to another seventy-two disciples in chapter 10. They, too, are directed to proclaim the Good News, to heal those in need of healing, and to confront evil. As Gerhard Lohfink notes, "[Jesus' disciples] are to do exactly what Jesus

---

40. Augustine, "Our Lord's Sermon," 17,832–33.

41. Pinckaers, *Sources*, 149.

42. Lohfink, *Jesus of Nazareth*.

does. They share his fate, his duties, his joys, and his sorrows."[43] This is what it means to be a disciple; and this is precisely how the early church fathers interpreted the discipleship of all believers.

The New Testament uses an evocative image to make this point. Consider three arguments. One, God is light. "Now this is the message that we have heard from him and proclaim to you: God is light, and in him there is no darkness at all. If we say, 'We have fellowship with him,' while we continue to walk in darkness, we lie and do not act in truth. But if we walk in the light as he is in the light, then we have fellowship with one another, and the blood of his Son Jesus cleanses us from all sin" (1 John 1:5–7). Two, Jesus is the light of the world and hence God, a remarkable claim to be sure. "Jesus spoke to them again, saying, 'I am the light of the world. Whoever follows me will not walk in darkness, but will have the light of life'" (John 8:12). Three, we, too, are the light of the world. "You are the light of the world. A city set on a mountain cannot be hidden. Nor do they light a lamp and then put it under a bushel basket; it is set on a lampstand, where it gives light to all in the house. Just so, your light must shine before others, that they may see your good deeds and glorify your heavenly Father" (Matt 5:14–16).

This final teaching follows immediately after Jesus' proclamation of the Beatitudes. It is not a separate teaching *per se*, but a further explication of the Beatitudes's implications for anyone who would be a disciple of Jesus. We are the light of the world. As such, we are challenged to share the light that is within us—the light of Christ, the light that is God—with the whole world. Discipleship holds implications for how we interact with others in all aspects of our lives, including our work lives. Indeed, this is the sense of Scripture embraced by the early church fathers.

As it pertains specifically to the nature of discipleship, the image of light may be even more powerful than the corresponding stories of the commissioning of the Twelve and the seventy-two in Luke's Gospel. It is all too easy to read Luke's "commissioning" stories functionally. We can all too easily focus on the tasks to be performed by the Twelve and the seventy-two disciples. In contrast, the image of light is anything but task-oriented. Again, God is light; Jesus is light; and we, too, are called to be light to the world. Discipleship is about who we are much more so than what we do "functionally" in the world, and this includes the "functions" we perform on the job.

43. Lohfink, *Jesus of Nazareth*, 84.

Again, however, how do we do this? How do we live the life of faithful discipleship as it is deconstructed in Matthew's version of the Beatitudes? How do we do so in a world that holds little regard for spiritual truths? In grappling with these questions, we would do well to note, perhaps, the proximity of Matthew's extended metaphor on light to the Beatitudes themselves. Again, the similes of salt and light follow Jesus' proclamation of the Beatitudes. The Beatitudes are a roadmap, in fact. In a very real sense, the Beatitudes can be thought of as a set of operating instructions for ongoing formation in the life of the disciple. Echoing the early church fathers, Pinckaers notes: "The Beatitudes go deeper than words and ideas. They confront us with the realities of human existence and show us what lies in our own depths. They force us into an interior solitude and put to us this personal, decisive question: Here and now, in the emptiness of this trial, where darkness reigns and discouragement lies in wait, do you dare to believe the word of the one who declared that the poor, the afflicted, and the persecuted are happy? Can you hope to find in all this wreckage a path to happiness, to the Kingdom? Can you leap over the wall? The Beatitudes teach us faith and courage. They put into our hearts an astounding hope."[44]

The eight Beatitudes enumerated in Matthew's Gospel will be examined individually in the several chapters that follow. From this point forward, our approach will be more reflective than didactic, since each of the Beatitudes speaks in a powerful way to the individual journey of discipleship.

44. Pinckaers, *The Pursuit of Happiness*, 35.

Chapter 6

"Blessed Are the Poor in Spirit" & "Blessed Are They Who Mourn"

As he was setting out on a journey, a man ran up, knelt down before him, and asked him, "Good teacher, what must I do to inherit eternal life?" Jesus answered him, "Why do you call me good? No one is good but God alone. You know the commandments: 'You shall not kill; you shall not commit adultery; you shall not steal; you shall not bear false witness; you shall not defraud; honor your father and your mother.'" He replied and said to him, "Teacher, all of these I have observed from my youth." Jesus, looking at him, loved him and said to him, "You are lacking in one thing. Go, sell what you have, and give to [the] poor and you will have treasure in heaven; then come, follow me." At that statement his face fell, and he went away sad, for he had many possessions. Jesus looked around and said to his disciples, "How hard it is for those who have wealth to enter the kingdom of God!" The disciples were amazed at his words. So Jesus again said to them in reply, "Children, how hard it is to enter the kingdom of God! It is easier for a camel to pass through [the] eye of needle than for one who is rich to enter the kingdom of God." They were exceedingly astonished and said among themselves, "Then who can be saved?" Jesus looked at them and said, "For human beings it is impossible, but not for God. All things are possible for God" (Mark 10:17–27).

THE EARLY CHURCH FATHERS understood the first Beatitude, i.e., "blessed are the poor in spirit," and the second, i.e., "blessed are they who mourn," to be related. In the view of the early church fathers, the kind of self-emptying implied in the first two Beatitudes—self-emptying to the very point of mourning—was required for true meekness to emerge in those who have been invited or called into a relationship with Jesus.

The wisdom of Matthew's first two Beatitudes is embodied in the compelling Gospel reading shared above. Jesus requires something more of the "rich young man" than mere adherence to the requirements of the Decalogue. He invites the rich young man to empty himself of his many material possessions and to do so to the point that it hurts. As a result, the rich young man "went away sad" for "he had many possessions."

Five reflections pertaining to the meaning of Matthew's first two Beatitudes follow. We will first examine the early church fathers's understanding of what it means to be "poor in spirit." This will be followed by an analysis of root sin as it has come to be understood in the broader tradition of the church. We will then consider the early church fathers's understanding of mourning as it pertains specifically to discipleship. The ongoing need for the kind of self-emptying recommended by the early church fathers will then be examined. Finally, we will consider a number of implications that follow from the preceding reflections. This will include implications that pertain to all aspiring disciples of Jesus and to managers and to nominal leaders more specifically.

Luke's version of the first Beatitude differs significantly from Matthew's. In Luke 6:30, Jesus identifies the poor as blessed. In contrast, Matthew's Jesus declares the poor *in spirit* to be favored by God. At first glance, Matthew seems to spiritualize Luke's version of the first Beatitude. Indeed, it is sometimes suggested that Matthew's version "waters down" an explicit concern for social justice articulated to such great effect in Luke's Gospel.

Matthew's understanding of poverty can be thought of as a powerful metaphor, however. Metaphorically, poverty can be understood as more than financial or material deprivation. In this expanded sense, poverty can be understood as any experience of loss. We know that all kinds of losses can be encountered over the course of a lifetime, including, for instance, the loss of employment, the loss of freedom, the loss of a relationship due to death or estrangement, and even the loss of one's youth. As human beings, we can suffer many different kinds of losses as we journey through life, some of which can be debilitating, even to the point of triggering a psychological or spiritual crisis.

The early church fathers did not understand Matthew's version of the first Beatitude as material deprivation or even as the experience of personal loss, however. According to the early church fathers, Jesus' understanding of spiritual poverty challenges us to empty ourselves of something very specific: sin. The understanding of serious sin detailed in the many confessors's manuals published in the wake of the Counter-Reformation differed considerably from the understanding of sin that so preoccupied the early church fathers, however. Whereas the confessors's manuals studied in the seminary system developed in the Catholic Church following the Council of Trent were oriented, by and large, to the Ten Commandments, the early church fathers were concerned about something far deeper. In the collective wisdom of the early church fathers, Matthew's Jesus was talking about something more fundamental than any particular violation of the Decalogue.

Today, this something other or something more is understood as root sin, the deep and underlying causes of our unhealthy attachments. Indeed, the early church fathers were convinced, it seems, that root sin is part and parcel of everyone's life. The early church fathers did, indeed, understand Matthew's first Beatitude metaphorically; for many of them, however, the metaphor implied by the term "poverty" pertained to the self-emptying of root sin rather than to the experience of loss understood more generally.

The early church fathers viewed pride as *the* root sin. Consider John Chrysostom's perspective in this regard: "The greatest of evils, and those which make havoc of the whole world, had their entering in from pride."[1] Chrysostom's contemporary Augustine agreed: "The poor in spirit are rightly understood here as meaning the humble and God-fearing, i.e., those who have not the spirit which puffeth up. Nor ought blessedness to begin at any other point whatever, if indeed it is to attain unto the highest wisdom; 'but the fear of the Lord is the beginning of wisdom'; for, on the other hand also, 'pride' is entitled 'the beginning of all sin.'"[2]

The intellectual heirs of the early church fathers tended to disaggregate root sin a bit further, typically into three or four categories. Thomas Aquinas thus identified four unhealthy and ultimately unsatisfying detours along the road to true happiness: wealth, pleasure, power, and honor.[3] In the sixteenth century, Ignatius of Loyola (1491–1556) resorted Aquinas's categories under three headings: riches, honor, and pride: "The

1. Chrysostom, "Homily XV," 22,391.
2. Augustine, "Our Lord's Sermon," 17,829.
3. Aquinas, "First Part of the Second Part, Question 2."

first step shall be that of riches; the second, that of honor; the third that of pride; and from these three steps [Lucifer] draws on to all the other vices."[4] According to Ignatius, but using contemporary language, all sin stems from one or more of three root sins: first, materialism or sensuality; second, pride; and, third, vanity. Writing from a purely philosophical perspective, Philippa Foote sorted "moral failings" into similar categories: worldliness and avarice, a synonym for materialism and sensuality, pride, and vanity.[5]

Two questions thus follow. First, is this understanding of root sin biblical? And second, is this ancient understanding of sin of any particular relevance to us today? Reading Matthew's version of Jesus' temptations in the desert in the light of the temptations to which Adam and Eve succumbed in the Garden of Eden (Gen 3:1–24) can be helpful with respect to our first question.

> Then Jesus was led by the Spirit into the desert to be tempted by the devil. He fasted for forty days and forty nights, and afterwards he was hungry. The tempter approached and said to him, "If you are the Son of God, command that these stones become loaves of bread." He said in reply, "It is written: 'One does not live by bread alone, but by every word that comes forth from the mouth of God.'" Then the devil took him to the holy city and made him stand on the parapet of the temple, and said to him, "If you are the Son of God, throw yourself down. For it is written: 'He will command his angels concerning you' and 'with their hands they will support you, lest you dash your foot against a stone.'" Jesus answered him, "Again it is written, 'You shall not put the Lord, your God, to the test.'" Then the devil took him up to a very high mountain, and showed him all the kingdoms of the world in their magnificence, and he said to him, "All these I shall give to you, if you will prostrate yourself and worship me." At this, Jesus said to him, "Get away, Satan! It is written: 'The Lord, your God, shall you worship and him alone shall you serve.'" Then the devil left him and, behold, angels came and ministered to him (Matt 3:1–11).

Before he was "led by the Spirit into the desert," Jesus had been baptized by John. As Matthew explains, "a voice came from the heavens, saying, 'This is my beloved Son, with whom I am well pleased'" (Matt 3:17). Jesus was thus affirmed as the beloved Son of the Father only to be

4. Loyola, "The Fourth Day," *The Spiritual Exercises*.

5. Foote, *Virtues and Vices*, 3.

dispatched into the desert for forty days of fasting. Jesus then experiences three temptations, all three of which bear a remarkable resemblance to the temptations experienced by Adam and Eve in the Garden of Eden.

In the first temptation, Jesus experiences intense hunger, and so the devil encourages him to turn the stones lying about into bread. The bread featured in this story reminds us of the forbidden fruit in the Garden of Eden, which so tempted Adam and Eve. Employing Ignatius of Loyola's understanding of root sin, the bread featured in Matthew's version of Jesus' temptations in the desert—like the forbidden fruit in the Garden of Eden—symbolizes our all too human desire for "stuff" and for un-healthy experiences of one kind or another. It symbolizes the unhealthy materialism and the sensuality to which we—as incarnated beings—are sometimes attracted, a debilitating root sin, in fact, that can lead to so many other sins and other dysfunction, all of which can wreak havoc in our lives. Jesus, it seems, had to be emptied of his temptations to materi-alism and sensuality. To become truly poor in spirit, he had to resist these powerful temptations to the point that he hungered for them.

In the second temptation, Jesus had to wrestle with the experience of abandonment. The Father—it must have seemed to Jesus—had deserted him just days after having pledged his love for Jesus. Recognizing this, the devil ridicules Jesus. He dismisses him as a fool just as the serpent ridi-culed Eve as a fool in the Garden of Eden. "You are so important Jesus, you are so very special," the devil seems to say. "Show us, Jesus. Throw yourself off of this cliff, so that we can see you being 'rescued' by the angels the Father will surely send on your behalf. Show us, Jesus. Show all of us." The devil pricks Jesus' vanity just as the serpent in the Garden of Eden pricks Eve's vanity. The devil appeals to Jesus' all too human need to feel loved and his all too human need to feel special or unique. This sug-gests that Jesus had to be emptied of a temptation to vanity, too. Jesus, it seems, had to be emptied of the all too human tendency to worship what others think and say about us.

In addition to feeling abandoned, Jesus must have felt powerless, and hence his third temptation. Again, the devil appeals to something that lies deep in so many of us. The devil appeals to Jesus' pride. He shows Jesus all the kingdoms of the world and promises all of them to Jesus if he will but "prostrate himself" in worship not to the Father but to the devil himself. Pride can manifest itself in the narcissistic conceit that we always know best. It can manifest itself, too, in the belief that we deserve the best for one reason or another. In a similar way, the devil promised

Adam and Eve that they would "be like gods" if they would but eat of the forbidden fruit. Like materialism and sensuality and like vanity, pride is a root sin that lies at the heart of considerable dysfunction in our world, a root sin to which the best and brightest and the most fortunate among us are particularly susceptible. For Jesus, pride proved the final barrier that stood between the Father's love he had experienced so intimately at the moment of his baptism on the one hand and the pursuit of the mission laid out for him on the other.

The fact that Adam and Eve proved susceptible to these three root sins speaks to their primordial nature and hence to our susceptibility as well; and the fact that Jesus had to wrestle with unhealthy materialism and sensuality, unhealthy vanity, and unhealthy pride speaks to the humanity he shared with us. These brief exegeses—one from the very beginning of the Jewish scriptures and one from the prelude to Jesus' three-year mission—also affirm the understanding of root sin espoused by the early church fathers and the spiritual writers who followed them.

The existential analysis introduced in chapter 1 and further developed in chapter 3 can be helpful in this regard as well. In one way or another, Jung, Tillich, Frankl, Heidegger, Sartre, Rahner, and other existential philosophers and theologians posited a universal aspiration to the experience of meaning. They further argued that this universal aspiration can sometimes be experienced by self-reflective individuals as a debilitating *angst*. Again, the universal horizons of birth, change, death, and the sense of rootlessness that attends to the human condition can engender an understanding of life as a project for which the desired end is the experience of meaning or authentic living. When the pursuit or achievement of this end is frustrated, discomfort, dissonance, and conflict can follow. In the view of a number of existential philosophers and theologians, life is most authentically experienced as a question that demands an answer. In this sense, life is inherently "empty." We are challenged to "fill" it, it seems, with that which gives meaning. As articulated by Viktor Frankl, a life-giving sense of meaning can be experienced in creative acts, in relationships of love, and in the stance we assume against circumstances over which we have little or no control.

All three of these possibilities lend themselves to a Christian interpretation, of course. The journey of discipleship, growth in the virtues, and the exercise of servant leadership can all be experienced as profoundly creative. An ever-deepening relationship with God and with other human beings, now recognized as brothers and sisters in Christ, can be deeply meaningful as well. And as we shall see, even the faithful stance we assume *vis-à-vis* dysfunction we experience in our families, in our workplaces, and in the public square can be intensely meaningful, too. Indeed, we can come to see these kinds of troubling experiences as a call to Christian witness or even as the experience of martyrdom.

The problem occurs when we attempt to fill the ontological emptiness that is part and parcel of the human condition with something that fails to engender an authentic experience of meaning. Too often, we seek to medicate this experience of life as a "question that demands an answer" or to counsel it into silence in succumbing to one or more temptations to unhealthy materialism or sensuality, unhealthy vanity, or unhealthy pride. Viewed from a Christian perspective, these root sins forestall the authentic experience of life into which we are invited by God.

A second question then follows: Is this ancient understanding of sin relevant to us today? In other words, does this remain a problem in our own time and place? In fact, the early church fathers viewed root sin as a very serious matter. Root sin violates the first commandment: "You shall have no other gods before me." Worshipping "stuff" or unhealthy experiences of one kind or another, i.e., materialism and sensuality; worshipping ourselves, i.e., pride; and worshipping what others think or say about us, i.e., vanity, can all be forms of idolatry. And idolatry, of course, is serious business, indeed!

This is why the early church fathers understood the first of Matthew's Beatitudes to be a prerequisite for all that followed in Jesus' Sermon on the Mount. An aspiring disciple must first be emptied so that she can then be filled and so that she can then serve as a true disciple of Jesus. Further, the early church fathers identified humility as the essential disposition to which we should aspire. According to John Chrysostom, "humility is the groundwork of all that is good, as in fact Christ saith, 'Blessed are the poor in spirit.' And here not simply, 'with humility of mind,' but, 'with all humility.'"[6] Gregory the Great agreed: "Let us consider how we are admonished by the precepts of our Redeemer, who says, Blessed are the poor in spirit; for theirs is the kingdom of heaven (Matt 55:3). Hence, also, he says by the prophet, 'On whom shall my Spirit rest, but on him that is humble, and quiet, and that trembleth at my words' (Isa 66:2)? Of a truth, when the Lord would bring back the hearts of his disciples, still beset with infirmity, to the way of humility, he said,

6. Chrysostom, "A Commentary on the Acts," 23,702.

Whosoever will be chief among you shall be least of all (Matt 20:27). Whereby it is plainly seen how he is truly exalted on high who in his thoughts is humbled."[7] The early church fathers recognized those who are humble as the poor in spirit to whom Jesus referred in his Sermon on the Mount. Indeed, the early church fathers recognized the universal applicability of the exchange between the rich young man and Jesus in the pericope that opened this chapter: "'Good teacher, what must I do to inherit eternal life?' Jesus answered him, 'Why do you call me good? No one is good but God alone.'" Those who are truly humble recognize that God is God and that they are not God. Drawing on the wisdom of the Jewish scriptures, this is what the early church fathers recognized as "fear of the Lord."

To this point in our analysis, we have noted that the early church fathers understood Matthew's version of the first Beatitude to involve the self-emptying of root sin. Like them and like those to whom they ministered, we who think of ourselves as aspiring disciples of Jesus are challenged to empty ourselves of sin, but not just of any manifestation of sin. We are challenged to go deeper. We are challenged to empty ourselves of our root sins.

We can now turn to Matthew's second Beatitude, i.e., "blessed are they who mourn." As noted above, the early church fathers understood the first two Beatitudes to be intimately connected. They did not understand the reference to mourning in Matthew's Gospel to pertain to any kind of grief, sorrow, or lamentation. Instead, the early church fathers understood Matthew's reference to mourning as mourning over sin, indeed, the serious kind of sin indicated metaphorically in Matthew's first Beatitude. According to John Chrysostom, "[Jesus] designated not simply all that mourn, but all that do so for sins."[8] Augustine agreed: "Mourning is sorrow arising from the loss of things held dear; but those who are converted to God lose those things which they were accustomed to embrace as dear in this world: for they do not rejoice in those things in which they formerly rejoiced; and until the love of eternal things be in them, they are wounded by some measure of grief."[9] Leo the Great concurred: "'Blessed are they which mourn, for they shall be comforted.' This mourning, beloved, to which eternal comforting is promised, is not the same as the

---

7. Gregory the Great, "Epistle XVIII," 38,824.

8. Chrysostom, "Homily XV," 22,392.

9. Augustine, "Our Lord's Sermon," 17,830.

affliction of this world: nor do those laments which are poured out in the sorrowings of the whole human race make anyone blessed. The reason for holy groanings, the cause of blessed tears, is very different. Religious grief mourns sin either that of others or one's own: nor does it mourn for that which is wrought by God's justice, but it laments over that which is committed by man's iniquity."[10]

We are thus invited to examine this particular understanding of mourning in terms of root sin. This is the point at which the intent of Matthew's first Beatitude is more fully revealed. It can be difficult to turn away from the idolatry of "stuff" and unhealthy experiences of one kind or another; it can be difficult to abandon pride and the worship of self; and it can be difficult to abandon the worship of what others think and say about us, i.e., vanity. As incarnated beings, most of us enjoy "stuff," sometimes to an unhealthy extent, and some of us like living on the edge, too; and too many of us think that we have it all figured out and that it is high time for us to be recognized as God's gift to the world; and we certainly like it when people hold us in high esteem, especially when they do so publicly. Giving all of this up is by no means easy. Self-emptying is very difficult, indeed.

The early church fathers recognized, it seems, that we cannot completely let go of our unhealthy attachments until we have mourned over them. This understanding can be explored psychologically as well. In the late 1960s, Elisabeth Kübler-Ross identified five stages of grief or mourning that attend the dying process: denial, anger, bargaining, depression, and acceptance.[11] She later extended her analysis to other kinds of loss. After years of research, Kübler-Ross concluded that an individual who has experienced a profound loss of one kind or another will often encounter difficulty in moving on with her life until she has grieved, that is, until she has mourned.

This kind of mourning, it seems, is part and parcel of the spiritual journey as well. It is one thing to foreswear materialism and sensuality, pride, and vanity. It is another thing entirely to progress to something more—to something better—without an adequate period of mourning for that which is being left behind either voluntarily or involuntarily.

Consider chastity as an example. A vow of chastity involves a foreswearing of certain sensual, material, and familial experiences, not the

10. Leo the Great, "Sermon XCV, A Homily on the Beatitudes," 38,458.
11. Kübler-Ross and Kessler, *On Grief and Grieving*.

least of which is conventional family life. Imagine, then, how the five stages of grief or mourning articulated by Kübler-Ross pertain to St. Augustine, an early church father who struggled mightily with this discipline. In his spiritual autobiography, *The Confessions*, Augustine prayed: "Grant me chastity and self-control, but please not yet."[12] Augustine, it seems, had yet to mourn his attachment to sex. At this point in his life, he was still "bargaining" with God. In a similar insight, Ronald Rolheiser, a contemporary spiritual writer, has noted that much of the dysfunction that some priests experience in their lives, most notably alcoholism, can be attributed to their failure to "bewail their virginity."[13]

The connection between the self-emptying of root sin that is demanded of us on the one hand and mourning on the other applies, of course, to all three of the root sins that are part and parcel of human existence. It applies to materialism and sensuality, to pride, and to vanity. The complete self-emptying of root sin, it seems, must be to the point of mourning. This is why the first two Beatitudes are presented in tandem here.

In fact, Matthew did not spiritualize or water down the first Beatitude or the second, for that matter. Jesus set a very high bar for his disciples as he invited them to journey with him, a bar that the rich young man in chapter 10 of Mark's Gospel was not yet ready to challenge; and so he mourned, not for the riches he was invited to surrender, but for his inability to do so.

The Greek word for this kind of self-emptying, the particular kind of poverty into which we are invited, is *kenosis*. This evocative word is featured, most notably, in Paul's Letter to the Philippians: "Have among yourselves the same attitude that is also yours in Jesus Christ, who, though he was in the form of God, did not regard equality with God something to be grasped. Rather, he emptied himself, taking the form of a slave, coming in human likeness; and found human in appearance, he humbled himself, becoming obedient to death, even death on a cross" (Phil 2:5–8). Poverty of spirit, i.e., self-emptying, applies not just to Jesus and not just to the apostles, and it applies to more than the "super-religious" among us today. *Kenosis* is required of all of us. As affirmed in the overview to the second part of our text, we are all called to holiness. We are all invited to journey with Jesus.

---

12. Augustine, *The Confessions*, 159.

13. Rolheiser, *The Holy Longing*, 156.

The early church fathers did not believe this kind of *kenotic* self-emptying to be a one-time experience. It requires an ongoing commitment. The need for this kind of sustained formation was asserted most poignantly by Gregory the Great, a father of the early church who moved uneasily between civil and ecclesial administration on the one hand and the contemplative life of the monastery on the other over the course of his eventful life. As pope, he lamented how easily he fell into sin.

> *Son of man, I have made you a watchman for the house of Israel.* Note that a man whom the Lord sends forth as a preacher is called a watchman. A watchman always stands on a height so that he can see from afar what is coming. Anyone appointed to be a watchman for the people must stand on a height for all his life to help them by his foresight.
>
> How hard it is for me to say this, for by these very words I denounce myself. I cannot preach with any competence, and yet insofar as I do succeed, still I myself do not live my life according to my own preaching.
>
> I do not deny my responsibility; I recognize that I am slothful and negligent, but perhaps the acknowledgment of my fault will win me pardon from my just judge. Indeed, when I was in the monastery I could curb my idle talk and usually be absorbed in my prayers. Since I assumed the burden of pastoral care, my mind can no longer be collected; it is concerned with so many matters.
>
> I am forced to consider the affairs of the church and of the monasteries. I must weigh the lives and acts of individuals. I am responsible for the concerns of our citizens. I must worry about the invasions of roving bands of barbarians and beware of the wolves who lie in wait for my flock. I must become an administrator lest the religious go in want. I must put up with certain robbers without losing patience and at times I must deal with them in all charity.
>
> With my mind divided and torn to pieces by so many problems, how can I meditate or preach wholeheartedly without neglecting the ministry of proclaiming the gospel? Moreover, in my position I must often communicate with worldly men. At times I let my tongue run, for if I am always severe in my judgments, the worldly will avoid me, and I can never attack them as I would. As a result, I often listen patiently to chatter. And because I too am weak, I find myself drawn little by little into idle conversation, and I begin to talk freely about matters

which once I would have avoided. What once I found tedious,
I now enjoy.

So who am I to be a watchman, for I do not stand on the
mountain of action but lie down in the valley of weakness? Truly
the all-powerful Creator and Redeemer of mankind can give
me in spite my weaknesses a higher life and effective speech;
because I love him, I do not spare myself in speaking of him.[14]

It seems that Gregory enjoyed gossip, an indication, perhaps, of the
root sin of vanity, the worship of what others think and say about us. We
gossip, in part, because we hope to look good in the eyes of those with
whom we share secrets. In his heartfelt confession, Gregory expresses a
clear desire to return to the monastery where he found it much easier
to embrace a poverty of spirit. He thus testifies to the ongoing need for
kenotic self-emptying in the life of the aspiring disciple. Gregory gives
voice, as well, to the unease experienced by so many Christian managers
and nominal leaders with respect to their demeanor and their behavior
in jobs that dismiss *kenosis* as irrelevant to our need to "get along" in the
"real world."

This understanding of the first two of Matthew's Beatitudes, i.e.,
"blessed are the poor in spirit" and "blessed are they who mourn," holds
profound implications for the way we live our lives as aspiring disciples
of Jesus. Most importantly, it promotes values that are countercultural,
especially in contemporary organizations of all kinds. Significant material rewards and status are associated with jobs at the summits of most
career ladders. Further, aspiring leaders often face a gauntlet of competitors while advancing into ever more responsible positions. Indeed, there
can be a considerable amount of rough and tumble along the way. Bitter
rivalries are not unknown. Climbing the corporate ladder is not for the
faint of heart or for wallflowers. Still further, those hoping for advancement are advised to do what they can to be noticed by those who hold
positions of power and to cultivate positive relationships with them.
As a result, collegiality, healthy ambition, and fair competition in the
workplace can all too easily succumb to the root sins of materialism and
sensuality, pride, and vanity. *Kenosis* is rarely recommended as a surefire
ticket to advancement in most of today's organizations.

The countercultural nature of Matthew's first and second Beatitudes
point, in fact, to the need for virtue. Certainly, the infused theological

14. International Commission on English in the Liturgy, "A Homily on Ezekiel,"
1,365–66.

virtue of faith plays a seminal role in suggesting the possibility of something other than the one or more ways of "being in the world" now celebrated in our culture. At this point in the aspiring disciple's journey, faith can best be understood as a preliminary response to an invitation, an initial response that addresses the individual's fundamental orientation to meaning, a concept described at some length in chapter 3. Consider as well the definition contained in the Catechism of the Catholic Church: "Faith is *man's response to God*, who reveals himself and gives himself to man, at the same time bringing man a superabundant light as he searches for the *ultimate meaning* of his life."[15]

Lacking moral virtue, it would be very difficult, too, for most of us to resist the intense demands now placed on managers and nominal leaders in many of today's organizations. Consider, again, the four cardinal virtues adopted into Christianity from their original homes in ancient Greece and Rome: prudence, justice, temperance, and fortitude or courage. It can take considerable fortitude or courage to acknowledge and then confront the powerful pull of materialism, sensuality, vanity, and pride. Further, resisting these temptations requires temperance, itself a virtue. Still further, prudence is essential. A prudent person rarely forgets who she is at her core. Gregory the Great sometimes forgot who he was and "whose he was," it seems. He gave in to gossip far too willingly. We could say the same, perhaps, about those who were ensnared in the Tuskegee syphilis study, the Ford Pinto scandal, the Nestlé infant formula controversy, the space shuttle *Challenger* disaster, and the clergy sexual abuse scandal that has so unsettled the Catholic Church over the course of the last three decades.

Could *kenotic* self-emptying to the point of mourning have made a difference in these instances? We will never know. Lacking the virtue of prudence, it is doubtful that those who were caught up in these several scandals could have resisted either the inertia of the instrumental values clearly embraced in their respective organizations or the intense pressures brought to bear on some of them. Each of these instances demanded moral discernment under very challenging circumstances. Whether one believes that virtues are unmerited gifts, finely honed habits, or some combination of the two, the hard work of *kenotic* self-emptying—again, to the point of mourning—can be very difficult indeed, lacking the virtues of courage, temperance, and prudence.

15. *Catechism* 26. Emphasis added.

That being said, it is important to note that Jesus did not celebrate "poverty of spirit" or "mourning" *per se*. He recommended prayer, fasting, and almsgiving, but condemned ostentation in performing these disciplines.

> Take care not to perform righteous deeds in order that people may see them; otherwise, you will have no recompense from your heavenly Father. When you give alms, do not blow a trumpet before you, as the hypocrites do in the synagogues and in the streets to win the praise of others. Amen, I say to you, they have received their reward. But when you give alms, do not let your left hand know what your right is doing, so that your almsgiving may be secret. And your Father who sees in secret will repay you. When you pray, do not be like the hypocrites, who love to stand and pray in the synagogues and on street corners so that others may see them. Amen, I say to you, they have received their reward. But when you pray, go to your inner room, close the door, and pray to your Father in secret. And your Father who sees in secret will repay you . . . When you fast, do not look gloomy like the hypocrites. They neglect their appearance, so that they may appear to others to be fasting. Amen, I say to you, they have received their reward. But when you fast, anoint your head and wash your face, so that you may not appear to others to be fasting, except to your Father who is hidden. And your Father who sees what is hidden will repay you (Matt 6:1–18).

As Pope Francis put it so graphically in his apostolic exhortation, *The Joy of the Gospel*, Jesus does not want us to walk around like "sourpusses."[16] Thomas Aquinas contended that the ultimate goal of the spiritual life is happiness, and not just happiness in the next life. We are invited to happiness in this life as well. God wants this for us. Following Augustine, Aquinas believed that God instilled the very desire for happiness in each of us. Happiness is from God. We may be emptied—voluntarily or involuntarily—of our unhealthy attachments, our idols, and our sins to the point of mourning, but this emptiness—this poverty of spirit to the point of mourning—is for a purpose. We are invited to make room for something more.

The need for formation in the first two of Matthew's Beatitudes as a necessary preparation for the full life of discipleship is clear. According to Luke, Jesus himself testified to this something more at the outset of his ministry. In addressing the assembly in a synagogue, he drew from

16. Francis, *Evangelii Gaudium*, 85.

the prophet Isaiah: "He has sent me to bring glad tidings to the lowly, to heal the brokenhearted, to proclaim liberty to captives and release to the prisoners, to announce a year of favor from the Lord and a day of vindication by our God, to comfort all who mourn, to place on those who mourn in Zion a diadem instead of ashes" (Isa 61:1–2). We are emptied of our unhealthy attachments, our idols, and our sins so that we can open ourselves to something more, indeed, so that we can open ourselves to something better. In mourning, our unhealthy attachments, our idols and our sins are reduced to "ashes."

This is one of the reasons why those who have been emptied of their unhealthy attachments, their idols, and their sins are blessed in a very real sense. "Those who mourn" have come to their senses. They know who they are and "whose they are." They have recognized their total dependence on God. Servais Pinckaers employed the image of a plow in making this point:

> We can compare the work of the Beatitudes to that of the plow in the fields. Drawn along with determination, it drives the sharp edge of the plowshare into the earth and carves out, as the poets say, a deep wound, a broad furrow. With the same movement it turns the earth over to uproot the weeds and prepares the ground for the seeds which will fall into the renewed soil to shelter there, germinate and fructify. In the same way the word of the Beatitudes penetrates us with the power of the Holy Spirit in order to break up our interior soil. It cuts through us with the sharp edge of trials and with the struggles it provokes. It overturns our ideas and projects, reverses the obvious, thwarts our desires, and bewilders us, leaving us poor and naked before God. All this, in order to prepare a place within us for the seed of new life, the seed of the gospel which will bear fruit a hundredfold at harvest time if we have known how to welcome it and guard it with the patience of faith and the tenacity of hope.[17]

17. Pinckaers, *The Pursuit of Happiness*, 36.

REFLECTION QUESTIONS: "BLESSED ARE THE POOR IN SPIRIT" AND "BLESSED ARE THEY WHO MOURN"

- Do I understand faith as a preliminary response to an invitation that addresses my fundamental orientation to the experience of meaning?

- Do I understand the role that root sin, i.e., materialism and sensuality, pride, and vanity, play in my life?

- Have I committed myself to *kenosis* or self-emptying in this regard?

- Where do I look for wisdom in confronting the day-to-day struggles I face with respect to my root sin(s)?

- What steps do I need to take to be more fully formed in the virtues of fortitude, prudence, and temperance, all of which are required in the struggle against root sin?

- What might this mean in terms of my work, key relationships in my life, and the challenges I face on a day-to-day basis? What new behaviors or disciplines will be required? What deep-seated behaviors will need to be abandoned?

Chapter 7

"Blessed Are the Meek"

When Jesus went into the region of Caesarea Philippi, he asked his disciples, "Who do people say that the Son of Man is?" They replied, "Some say John the Baptist, others Elijah, still others Jeremiah or one of the prophets." He said to them, "But who do you say that I am?" Simon Peter said in reply, "You are the Messiah, the Son of the living God." Jesus said to him in reply, "Blessed are you, Simon son of Jonah. For flesh and blood has not revealed this to you, but my heavenly Father . . . From that time on, Jesus began to show his disciples that he must go to Jerusalem and suffer greatly from the elders, the chief priests, and the scribes, and be killed and on the third day be raised. Then Peter took him aside and began to rebuke him, "God forbid, Lord! No such thing shall ever happen to you." He turned and said to Peter, "Get behind me, Satan! You are an obstacle to me. You are thinking not as God does, but as human beings do" (Matt 16:13–23).

A T FIRST GLANCE, THIS disconcerting story may seem to have little to do with meekness. After all, we tend to think of meekness as an obsequious stance assumed *vis-à-vis* others, a stance characterized by inordinate modesty, unpretentiousness, or even self-effacement. As we shall see, the early church fathers understood the third Beatitude, i.e., "blessed are the meek," differently. Meekness does not pertain to our disposition toward other human beings so much as to our disposition toward God.

With this in mind, we will first consider how meekness was exemplified in the life of Jesus. We will then be in a position to appreciate the import of Peter's jarring encounter with Jesus more fully. This will be followed, in turn, by a brief reflection on the relationship shared by Matthew's first two Beatitudes, i.e., "blessed are the poor in spirit" and "blessed are those who mourn" on the one hand and his third on the other. As we shall see, a radical openness to God's hopes and dreams for us is only possible to the extent that we have acknowledged our vulnerability to temptation. We will then tap the wisdom of the church as it pertains to the way in which God works in our lives. How is it even possible for us to know God's hopes and dreams for us? Finally, we will consider three implications that follow from these reflections for aspiring disciples of Jesus and for managers and nominal leaders in contemporary organizations more specifically.

There are moments in the Gospels in which Jesus is portrayed as modest and unpretentious. His openness to children (Luke 18:15–17 and Matt 19:13–14) and to the bereaved (Luke 7:11–15) come to mind, and so, too, his passion and death, which are recorded at great length in all four of the Gospels. These stories underwrite the image of Jesus as meek as we tend to understand the term.

There are other stories in the Gospel tradition, however, that belie this all too familiar portrayal of Jesus. Consider, for instance, his withering denunciation of the scribes and Pharisees in Matthew 23:1–12. Consider, too, Jesus' violent expulsion of the scribes and Pharisees from the marketplace that served pilgrims who visited the temple: "Since the Passover of the Jews was near, Jesus went up to Jerusalem. He found in the temple area those who sold oxen, sheep, and doves, as well as the money-changers seated there. He made a whip out of cords and drove them all out of the temple area, with the sheep and oxen, and spilled the coins of the money-changers and overturned their tables, and to those who sold doves he said, 'Take these out of here, and stop making my Father's house a marketplace.' His disciples recalled the words of Scripture, 'Zeal for your house will consume me'" (John 2:13–17). As portrayed in these incidents, Jesus—at times—was anything but modest, unpretentious, and self-effacing.

Given this, we would do well, perhaps, to rethink meekness as it pertains to Jesus and hence to our own lives as aspiring disciples of Jesus. In doing so, we will begin at the end of the story and work our way back into Jesus' ministry. Consider, first, Mark's account of Jesus' experience of abandonment in the Garden of Gethsemane the night before he was tortured and killed.

Then they came to a place named Gethsemane, and he said to his disciples, "Sit here while I pray." He took with him Peter, James, and John, and began to be troubled and distressed. Then he said to them, "My soul is sorrowful even to death. Remain here and keep watch." He advanced a little and fell to the ground and prayed that if it were possible the hour might pass by him; he said, "Abba, Father, all things are possible to you. *Take this cup away from me, but not what I will but what you will.*" When he returned he found them asleep. He said to Peter, "Simon, are you asleep? Could you not keep watch for one hour? Watch and pray that you may not undergo the test. The spirit is willing but the flesh is weak." Withdrawing again, he prayed, saying the same thing. Then he returned once more and found them asleep, for they could not keep their eyes open and did not know what to answer him. He returned a third time and said to them, "Are you still sleeping and taking your rest? It is enough. The hour has come. Behold, the Son of Man is to be handed over to sinners. Get up, let us go. See, my betrayer is at hand" (Mark 14:32–42, emphasis added).

It is entirely plausible to describe the Jesus portrayed in this account as modest, unpretentious, and self-effacing; but do these attributes—these supposed synonyms for meekness—actually demonstrate meekness? An alternative interpretation holds that Jesus' disposition in the Garden of Gethsemane demonstrates not meekness as we tend to understand the term but Jesus' complete and total submission to the Father's will. Again, "not what I will but what you will." Jesus' disposition in the Garden is better understood, perhaps, as an expression of his radical submission to the Father's hopes and dreams for him.

Viewed from this perspective, Jesus did not bargain with the Father from a position of weakness. On the contrary, he acquiesced to the Father from a position of great strength, a position of great strength underwritten, in fact, by tremendous courage and self-sacrificial love. What was being asked of Jesus was undoubtedly difficult, more so than we can imagine, perhaps, but he said "yes" to the Father, a "yes" that was anticipated in Mary's "yes" to the angel Gabriel when she was asked to take up another seemingly impossible task. The "yes" in each of these instances can be understood as an act of remarkable courage and as an incredible display of strength, too.

We can now read this alternative understanding of Jesus' display of meekness back into his ministry. Recall that Gerhard Lohfink distilled

Jesus' three-year ministry into three distinct tasks: Jesus proclaimed the reign of God; he healed; and he confronted evil. That being said, there is considerable evidence that Jesus embraced preaching as his number one priority. Donald Senior and other Scripture scholars have observed that Jesus tended to initiate the action in proclaiming the good news. In contrast, others seem to have prompted Jesus' miracles of healing and exorcism. More often than not, sinners, the disabled, the possessed, and the distraught sought Jesus out and solicited his interventions in their lives. Indeed, Donald Senior describes Jesus as something of a "reluctant" miracle worker.[1] Consider one such incident from Mark's Gospel.

> When it was evening, after sunset, they brought to him all who were ill or possessed by demons. The whole town was gathered at the door. He cured many who were sick with various diseases, and he drove out many demons, not permitting them to speak because they knew him. Rising very early before dawn, he left and went off to a deserted place, where he prayed. Simon and those who were with him pursued him and on finding him said, "Everyone is looking for you." He told them, "Let us go on to the nearby villages that I may preach there also. *For this purpose have I come.*" So he went into their synagogues, preaching and driving out demons throughout the whole of Galilee. A leper came to him [and kneeling down] begged him and said, "If you wish, you can make me clean." Moved with pity, he stretched out his hand, touched him, and said to him, "I do will it. Be made clean." The leprosy left him immediately, and he was made clean. Then, warning him sternly, he dismissed him at once. Then he said to him, "See that you tell no one anything, but go, show yourself to the priest and offer for your cleansing what Moses prescribed; that will be proof for them." The man went away and began to publicize the whole matter. He spread the report abroad so that it was impossible for Jesus to enter a town openly. He remained outside in deserted places, and people kept coming to him from everywhere (Mark 1:40–45, emphasis added).

Note two frequently missed aspects of this familiar story. First, Jesus leaves town without telling anyone, including his disciples. It seems that Jesus has had enough of the demands put upon him by those who are so in need of healings and exorcisms. Jesus clearly hoped to get on with what he perceived to be his primary mission: preaching the good news of the

---

1. Senior, *Jesus: A Gospel Portrait*, 112–16; Meier, *A Marginal Jew*, 548–51; and Lohfink, *No Irrelevant Jesus*, 58.

Father's love. "For this purpose have I come," he declares. Second, Jesus tells the leper to "tell no one." At first glance, this directive is perplexing. After all, Jesus' healings and exorcisms were drawing crowds. They were providing him with an audience. At this point in the story, Jesus seems to be squandering a potentially valuable marketing opportunity. His reluctance to take advantage of this opportunity makes sense, however, if we consider the implication of his having touched a leper. Jesus knew that he would have had to submit to an elaborate cleansing ritual if word of this healing got out, an elaborate cleansing ritual that would have delayed his preaching. Again, Jesus clearly wants to get on with the task at hand.

Jesus' celebrity over the course of his three-year ministry can be attributed less, it seems, to his proclamation of the Father's love than to his healings and exorcisms. Nevertheless, it is clear that Jesus was more than willing to forego celebrity—a degree of popularity that can feed temptations to unhealthy materialism and sensuality, to unhealthy vanity, and to unhealthy pride—for a task that all too often evoked the bitter wrath of others. Consider the reception he received in his own hometown.

> [Jesus] came to Nazareth, where he had grown up, and went according to his custom into the synagogue on the sabbath day. He stood up to read and was handed a scroll of the prophet Isaiah. He unrolled the scroll and found the passage where it was written: "The Spirit of the Lord is upon me, because he has anointed me to bring glad tidings to the poor. He has sent me to proclaim liberty to captives and recovery of sight to the blind, to let the oppressed go free, and to proclaim a year acceptable to the Lord." Rolling up the scroll, he handed it back to the attendant and sat down, and the eyes of all in the synagogue looked intently at him. He said to them, "Today this Scripture passage is fulfilled in your hearing" . . . When the people in the synagogue heard [his teaching], they were all filled with fury. They rose up, drove him out of the town, and led him to the brow of the hill on which their town had been built, to hurl him down headlong. But he passed through the midst of them and went away (Luke 4:17–30).

To the extent that he was, in fact, a reluctant healer who eschewed celebrity in favor of the principal task set before him by the Father, why, then, did Jesus deign to consider the leper's request for healing in the first place? The Gospel tradition is suggestive in this regard, too. Jesus could not say "no," it seems, to those whom he recognized as brothers and sisters. Over the course of his three-year ministry, Jesus made himself radically available to those who sought healing. This is why some refer to Jesus' healings as a sustained ministry of interruptions.

We are now in a position to further define Jesus' meekness as something other than inordinate modesty, unpretentiousness, or self-effacement. Indeed, Jesus' meekness can more accurately be described in terms of his radical submission to the Father's will *and* to his radical availability to others.

Jesus' rebuke of Peter in the Gospel story that opened this chapter now makes more sense. Peter hails Jesus' celebrity: "You are the Messiah, the Son of the living God." In doing so, however, Peter clearly hoped to ensnare Jesus in a cocoon—or in a straitjacket, perhaps—of fame and fortune: "God forbid, Lord! No such thing shall ever happen to you." Although Peter might have expected his words to be received as affirming, Jesus had already surrendered himself to the Father's hopes and dreams. Jesus had emptied himself while in the desert and had aligned himself completely to the Father's will, and hence his scathing rebuke of Peter: "Get behind me, Satan! You are an obstacle to me. You are thinking not as God does, but as human beings do." Jesus was having none of it!

Viewed from this perspective, Jesus' denunciation of the scribes and the Pharisees and his violent cleansing of the temple align well with the Father's hopes and dreams for him. In excoriating the religious leaders of his day and in purging the temple courtyard of those who were extorting their fellow Jews, Jesus was acting meekly in the sense that he had subordinated his will so completely to the Father's hopes and dreams. Indeed, Jesus' displays of meekness could be anything but meek as we tend to understand the term today. His meekness was expressed, instead, in submitting himself entirely to the Father's will and in his radical availability to others.

We are now in a position to examine the relationship shared by the first two Beatitudes, i.e., "blessed are the poor in spirit" and "blessed are they who mourn, on the one hand and the third Beatitude, i.e.,, "blessed are the meek," on the other. Recall that the early church fathers viewed the Beatitudes not as discrete dispositions or attributes but as a progression in which each Beatitude built, in turn, upon those that preceded it. In the view of the early church fathers, the blessings associated with Matthew's third Beatitude can only be realized to the extent that we acknowledge and then master our proclivities to sin. The first and second Beatitudes invite us to empty ourselves of our idolatries. They invite us to empty ourselves of our unhealthy attachments to "stuff" and unhealthy experiences of one kind or another, our unhealthy attachments to ourselves, and our unhealthy attachments to what the world thinks and says about us; and, if this requires mourning, so be it. Such is the way of the cross. We empty ourselves, not just to rid ourselves of our idolatries, however. We empty ourselves so that we can be filled up, instead, by the Father's hopes and dreams for us. Clement of Alexandria (150–215) put it this way: "The meek are those who have quelled the battle of unbelief in the soul, the battle of wrath, and lust, and the other forms that are subject to them."[2]

Again, the early church fathers equated humility, i.e., a virtue associated with those who strive for spiritual *kenosis*, with "fear of the Lord," the recognition that God is God and that we are not God. According to Augustine, humility opens us up to God's hopes and dreams for us, a stance he associated with true piety: "Piety corresponds to the meek: for he who inquires piously honours Holy Scripture, and does not censure what he does not yet understand, and on this account does not offer resistance; and this is to be meek: when it is said, 'Blessed be the meek.'"[3]

This understanding of Matthew's third Beatitude prompts at least two questions, however. First, how precisely does God work in our lives? In other words, how does God fill our hearts? And how does he move us to action? And, second, how can we possibly know God's hopes and dreams for us? These kinds of questions have preoccupied spiritual writers for millennia, of course. Although they move well beyond the more narrow focus of this text, the broad outlines of key positions staked out in this regard will be noted so that we can more fully appreciate the import of Matthew's third Beatitude.

How, then, does God work in our lives? How does God fill the "spiritual space" that opens up in us as we become increasingly "poor in spirit" even to the point of mourning our deeply rooted tendencies toward sin? How does God move us and those around us in terms of our dispositions and our actions? It is only a slight exaggeration to suggest that most Christians volley back and forth rather comfortably between a neo-deist belief that God has little to do with our lives outside of our attendance at religious services on Sunday and our nominal conformance to the requirements of the Decalogue on the one hand and an understanding of God as a kind of cosmic puppet master who controls every aspect of our lives on the other.

2. Clement of Alexandria, "The Stromata," 2,218.
3. Augustine, "Our Lord's Sermon," 18,833.

In truth, the Jewish scriptures are not particularly helpful in sorting through these and other perspectives in this regard, particularly as they pertain to the problem of human suffering. The Deuteronomist tradition associated positive outcomes in this life with strict adherence to the law, and the Priestly tradition attributed earthly blessings, instead, to ritual sacrifice. These competing points of view both assumed that good things happen to good people and bad things to bad people. Indeed, God even rewards and punishes to the "third and fourth generation" (Deut 5:9)! According to these traditions, God even intervenes in our lives for his own purposes, irrespective of our own "goodness" or "badness." For instance, he "hardened" Pharaoh's heart in the Book of Exodus and, elsewhere in the Jewish scriptures, the hearts of whole peoples. Even the Book of Job, a text that thematically addresses the problem of undeserved suffering, can be problematic. God is baited by Satan into using Job to prove a point. In the end, Job is subjected not to comfort but to a rant of truly biblical proportions. It is little wonder that Christianity has struggled with the problem of suffering over the course of two millennia!

Jesus seems to have rejected this all too simple cause-and-effect theodicy At the same time, Jesus clearly affirmed the efficacy of prayer and hence God's willingness to intervene in our day-to-day lives: "Again, I say to you, if two of you agree on earth about anything for which they are to pray, it shall be granted to them by my heavenly Father. For where two or three are gathered together in my name, there am I in the midst of them" (Matt 18:19–20).

Given this, we would do well, perhaps, to acknowledge that the way in which God moves our hearts and minds and the hearts and minds of those with whom we journey remains something of a mystery. Indeed, the Book of Tobit may be a more accurate description of the precise way in which God intervenes in our lives. Tobit is a charming story that revolves around three appealing characters: Tobit himself, an elderly man who is suddenly blinded; his dutiful son, Tobiah; and Sarah, a young woman who is beset by a demon named Asmodeus. Raphael, an angel who conceals his true identity until the very end of the story, accompanies Tobiah on a hazardous journey to retrieve funds owed to his father. Along the way, Raphael protects Tobiah from injury, introduces him to Sarah, whom he will eventually marry, and secures an ointment that will be used to restore Tobit's sight.

The theodicy implicit in this engaging story rejects both the unreflective neo-deism that is all too common in our world and the rather naive understanding of God as a kind of cosmic puppet master, too. The Book of Tobit suggests that God is neither indifferent to us nor arbitrary in his interactions with us. God cares for us and responds to our prayers, but he does so in subtle ways: through inspirations discerned by those who are fully attuned to his voice, i.e., the meek, through the gifts he shares with us, and through the actions of others whom we encounter over the course of our journeys.

How then does God work in our lives? Drawing on the philosophy of John Macmurray and Karl Rahner's theology of grace, William A. Barry argues that "the one action of God includes the free actions of all human beings . . . Our faith and our experience tell us that we really are free agents, not pawns in the great chess game of creation. If our actions are truly free, then, again in some mysterious fashion, God's one action includes them and adjusts to them in order to attain God's intention."[4] This view is reflective, too, of Jesus' prayer on behalf of his disciples: "As you sent me into the world, so I sent them into the world. And I consecrate myself for them, so that they also may be consecrated in truth. I pray not only for them, but also for those who will believe in me through their word, *so that they may all be one, as you, Father, are in me and I in you, that they also may be in us*, that the world may believe that you sent me" (John 17: 18–21, emphasis added); and, with respect to suffering specifically, it is reflective, as well, of Martin Luther King Jr.'s memorable turn of phrase: "The arc of the moral universe is long, but it bends toward justice."

Our second question is just as challenging. How can we know God's hopes and dreams for us? Catholic moral teaching has long posited the existence of natural law, a variously defined set of moral principles that are intuitively knowable by all right-thinking people of all times and places, including non-Christians. This is in keeping with Paul's teaching in his Letter to the Romans: "When the gentiles who do not have the law by nature observe the prescriptions of the law, they are a law for themselves even though they do not have the law. They show that the demands of the law are written in their hearts" (Rom 2:14–15). According to proponents of natural law theory, God has instilled a certain orientation to moral behavior in each of us. Although Protestant theologians have tended to reject the very idea of natural law as insufficiently cognizant of sin and its corroding influence on conscience, we have noted, too, the somewhat

4. Barry, *Spiritual Direction*, 15.

analogous concept of the "inner light," which seems to have underwritten so much of Robert Greenleaf's work. In this view, the perception of God's hopes and dreams for us is directly available to those among us who are properly disposed. In this view, ready access to God's hopes and dreams for us can be attributed less to human nature and less to virtue honed by habit than to prayer and to a personal relationship with God. In keeping with these several perspectives, the meek can be understood either as those who are fully attuned to the law written on every human being's heart or to the inner light of conscience.

Again, however, the early church fathers understood Matthew's version of the Beatitudes as a progression in holiness. The necessary attunement noted above can be attributed to the first two of Matthew's Beatitudes: "blessed are the poor" and "blessed are they who mourn" their abandonment of their deeply rooted sin. *Kenotic* self-emptying is essential if one is to be truly open to God's hopes and dreams.

Beyond this, careful discernment is required. This brings us back, however, to a question we have encountered in various guises at several points in this text: Is this "discernment of spirits," as it is referred to in the New Testament and in the Christian tradition more generally, like virtue, entirely unmerited, or is it developed through conscious and intentional formation, or via some combination of the two? According to Michael J. Buckley, "[the discernment of spirits] was understood as an infused gift of the Spirit or as a connatural sensibility issuing from a committed Christian life or as knowledge learned from study or an intermixture of all three. It was consequently classified as an art or as a doctrine, and the experiences out of which it issues have historically included the radical and transformational gift of the Spirit, a life of spiritual discipleship, and the disciplined inquiry into the criteria by which diverse religious influences may be recognized."[5] It may be sufficient for our purposes to simply acknowledge that the discernment of spirits requires our cooperation.

Again, the topic of spiritual direction goes beyond the scope of this text. That being said, several of the early church fathers had a lot to say about the "discernment of spirits," and their work would prove foundational for the spiritual directors who followed them. This includes Augustine and John Climacus. Augustine certainly viewed his life as a progression in the life of virtue and associated his journey of faith with the ascent unfolded in Matthew's version of the Beatitudes. It is important

---

5. Buckley, "Discernment of Spirits," 279.

to note, as well, that he attributed his conversion, in part, to the mentor-ship of Ambrose, the Bishop of Milan.[6] John Cassian (360–435) agreed on the need for spiritual direction.

> True discretion, said [Abbot Moses], is only secured by true hu-mility. And of this humility the first proof is given by reserving everything (not only what you do but also what you think) for the scrutiny of the elders, so as not to trust at all in your own judgment but to acquiesce in their decisions in all points, and to acknowledge what ought to be considered good or bad by their traditions. And this habit will not only teach a young man to walk in the right path through the true way of discretion, but will also keep him unhurt by all the crafts and deceits of the en-emy. For a man cannot possibly be deceived, who lives not by his own judgment but according to the example of the elders, nor will our crafty foe be able to abuse the ignorance of one who is not accustomed from false modesty to conceal all the thoughts which rise in his heart, but either checks them or suffers them to remain, in accordance with the ripened judgment of the elders. For a wrong thought is enfeebled at the moment that it is discov-ered: and even before the sentence of discretion has been given, the foul serpent is by the power of confession dragged out, so to speak, from his dark underground cavern, and in some sense shown up and sent away in disgrace.[7]

At least three implications follow from this reflection on Matthew's third Beatitude. First, our understanding of meekness needs to be re-conceived as a radical openness to God's hopes and dreams for us. As a consequence, the humility so prominently celebrated in the tradition of the early church fathers needs to be directed away from our relationship with others; the Christian virtue of humility should be oriented, instead, to God. God is God and we are not God! From this perspective, meek-ness understood as inordinate modesty, unpretentiousness, or even self-effacement *vis-à-vis* others may or may not be appropriate in the case of any particular individual. Other dispositions may be required.

This broader understanding of meekness is aptly reflected in John the Baptist's citation of the prophet Isaiah: "Every valley shall be filled and every mountain and hill shall be made low. The winding roads shall be made straight, and the rough ways made smooth" (Luke 3:5). In ori-enting ourselves in a radical way to God's purposes, some of us may need

6. Augustine, *The Confessions*, 93–95.

7. Cassian, "Second Conference," 37,323

to be brought down a notch or two, while others among us may need to be raised up. Indeed, this is the sense in which Stephen Bevans and Roger Schroeder—drawing on the work of Judith Plaskow—have argued that meekness—at least as our culture tends to understand the term—does not serve women particularly well.

> The root of sin [in Western theology] is pride, self-assertion, and self-will, and the corresponding Christian task is to undergo the discipline of humility, self-effacement and self-sacrifice. But while such *kenosis* is liberating in the lives of those who have power and prestige (that is, men), it is actually oppressive for women, who are thus encouraged to remain in situations in which they continue to be dominated by men and a male-oriented culture . . . What women need to recognize is that holiness for them often entails pride in themselves, self-assertion, and the development of an authentic sense of self. While the asceticism required of men involves the way of humility, the asceticism required of women might very well involve a discipline whereby they learn to acknowledge their own worth, dignity, and power.[8]

The same may be true of others who are discounted or abused in one way or another in our own time and place. This is not what God wants. God does not desire the marginalization of anyone. This is the sense, too, in which it may sometimes be possible to interpret self-assertion and certain oppositional behaviors as meekness, indeed, as faithful expressions of an individual's radical abandonment to God's hopes and dreams for her.

To the extent that this may be true, a number of uncomfortable questions follow for managers and nominal leaders in many of today's organizations: To what extent can God's hopes and dreams be detected in the discordant voices I hear both inside and outside the organization for which I work? Are the discordant voices I am so tempted to dismiss as oppositional—in truth—prophetic in nature? Indeed, do they represent the kind of "zeal" described in John 2:13–17? And have I dismissed certain voices as self-serving that can better be understood as faithful to God's purposes?

Second, it is essential for aspiring disciples of Jesus to cultivate a rich mix of spiritual disciplines and practices. Attuning oneself to God's hopes and dreams is the essential work of a lifetime; and this essential work is

8. Bevans and Schroeder, *Prophetic Dialogue*, 98.

a matter of sustained formation rather than a kind of "one and done" intellectual exercise or a matter reserved exclusively for Sunday mornings. Fortunately, our tradition provides a whole host of tools that can be helpful, including the daily reading of Scripture, other spiritual reading, spiritual journaling, *lectio divina* and other forms of prayer, and the daily *examen*, all of which require time, persistence, and great patience, itself a distinctly countercultural value. The counsel provided in Psalm 37 is pertinent in this regard: "Be still before the Lord; wait for God." God works in God's own time.

As we have seen, spiritual mentors or directors can also play an important role in the discernment of spirits. It can be difficult, indeed, to determine what is from God and what is from our own desires and expectations or, perhaps, from the evil one. We know that human beings can be powerful rationalizers. Given this, the theological virtue most closely associated with discernment is hope, the anticipation that God will provide us with sufficient direction and the wherewithal to realize his hopes and dreams for us. At this point in the aspiring disciple's journey, hope tends to be tentative, however. Interestingly, the Catechism of the Catholic Church describes hope as both a "desire" and an "expectation."[9] Hope is experienced at this point as a fervent desire rather than as a confident expectation. The corresponding cardinal virtue with respect to discernment is prudence.

Finally, aspiring disciples of Jesus who work in all kinds of contemporary organizations must simply accept the fact that meekness is and will likely remain profoundly countercultural. There is no place for meekness in the instrumental and largely transactional language games examined in chapters 2 and 5 of this text.

REFLECTION QUESTIONS: "BLESSED ARE THE MEEK"

- Do I experience hope as a fervent desire for a deep and abiding relationship with God?
- What practices in my life are oriented to the development of a relationship with God and to knowing God's hopes and dreams for me

9. *Catechism*, 882.

and his hopes and dreams for those with whom I journey? Am I faithful to these practices?

- What new practices and disciplines in this regard may be needed for me to better discern God's hopes and dreams for me?

- How do I sense God's presence in my life?

- What steps do I need to take in order to be more fully formed in the virtue of prudence, which is essential to discerning God's hopes and dreams for me?

- Do I have a sense of what God is asking of me now in terms of my work, key relationships in my life, and the challenges I face on a day-to-day basis? If not, have I truly emptied myself of my root sin(s) and so opened myself to God's hopes and dreams for me? Further, what can I do to engender a better sense of what God may be asking of me at this point in my journey?

- Am I prepared for the sacrifices that God's hopes and dreams for me and for those with whom I journey might require?

Chapter 8

"Blessed Are They Who Hunger and Thirst for Righteousness" & "Blessed Are the Merciful"

Because [the scholar of the law] wished to justify himself, he said to Jesus, "And who is my neighbor?" Jesus replied, "A man fell victim to robbers as he went down from Jerusalem to Jericho. They stripped and beat him and went off leaving him half-dead. A priest happened to be going down that road, but when he saw him, he passed by on the opposite side. Likewise a Levite came to the place, and when he saw him, he passed by on the opposite side. But a Samaritan traveler who came upon him was moved with compassion at the sight. He approached the victim, poured oil and wine over his wounds and bandaged them. Then he lifted him up on his own animal, took him to an inn and cared for him. The next day he took out two silver coins and gave them to the innkeeper with the instruction, 'Take care of him. If you spend more than what I have given you, I shall repay you on my way back.' Which of these three, in your opinion, was neighbor to the robbers' victim?" He answered, "The one who treated him with mercy." Jesus said to him, "Go likewise" (Luke 10:29–37).

SOME BACKGROUND MAY BE helpful before we examine the familiar story of the Good Samaritan in some detail. It is sufficient for the moment to note the parable's explicit orientation to behavior. We are told little about the Good Samaritan's background, his spirituality, or his motivation for responding as he did. Instead, Jesus describes what the Good Samaritan does and what it means. The first three Beatitudes, i.e., "blessed are the poor in spirit," "blessed are they who mourn," and "blessed are the meek," each hold behavioral implications, of course, but they are, for the most part, dispositional in nature. As we shall see, a pivot to behavior is evident in the case of Matthew's fourth and fifth Beatitudes.

The early church fathers recognized the centrality of action. In their view, Jesus promoted inner transformation, but expected, nonetheless, that this *metanoia* or *shub* would translate into concrete action. The contrast between righteousness on the one hand and iniquity on the other is thus a common theme in the writings of the early church fathers, and so, too, the need to practice charity and to forgive. Righteousness and mercy both pertain to explicit behaviors.

Given this focus on what the Reformers of the sixteenth century dismissed as "works," we will briefly revisit the theological dispute that has been addressed at several points in this text, a dispute that separates the soteriology of the Catholic and Orthodox churches on the one hand and the *sola gratia* soteriology embraced by the Reformers on the other. In doing so, we will affirm once again the belief that righteousness is God's work. We will then explore the early church fathers's understanding of the relationship between the first three of Matthew's Beatitudes and the fourth and fifth Beatitudes, i.e., "blessed are those who hunger and thirst for righteousness" and "blessed are the merciful." This will be followed, in turn, by a reframing of the concept of righteousness in terms of "right relations," a reframing that is fully reflective, nonetheless, of the early church fathers's understanding of righteousness. We will then assess Jesus' understanding of mercy. Finally, we will consider several implications that the foregoing reflections may hold for all who aspire to discipleship and for Christian managers and nominal leaders more specifically.

Matthew's fourth and fifth Beatitudes were problematic for the Reformers because they both seem to suggest a theology of "works," a soteriology that the Reformers had rejected in no uncertain terms. Luther, Zwingli, and Calvin pointed in a particular way to Paul's Letter to the Romans in promoting faith in Jesus as a response to God's unmerited grace as the sole path to salvation.

We need not belabor this theological fault line since we have already addressed it in some detail. Suffice it to say that the Catholic view on this question now endorses—to a substantial degree—the Reformers's critique in this regard. See, for instance, the 1999 Joint Declaration on the Doctrine of Justification by the Lutheran World Federation and the

Catholic Church.[1] The Catholic perspective holds, nonetheless, that each of us has a role to play. God invites our active engagement in the work of salvation and provides us with the graces needed to respond positively to the many gifts we have received. A footnote in the New American Bible makes this clear: "Here [Matt 3:14–15], as in Matt 5:6 [and] 6:33, righteousness seems to mean the saving activity of God. To fulfill all righteousness is *to submit* to the plan of God for the salvation of the human race."[2]

In including "hunger and thirst" in the fourth Beatitude, Jesus—or members of Matthew's community who celebrated Jesus' Sermon on the Mount—may, in fact, have had Psalm 107:1–9 in mind. Note the ultimate source of the satisfaction that comes to those who hunger and thirst for something more: "Give thanks to the Lord who is good, whose love endures forever . . . Yes, *some had lost their way in a barren desert; found no path toward a city to live in.* They were hungry and thirsty; their life was ebbing away. In their distress, they cried to the Lord who rescued them in their peril, so they reached a city to live in. Let them thank the Lord for such kindness, such wondrous deeds for mere mortals. For *he satisfied the thirsty, filled the hungry with good things*" (emphasis added). When we "submit to the plan of God for the salvation of the human race" and when we cooperate with God in pursuing righteousness, we are doing God's work.

We are now in a position to examine the relationship shared by the first three Beatitudes on the one hand and the fourth and fifth Beatitudes on the other. Recall that the early church fathers viewed the Beatitudes as a progression in the life of discipleship, a progression in which each Beatitude is built, in turn, upon the settled foundations of those that preceded it. To this point in the journey, the aspiring disciple has wrestled—always at God's invitation and always with and through God's grace—with her root sin. She has emptied herself—to the extent possible—of her unhealthy attachment to "stuff" and to unhealthy experiences of one kind or another, to her unhealthy attachment to herself, and to her unhealthy attachment to the opinions of others. The aspiring disciple has emptied herself even to the point of mourning these unhealthy attachments. Further, this *kenotic* experience—this new poverty of spirit, in fact—has

---

1. *Joint Declaration.*
2. Senior, *The Catholic Study Bible*, 1,256. Emphasis added.

engendered a radical openness to God's hopes and dreams for her, a radical openness defined here as "meekness."

As a result, the blinders have now been removed. The disciple on the journey now sees, not through eyes dimmed by materialism and sensuality, pride, and vanity, but through God's eyes. She sees, in fact, a world in need of healing. She sees a world in need of God's mercy. This is the point at which the aspiring disciple moves into discipleship proper, the point at which she moves from having been invited into a relationship with Jesus to being sent into the world to continue his work. Indeed, this is the point at which she experiences a heretofore unrecognized hunger and thirst for righteousness and for mercy. Pinckaers explains this development as follows: "The chief difficulty to be overcome is our extreme dependence upon earthly nourishment, which renders us insensible to that which is spiritual . . . We do not appreciate spiritual goods until we have tasted them; it is experience which arouses our desire for them and makes us seek them . . . In order to discover the depth of this desire and to strengthen it, we need to resist the fallacious attraction of earthly goods—not only food and drink, but also money, pleasure, and vanities—and force ourselves to go hungry in their regard so as to be freed from their excessive hold on us. We need to make room within ourselves for a nobler desire. This work of detachment is effected by poverty and suffering."[3] In describing this formational process, Pinckaers is following the lead of the early church fathers. According to John Chrysostom, Jesus invited his disciples to "transfer" their "covetousness" for worldly goods to a "new freedom," a new "hunger and thirst," in fact, "for righteousness."[4] Augustine agreed: "'Blessed are they which do hunger and thirst after righteousness: for they shall be filled.' They will therefore be filled with that food of which the Lord himself says, 'My meat is to do the will of my Father,' which is righteousness; and with that water, of which whosoever 'drinketh,' as he also says, it 'shall be in him a well of water, springing up into everlasting life.'"[5]

The progression is clear. *Kenosis* leads to a new awareness of God's hopes and dreams for us, which awakens, in turn, a previously unrecognized hunger and thirst for righteousness and for mercy. We should not think of this progression as a one-way street or as a linear progression,

---

3. Pinckaers, *The Pursuit of Happiness*, 94.

4. Chrysostom, "Homily XV," 22,395.

5. Augustine, "Our Lord's Sermon," 17,830.

however. More often than not, the process is iterative. The disciple's journey can include detours along the way, detours John of the Cross referred to as spiritual "dryness." These sidesteps can even be experienced as "dark nights of the soul."[6] A spiral process is described in the spiritual direction literature as well. In this view, more and more self-emptying can lead to ever more attentiveness to God's work in our lives, which can lead, in turn, to ever more attentiveness to the needs of others.

To this point, we have yet to define two key terms: "righteousness" and "mercy." Each will be addressed in turn. Protestants often speak of righteousness. In doing so, they call attention to the store of grace—entirely attributable to Jesus—out of which individual Christians are "justified" or saved. In contrast, Catholics tend to equate righteousness with justice prosaically understood as "getting your just deserts." This narrow understanding of righteousness is underwritten by the use of "justice" in the place of "righteousness" in some translations of the New Testament.

The term 'justice' is highly problematic, however. Most importantly, it positions righteousness and mercy in opposition to each other. "Getting your just deserts" is the very opposite of mercy, which can be understood as "getting something other than your just deserts." As we shall see, this tension is resolved when we reclaim the understandings of righteousness and mercy espoused by Jesus.

To be righteous can be better understood as being in a "right relationship." In this view, we are righteous when we are in right relationship with God and when we are in right relationship with ourselves and with others. The root of this more expansive understanding of righteousness can be located in the idea of covenant, an ancient regulatory construct that was transferred into the emergent idea of church found in Luke's Gospel and in the Acts of the Apostles. The Jewish people's covenant with God gave their lives meaning. It also defined and circumscribed their relationships with God, with each other, and with strangers, too, perspectives that were clearly taken up in the New Testament.

Is this how Jesus thought about righteousness, however? It seems so. Jesus healed and expelled demons in order to restore those who were ill and those who were possessed back to their families and their communities. Jesus' encounter with the widow of Nain in Luke's Gospel is a case in point. Jesus recognized that an abiding relationship shared by an only son and his mother had been disrupted. He was "moved with pity" and

6. John of the Cross, *The Collected Works*, 375–77.

so "gave the young man back to his mother" (Luke 7:13–15). The story of the Gerasene demoniac in Mark's Gospel makes the same point. "Go home," Jesus tells the young man (Mark 5:18–20). "Go home!" Jesus restored those whom he encountered back to right relationship with themselves, to right relationships with others, and, through the forgiveness of their sins, to right relationship with God. Jesus, it seems, associated righteousness with healing. Recall, again, Psalm 107: "They reached a city to live in." We can think of this city as a realm of right relationships, right relationships with God, with ourselves, and with others.

As Christians, we have a role to play with respect to righteousness re-conceived—or re-appropriated, perhaps—as right relationship. We can help restore wellbeing and right relationships with a word of good counsel. We can promote right relationships within and between communities through sharing, i.e., through charity. We can engender right relationships among those who have been estranged from one another, thus promoting reconciliation. As servant-leaders, we can encourage and help sustain right relationships among those who labor in various work and ministry settings. We can promote right relationships by enabling others to respond more fully to their own unique callings. And we can engender right relationships when we name evil for what it is and work to dispel it. Few of us "expel demons" as such, but we are challenged—more often than we would like, perhaps—to confront dysfunction in our families, in our workplaces, in our communities, and in the world as a whole.

It is important to note that right relationships—as they are described here—are shared by people *with* God and *with* other people. These relationships cannot be defined in terms that are exclusively formal, legal, or transactional in nature. Instead, they can only be motivated by and oriented to love, i.e., *agape*. According to Justin Martyr (100–165), one of the earliest of the church fathers, "all righteousness is divided into two branches, namely, in so far as it regards God and men . . . Whoever, says the Scripture, loves the Lord God with all the heart, and all the strength, and his neighbour as himself, would be truly a righteous man."[7] This understanding of righteousness as right relationship is profoundly scriptural, in fact. According to Pinckaers, "justice in Scripture differs from our justice because it establishes strongly personal relationships, first of all between God and his people through the covenant and the law which teach us the ways of God and show us his mercy; but then also between

7. Justin, "Dialogue of Justin," 622.

men, teaching us to respect one another and to cultivate just relationships which will result in peace and concord."[8]

We are now in a position to consider the parable of the Good Samaritan from Luke's Gospel. It is important to note that the priest and the Levite who passed by the injured man are defined in terms of their social and religious roles. We know nothing of their attitudes as such. Did they fear being robbed and beaten themselves? Did they shrink away from the ritual impurity that could have resulted from touching a dead body? Did they dread the inconvenience of a ritual cleansing? Did they think that attending to the injured man was beneath their lofty status as religious functionaries? Or did they simply not want to be bothered? We do not know. We can safely say, however, that their respective responses to the injured man were impersonal and lacking in love.

In contrast, Jesus describes the Good Samaritan as having been "moved with compassion," that is, as having been moved by love oriented to action, i.e., *agape*. The question that prompted this parable is worth noting as well: "Who is my neighbor?" Neighbors are people—or, better yet, "persons"—with whom we are invited into relationship.

Righteousness understood as being in right relationship, not just with God, but with other persons, too, obviates the perceived tension noted at the outset of this reflection between righteousness understood as justice, i.e., "getting your just deserts," and mercy, i.e., "getting something other than your just deserts." As we shall see, an awakened perception of the world's need for the restoration of right relationships demands a renewed commitment to mercy as well. As affirmed in Psalm 85, this is the point at which "mercy and justice shall meet" and "justice and peace shall kiss."

How then should we understand mercy? It is important to note, first, that the mercy we share is God's mercy. We are merciful because God has been merciful to us. Further, Jesus' understanding of God's mercy was incomprehensively large and bounteous. According to Jesus, God's mercy far transcends our truncated understanding of mercy. Beyond this, three observations are in order.

First, the early church fathers encouraged their congregants to expand the pool of resources from which most of them drew in pursuing their charitable endeavors. The early church fathers recognized charity as a non-optional expression of mercy. John Chrysostom, in particular,

---

8. Pinckaers, *The Pursuit of Happiness*, 98.

excoriated greed and stinginess. The early church fathers recognized that all that we are and all that we have, i.e., our time, our talent, and our treasure, too, comes from God. With this in mind, Clement of Alexandria insisted that all "God's gifts are for the common good."[9] Charity that is fully reflective of God's mercy must come from something more than our perceived surplus.

Second, motive matters, hence our need to journey to the fifth Beatitude through the progressive discipline of the first four. Christian discipleship demands inner transformation. Christian charity, for instance, should be motivated by something more than the desire to look good in one's own eyes, i.e., pride, or in the eyes of others, i.e., vanity; and it should be motivated, too, by something more than the sense of *noblesse oblige* sometimes professed by those who enjoy substantial means and status. Christian charity should be founded, instead, on love. Irenaeus (130–202) invoked the image of "one's neighbor" in making this argument: "As God, when teaching them his will in Hosea the prophet, said, 'I desire mercy rather than sacrifice, and the knowledge of God more than burnt offerings . . .' Those, then, are the perfect who have had the Spirit of God remaining in them, and have preserved their souls and bodies blameless, holding fast the faith of God, that is, that faith which is [directed] towards God, and *maintaining righteous dealings with respect to their neighbors.*"[10] Our charitable endeavors may even be sinful unless they are founded on loving relationships that are grounded, in turn, in our shared identity as God's sons and daughters. Consider John Chrysostom's warning in this regard, a warning drawn from a reflection on the parable of the Pharisee and the tax collector (Luke 18:9–14):

> How great is the gain of humbleness of mind, and how great the damage of pride . . . For what was worse than the publican? Even if he was removed from greed of gain and robbery, he had rooted over his soul the mother of all evils—vain-glory and pride . . . Just as a ship, after having run through innumerable surges, and having escaped many storms, then in the very mouth of the harbor having been dashed against some rock, loses the whole treasure which is stowed away in her—so truly did this Pharisee, after having undergone the labors of the fasting, and of all the rest of his virtue, since he did not master his tongue, in the very harbor underwent shipwreck of his cargo.

9. Clement of Alexandria, "The Stromata," 2,130.
10. Irenaeus, "Against Heresies," 1,229. Emphasis added.

For the going home from prayer, whence he ought to have derived gain, having rather been so greatly damaged, is nothing else than undergoing shipwreck in harbour.[11]

Third, charity alone does not do justice to Jesus' understanding of mercy. Again, the mercy Jesus extended to those whom he encountered seems to have been more closely related to his healing ministry than to almsgiving *per se*. Jesus' physical healings were rarely stand-alone events. They were often accompanied by the forgiveness of sins. In Jesus' mind, mercy clearly encompassed both charity *and* forgiveness. The interrelationships of these three terms, i.e., mercy, charity, and forgiveness, is most evident in Luke's Gospel: "Be merciful, just as [also] your Father is merciful. Stop judging and you will not be judged. Stop condemning and you will not be condemned. Forgive and you will be forgiven. Give and gifts will be given to you; a good measure, packed together, shaken down, and overflowing, will be poured into your lap. For the measure with which you measure will in return be measured out to you" (Luke 6:36–38). In fact, the promise of abundance in this pericope identifies it as a Lukan analogue to Matthew's fourth and fifth Beatitudes. Those who are merciful, those who share generously of themselves, and those who forgive others will be satisfied.

The biblical record suggests that Jesus knew something important about forgiveness. Our inability to forgive others stunts our growth, and so, too, our inability to forgive ourselves. Jesus seems to have known that unresolved hurt, anger, and guilt can function like straightjackets, unbreakable bindings, in fact, that can inhibit our ability to experience joy and to love.

This is evident in the story of the paralyzed man in Mark's Gospel (2:1–12) and in Luke's Gospel (5:17–26), too. The man was tied to a mat that was being let down through the roof of a house in which Jesus was healing people. The man was seeking healing, of course, but the mat in this story can be understood symbolically, too. Indeed, the mat can be understood as representing the kind of unresolved hurt, anger, and guilt that can so immobilize us. The paralyzed man is tied down. He cannot move; and, as a result, he is unable to experience joy or to love. Indeed, the paralyzed man is seeking release from the unresolved hurt, anger, and guilt—the sins, in fact—that have immobilized him.

---

11. Chrysostom, "Homily Concerning Lowliness," 21,639.

This kind of analogizing may sound strange to our ears, long accustomed as we are—as children of the Enlightenment—to literal thinking, but this is precisely how the early church fathers interpreted Scripture. Consider Augustine's exegesis pertaining to the story of the paralytic's healing: "All the limbs [of the paralytic's soul] are lifeless, it is empty of every good work, burdened with its sins, and weak from the illness brought on by its evil desires. Since all its limbs are helpless, and the paralysis is interior, [he] cannot come to the physician [by himself]."[12]

Jesus shows mercy to the man; he forgives him and he heals him, too. There is a catch, however, the very same catch we invoke every time we recite the Lord's prayer: "Forgive us our trespasses as we forgive those who trespass against us." To receive mercy, we must show mercy. To be forgiven, we must forgive. To be healed, we must bring healing when and where we can. To be made whole again, we must help others become whole.

In the case of the paralyzed man, being healed does not mean that the paralysis never happened. Understood metaphorically, it does not mean that serious sin has never been committed, that the hurt has never been experienced, or that the offense can be forgotten. Jesus tells the healed man to pick up his mat and take it home, however. His mat, it seems, will always be with him. The man's hurt, his anger, and his guilt will always be there, but there is a difference now. The man is carrying the mat. He is no longer being carried by it. He is no longer being carried by his hurt, his anger, and his guilt. He is now carrying the pain that had tied him down for so long. The man—the *formerly* paralyzed man—has been healed.

Understanding forgiveness as a constitutive part of mercy holds implications for us, of course. Hurt invites reparations; anger invites reconciliation; and guilt invites personal acceptance and public acknowledgement. The larger lesson is this, however: we are merciful because we, too, are in need of mercy; we share because all that we are and all that we have comes from God; we forgive because we, too, hope for forgiveness; and we bring healing when and where we can because we, too, are in need of healing.

The implications that follow from the foregoing analyses are significant, especially for those who exercise managerial responsibilities in organizations. Recall that the early church fathers understood Matthew's

12. International Commission on English in the Liturgy, "On Pastors by Augustine," 286.

Beatitudes as a progression in discipleship; and recall, too, that the Catholic Church and many Protestants, as well, now affirm that all are called to holiness. Then note the contrast between the weaknesses associated with the dominant language games of contemporary management theory and practice, i.e., their circumscribed understanding of human motivation and their orientation to instrumental ends variously disclosed as profit, efficiency, one or more particular policy goals, effectiveness, results, the optimal use of resources, the maximization of shareholder wealth, and conformance to specifications, on the one hand and the values and intellectual commitments embodied in Matthew's fourth and fifth Beatitudes, i.e., a commitment to the development of right relationships with God, with ourselves, and with other persons and mercy understood as charity, inner transformation, and forgiveness, on the other; and note, as well, the non-negotiability of these seminal Christian intellectual commitments and values. There is no avoiding the conclusion that dissonance can all too easily ensue in the lives of disciples of Jesus who exercise managerial responsibilities of one kind or another due to the incommensurate value systems that claim their allegiance.

For a disciple, however, there should be no doubt as to which of these competing value systems should take precedence. Augustine put it well: "I must distinguish carefully between two aspects of the role the Lord has given me, a role that demands a rigorous accountability, a role based on the Lord's greatness rather than on my own merit. The first aspect is that I am a Christian; the second, that I am a leader. I am a Christian for my own sake, whereas *I am a leader for your sake*; the fact that I am a Christian is to my own advantage, but *I am a leader for your advantage*."[13] Augustine recognized that he was a Christian first and that his commitments in this regard should inform the exercise of his responsibilities as a leader.

In fact, Augustine's understanding of leadership anticipated language employed by Robert Greenleaf. Again, "the servant-leader is servant first . . . It begins with a natural feeling that one wants to serve, to serve *first*. Then conscious choice brings one to aspire to lead. The person is sharply different from one who is *leader* first, perhaps because of the need to assuage an unusual power drive or to acquire material possessions."[14] Like Greenleaf, Augustine would certainly have rejected

13. International Commission on English in the Liturgy, "On Pastors by Augustine," 255. Emphasis added.

14. Greenleaf, *Servant Leadership*, 27.

the remarkably thin understandings of human nature professed by most of today's managerial language games and so, too, their instrumental ethic.

The exemplar in this regard—for both Greenleaf and Augustine—was clearly Jesus. We would thus do well to consider the defining moment in John's Gospel in which Jesus washed his disciples's feet.

> Before the feast of Passover, Jesus knew that his hour had come to pass from this world to the Father. He loved his own in the world and he loved them to the end . . . So, during supper, fully aware that the Father had put everything into his power and that he had come from God and was returning to God, he rose from supper and took off his outer garments. He took a towel and tied it around his waist. Then he poured water into a basin and began to wash the disciples' feet and dry them with the towel around his waist. He came to Simon Peter, who said to him, "Master, are you going to wash my feet?" Jesus answered and said to him, "What I am doing, you do not understand now, but you will understand later." Peter said to him, "You will never wash my feet." Jesus answered him, "Unless I wash you, you will have no inheritance with me." Simon Peter said to him, "Master, then not only my feet, but my hands and head as well . . ." So when he had washed their feet [and] put his garments back on and reclined at table again, he said to them, "Do you realize what I have done for you? You call me 'teacher' and 'master,' and rightly so, for indeed I am. If I, therefore, the master and teacher, have washed your feet, you ought to wash one another's feet. I have given you a model to follow, so that as I have done for you, you should also do" (John 13:1–15).

Following the example of Jesus is by no means easy. The theological virtue foregrounded at this point in the disciple's journey is charity, of course; and the cardinal virtues associated most closely with Matthew's fourth and fifth Beatitudes are prudence, i.e., right judgement, fortitude or courage, and justice.

Consider, too, the implications this analysis holds for our understanding of the moral and the just. Again, the moral can be defined as how one thinks about and acts toward oneself and toward others as persons; and the just can be understood as a particular kind of moral behavior that pertains to how life's benefits and burdens should be shared among individuals recognized as persons and communities comprised of persons. If I think of myself first as a Christian, organizational imperatives should be filtered through the intellectual commitments and values I hold *as* a Christian; and, if I think of all other persons as fellow sons and daughters of God to whom and for whom I am responsible, I am obligated to consider and attend to their unique journeys of discipleship—as well as to my own—to the extent I can. Again, Greenleaf argued that this "standard of care" should apply to all who are "touched" in any way by an organization.[15] At a minimum, therefore, I should avoid—again, to the extent I can—any actions that could impede their journeys. As Greenleaf put it, "the best test, and difficult to administer, is this: Do those served grow as persons? Do they, *while being served*, become healthier, wiser, freer, more autonomous, more likely themselves to become servants? *And*, what is the effect on the least privileged in society? Will they benefit or at least not be further deprived."[16]

Most importantly, the filtering or buffering function that Christian intellectual commitments and values can serve can encourage true leadership to emerge. Again, "authentic leadership" is defined here as the balanced exercise of one or more managerial functions in service to a broad array of stakeholders in a manner constrained by the leader's internalized virtues and informed by values and intellectual commitments drawn from a larger belief system, but oriented, nonetheless, to ends sanctioned by the organization or by society. As noted throughout this text, this understanding of leadership can be distinguished from functional management in four ways: it is oriented to service; it takes into consideration the needs of a broad array of stakeholders; it is constrained by virtues internal to the leader; and its exercise is oriented to values and intellectual commitments drawn from a larger belief system.

We are now in a position to reimagine the model introduced in chapter 4. See figure 11.

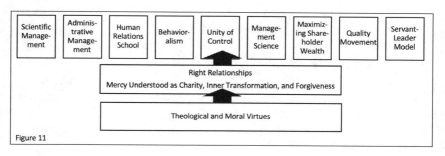

Figure 11

15. Greenleaf, *Servant Leadership*, 68.

16. Greenleaf, *Servant Leadership*, 27.

Christian managers must work in the world. Indeed, they are embedded in the managerial language games sanctioned by the organizations that employ them. For disciples of Jesus, however, Christian virtues oriented to Christian intellectual commitments or values should serve as a kind of preliminary filter through which actions impacting a broad array of stakeholders, i.e., persons and communities of persons, can be examined. These values and intellectual commitments can thus provide a potential defense against the enclosed and sometimes suffocating worldviews promoted in today's dominant language games and the stresses associated with decision-making in contemporary organizations, too. To this end, the box generically labeled "Christian intellectual commitments" in the middle of the model presented in chapter 4 has now been replaced by a box featuring the Christian values examined in this chapter: a commitment to the development of right relationships and mercy understood as charity, inner transformation, and forgiveness.

This understanding of righteousness and mercy also pertains to the public square. Pinckaers's insights regarding the Beatitudes and the potential they hold for the life we share in common extends beyond the more narrow—albeit foundational—confines of family and employment: "In regard to others, justice inclines us to carry out our allotted tasks conscientiously, especially those connected with our profession, for this may benefit many other people and lead us eventually to assume public functions which, beyond our legitimate concern for our own particular interests, we will perform with an eye to the common good."[17]

Because we live in a pluralistic society, however, Christian intellectual commitments and Christian values cannot be assumed to be universal. With respect to decision-making, we move from the leader as a sole practitioner who labors in an organization—a sole practitioner at least in terms of her moral responsibilities—to a community of decision-makers in the public square. A more generalized set of values, i.e., a moral system, in fact, which is based on an existential understanding of human persons as meaning-seeking beings, an understanding of the good as the experience of meaning, an understanding of the moral as the full recognition of the inherent dignity that attaches to all persons, and an understanding of justice as opportunity, was thus proposed in chapter 5 in place of the explicitly Christian set of intellectual commitments and values detailed above.

---

17. Pinckaers, *The Pursuit of Happiness*, 103.

Although not distinctively Christian in nature, this articulated moral framework is fully compatible with the broader wisdom literature cited by Greenleaf and other proponents of the servant-leader model. More to the point, meaning, dignity, and opportunity are Christian values, too. Given this, it should be possible for Christian leaders in the public square—Christian leaders who espouse a commitment to the development of right relationships and mercy understood as charity, inner transformation, and forgiveness—to enter into productive conversations with non-Christians and with their nominally Christian neighbors, too.

REFLECTION QUESTIONS: "BLESSED ARE THEY WHO HUNGER AND THIRST FOR RIGHTEOUSNESS" AND "BLESSED ARE THE MERCIFUL"

- How do I view others in my life? Do I see them primarily as opportunities or as obstacles or constraints? Do I see them as "things" valued primarily for their "handiness" to me? Or do I recognize them as fellow sons and daughters of God?

- If I struggle in this regard, have I truly emptied myself of my root sin(s) and so opened myself to God's hopes and dreams for me?

- Where in my life do relationships need to be mended? In and among those with whom I work? In and among those who are impacted directly or indirectly by my work? In my family? In my church? In my community? In the world?

- How do I understand my time, talent, and treasure? Do I see them as gifts from God, all of which should be ordered to the common good? If not, have I emptied myself sufficiently of my own root sin(s) and so opened myself to God's hopes and dreams for me in this regard?

- How do I understand "mercy"? Is it mine to give or is it better understood as God's mercy, which I am invited to share with others?

- How am I in need of forgiveness? What acts of mercy do I hope for?

- Who in my work relationships, in my personal relationships, and in my many other relationships in the world needs forgiveness? How am I challenged to share God's mercy with them? What will this require of me?

- How can I better form myself in the virtues of fortitude, justice, and prudence so that I can be ever more faithful in sharing God's mercy with others?

Chapter 9

"Blessed Are the Clean of Heart"

Now when Jesus was in Bethany in the house of Simon the leper, a woman came up to him with an alabaster jar of costly perfumed oil and poured it on his head while he was reclining at table. When the disciples saw this, they were indignant and said, "Why this waste? It could have been sold for much, and the money given to the poor." Since Jesus knew this, he said to them, "Why do you make trouble for the woman? She has done a good thing for me. The poor you will always have with you; but you will not always have me. In pouring this perfumed oil upon my body, she did it to prepare me for burial. Amen, I say to you, wherever this gospel is proclaimed in the whole world, what she has done will be spoken of in memory of her" (Matt 26:6–13).

THIS COMPELLING STORY SPEAKS to the inner integrity and servant identity of the nameless woman, a true disciple of Jesus. She is rendered anonymous, perhaps, so that each of us can envision ourselves in her place. The woman can thus be considered an exemplar with respect to the sixth Beatitude, i.e., "blessed are the clean of heart," and so, too, Jesus, of course.

Five arguments will be advanced in this chapter. First, our received understanding of purity or cleanliness of heart is far too limited. It does not capture the full sense of the sixth Beatitude as it was understood by the early church fathers. Second, purity or cleanliness of heart is better understood as singleness of purpose or integrity. Third, the journey to this all important sixth Beatitude—another pivot point, in fact—must proceed through the five Beatitudes that proceeded it in Matthew's

Gospel. Again, the early church fathers understood the Beatitudes as a progression in the journey of faith. Fourth, the sixth Beatitude is better understood as a gift, a gift shared with some disciples, it seems, sometimes to a deep and abiding degree and sometimes fleetingly, but not with others. And, fifth, the ideal of purity or cleanliness of heart, nevertheless, holds implications for all Christians and, more specifically for our purposes, for managers and nominal leaders in contemporary organizations.

Purity or cleanliness of heart came to be associated with sexual purity in the late Middle Ages. This was likely so for three closely related reasons. As noted in the introduction to part II, the several Beatitudes came to be viewed as discrete and hence unrelated prescriptions for a blessed life during this time period. Given this, there was no need for the sixth Beatitude to carry the full weight of the five that preceded it. As a result, the sixth Beatitude could be carved out for a particular purpose: the ideal of sexual purity. Further, this narrow focus attained a particular salience—an enduring preoccupation, in fact—in the Catholic Church of the late Middle Ages and early modern period, a church that had committed itself to the ideals of celibacy and sexual continence. Still further, as Matthew's Beatitudes were increasingly viewed as optional or supererogatory in nature, they were increasingly associated with clergy and with men and women religious, most of whom had "given up house [and] brothers [and] sisters [and] mother [and] father [and] children [and] lands" for Jesus' sake and "for the sake of the gospel" (Mark 10:29). The laity—the rank and file of the highly structured church of this time period—were referred, instead, to the proscriptive dictates of the Decalogue: "you shall not commit adultery" and "you shall not covet your neighbor's wife" (Deut 5:18–21).

Although the church has come a long way with respect to its understanding of Matthew's sixth Beatitude, this older perspective persists. At their November 2015 General Assembly, the bishops of the United States approved a formal statement on pornography entitled *Create in Me a Clean Heart: A Pastoral Response to Pornography*.[1] In keeping with our reflection on Matthew's first two Beatitudes, this document might have been more appropriately entitled *Make Me Poor in Spirit, Lord: Help Me Mourn My Sins*. After all, an addiction to pornography can be understood as a manifestation of the root sins of materialism and sensuality, i.e., the worship of "stuff" and unhealthy experiences of one kind or another.

---

1. United States Conference of Catholic Bishops, *Create in Me*.

In contrast, the early church fathers tended to associate the sixth Beatitude's reference to purity or cleanliness with all kinds of serious sin. According to John Chrysostom, "He here calls 'pure,' either those who have attained unto *all virtue*, and are not conscious to themselves of *any evil* . . . For there is nothing which we need so much in order to see God, as this last virtue."[2] Ambrose agreed: "In these two points, then, consist the excellence of the soul: so that thy soul, trained in good thoughts, and with a pure heart, first, may see what is true and virtuous . . . and may decide that only to be good which is virtuous and, next, may never be disturbed by *business of any kind*, nor get tossed about by *any desires*."[3]

Indeed, the early church fathers tended to interpret Matthew's sixth Beatitude as singleness of heart or singleness of purpose or—to use a more contemporary term—integrity. According to Augustine, "as is written elsewhere, 'in singleness of heart seek him,' for that is a pure heart which is a single heart."[4] Further, "nothing cleanses but the undivided and single-minded striving after eternal life from the pure love of wisdom alone."[5] According to Daniel J. Harrington, the term "'pure of heart' in Matthew's Gospel characterizes people of integrity whose moral righteousness extends to their inmost being and whose actions and intentions correspond."[6]

In a very real sense, the sixth Beatitude represents another pivot point in the progression of faith now evident in Matthew's version of the Beatitudes. In the fourth and fifth Beatitudes, i.e., "blessed are they who hunger and thirst for justice" and "blessed are the merciful," we moved beyond the preliminary work of the first three Beatitudes, i.e., "blessed are the poor in spirit," "blessed are they who mourn," and "blessed are the meek," to see the world more nearly as God sees the world—the very meaning of *theoria* in Aristotle's epistemology[7]—a world in which relationships have gone awry, indeed, a world very much in need of mercy. We thus pivoted away from the interior work of the first three Beatitudes—the "sharp edge of the plowshare," to use Pinckaers's language—to action in the fourth and fifth Beatitudes.

2. Chrysostom, "Homily XV," 22,396. Emphasis added.

3. Ambrose, "On the Duties," 35,752. Emphasis added.

4. Augustine, "Our Lord's Sermon," 17,830.

5. Knight, "On the Sermon on the Mount."

6. Harrington, *The Gospel of Matthew*, 79.

7. Ten Klooster, *Thomas Aquinas*, 76.

With the sixth Beatitude, we pivot again, but this time away from discipleship understood as a "work in progress" to something more, to a fuller or more complete sense of discipleship, in fact. The clean of heart can thus be described as those who have completely emptied themselves of their unhealthy attachments and false idols. They have mourned their root sins. The clean of heart are those who are truly meek and have thus abandoned themselves completely to God's hopes and dreams for them. Finally, the clean of heart see the world day in and day out as God sees the world. They do so, however, with an extraordinary clarity and a remarkable consistency that exhibits true purity or singleness of heart. As Harrington puts it, their "actions and intentions correspond" with each other.

We have reached the point at which a model may be helpful. Using a medieval taxonomy, we could describe the first three Beatitudes as a kind of apprenticeship, the fourth and fifth Beatitudes as journeyman status, and the sixth, seventh, and eighth Beatitudes as master-class discipleship. This tired taxonomy belongs to the male-dominated world of guilds, however, a world that no longer exists. We would thus do well to abandon this language in favor of terminology that better reflects the relational nature of discipleship. Those who are in the process of embracing a poverty of spirit—even to the point of mourning their root sins—and those who are in the process of opening themselves up to God's hopes and dreams for them, i.e., the meek, can thus be described as aspiring disciples; and those whose eyes have been opened to the needs of the world and who are now responding to those needs can be described as true disciples. As noted in the introduction to part II of this text, Jesus' closest associates were challenged to do exactly as he did: they were sent out to proclaim the Father's love, to bring healing when and where they could, and to confront evil.[8] Finally, the clean of heart and peacemakers, including those who suffer for their peacekeeping efforts, can be understood as friends of God. This follows from Jesus' declaration in John's Gospel: "I no longer call you slaves, because a slave does not know what his master is doing. I have called you friends, because I have told you everything I have heard from my Father" (John 15:15).

See figure 12.

---

8. Lohfink, *Jesus of Nazareth*.

Friend or Artist (i.e., Master)	Foregrounded Theological Virtue(s)	Foregrounded Moral Virtue(s)
8. Blessed are they who are persecuted for the sake of righteousness. 7. Blessed are the peacemakers.	Charity	• Prudence • Justice • Fortitude
6. Blessed are the clean of heart.	• Hope • Faith	• Temperance • Prudence
Disciple (i.e., Journeyman)		⬆
5. Blessed are the merciful. 4. Blessed are they who hunger and thirst for righteousness.	Charity	• Prudence • Justice
Aspiring Disciple (i.e., Apprentice)		⬆
3. Blessed are the meek.	Hope	• Prudence
2. Blessed are they who mourn. 1. Blessed are the poor in spirit.	Faith	• Temperance • Prudence • Fortitude

Figure 12

These friends of God can also be described as artists. Indeed, there is a certain grace evident in those who have arrived at this point in their spiritual journeys, a certain way of being in the world that we associate with the moral virtues of prudence, i.e., the "disposition to discern the good and choose the correct means to accomplish it,"[9] and temperance, i.e., the disciplined control of the passions, all of which leave us vulnerable to root sin. Aquinas recognized the analogous relationship shared by the arts and the moral virtue of prudence: "Art is the *right reason of things to be made* whereas prudence is the *right reason of things to be done* . . . The various kinds of things made by art are all external to man . . . but prudence is right reason about human acts themselves."[10]

In one who is clean of heart, this disposition is artistically expressed as a fundamental part of her identity. She is truly blessed! Prudence is expressed as *phronesis* or practiced living. This is the point in the spiritual journey at which Jesus' consoling words in Matthew's Gospel are fully realized: "Take my yoke upon you and learn from me, for I am meek and humble of heart; and you will find rest for yourselves. For my yoke

9. *Catechism*, 895.

10. Pegis, *Introduction to St. Thomas*, 573–74.

is easy and my burden light" (Matt 11:29–30). As we shall see, "easy" in this context pertains more to the clarity of the choice to be made in any given situation than to the relative complexity of the task at hand or the extent to which demands associated with any given decision may weigh upon us. This is the point, instead, at which the blessed individual's "actions and intentions correspond," the point at which the discomfort, conflict, and dissonance she may have long experienced as a disciple of Jesus who lives nonetheless in the complex world of secular organizations may find some resolution. Jesus thus comforted his disciples who were worried about a coming persecution: "When they lead you away and hand you over, do not worry beforehand about what you are to say. But say whatever will be given to you at that hour. For it will not be you who are speaking but the Holy Spirit" (Mark 13:10–11). Jesus was confident that his disciples—his friends, in fact, friends who would in time become accomplished artists in the journey of faith—would have the right words when the moment arrived.

Two caveats are in order before we revisit the story of the anonymous woman with the alabaster jar. First, it is clear that the theological virtues of faith, hope, and charity are internalized at a deeper, more integral level in the case of the sixth, seventh, and eighth Beatitudes. As detailed in chapter 6, faith is associated with the first and second Beatitudes, i.e., "blessed are the poor in spirit" and "blessed are they who mourn," but faith is experienced at this initial stage in the journey of discipleship as a tentative response to an invitation, an invitation that appeals to the individual's search for meaning in her life. For the clean of heart, faith seems to be experienced differently. For the clean of heart, faith is experienced as sure knowledge or as the call and response of one who loves to one who is loved. As affirmed by Aquinas, "it is by faith that the intellect apprehends what it hopes for and loves. Hence, in the order of generation, faith must proceed hope and charity."[11]

Similarly, the infused theological virtue of hope is associated with the third Beatitude, i.e., "blessed are the meek." Hope is experienced in this preliminary stage of the spiritual journey, however, more as a "desire" than as an "expectation" *per se*. In contrast, the clean of heart experience hope as great confidence in God's providential love.

Further, as we have seen, the virtue of charity is associated with the fourth and fifth Beatitudes, i.e., "blessed are those who hunger and thirst

---

11. Pegis, *Introduction to St. Thomas*, 596.

for righteousness" and "blessed are the merciful." At these stages in the spiritual journey, the blinders have been removed. True discipleship begins as the now triply blessed individual sees the world more nearly as God sees the world, a world greatly in need of healing and mercy. She hungers and thirsts for righteousness. Similarly, cleanliness of heart—a new disposition, indeed, a new way of being in the world—seems to engender an even deeper commitment to the development of right relationships, now in the form of peacemaking.

We must remember, of course, that the three theological virtues underwrite and inform each other. Nevertheless, in terms of their foregrounding, a twofold movement is indicated: first, faith, i.e., the first and second Beatitudes; hope, i.e., the third Beatitude; and charity, i.e., the fourth and fifth Beatitudes; and, only then, deeper faith and more confident hope, i.e., the sixth Beatitude; and, finally, a true passion for charity understood as peacemaking, i.e., the seventh and eighth Beatitudes. We can also detect a recurring movement from disposition to action. Whereas the dispositional work of the first three Beatitudes leads to action in the fourth and fifth Beatitudes, the dispositional work of the sixth Beatitude leads to action in the seventh and eighth Beatitudes.

Our second caveat pertains to the end or *telos* of the hope that so animates the clean of heart. In truth, the early church fathers professed very different perspectives on the theological virtue of hope. No consensus was achieved in this regard. Those who exhibited gnostic tendencies promoted superior knowledge; others promised rewards in the afterlife; and still others associated the sixth Beatitude with contemplation or the beatific vision. This latter view is evident, for instance, in Augustine's appeal to the "pure love of wisdom alone." Indeed, a strong case can be made for contemplation as the *telos* of hope in the writings of the early church fathers and in the scholarly work of those who followed them. This should not be surprising given the profound influence of monasticism—a particular way of being in the world explicitly oriented to contemplation—in the development of Christian spirituality. Further, an even stronger case for contemplation as *the* end or *telos* of the spiritual life could be made if Matthew had only recorded six Beatitudes. The contemplative orientation of the sixth Beatitude is followed, however, by the clear action orientation of the seventh and eighth Beatitudes, i.e., "blessed are the peacemakers" and "blessed are they who are persecuted."

Bypassing the views of the early church fathers in this regard, Aquinas followed Aristotle in postulating *eudaemonia* or human flourishing as the overarching goal of human existence. Indeed, Aquinas rejected the view that the several blessings associated with the Beatitudes can only be realized in the next world. He associated the Beatitudes with happiness and argued that human flourishing can be experienced in this life as a foretaste of the blessings to come in the afterlife,[12] hence the seventh and eighth Beatitudes.

In chapter 3, we drew on existential thinking to postulate an understanding of *eudaemonia* or human flourishing as the experience of meaning in one's life. Aquinas did not have access to the existential thought of the twentieth century, of course. Given this, some may wonder if this more contemporary understanding can even be considered Christian. To address this concern, the seminal work of the notable Jesuit scholar Karl Rahner was cited in chapter 3. In fact, the idea that the experience of meaning in one's life can be understood as human flourishing is well established in Catholic teaching. See, for instance, *Gaudium et Spes*, one of the most important of the sixteen documents promulgated at the close of the Second Vatican Council: "In the face of modern developments, there is a growing body of people who are asking the most fundamental of all questions or are glimpsing them with keener insight: What is humanity? What is the meaning of suffering, evil, death, which have not been eliminated by all of this progress? What is the purpose of these achievements, purchased at so high a price? What can people contribute to society? What can they expect from it? What happens after this earthly life has ended?"[13] This existential outlook is reflected in the *Catechism of the Catholic Church* as well: "By love, God has revealed himself and given himself to man. He has thus provided the definitive, superabundant answer to the questions man asks himself about the meaning and purpose of his life."[14]

Consistent with an ontology that defines human beings as intelligent or rational creatures, the Catholic Church continues to privilege Aristotle's understanding of human purpose as the pursuit of happiness.[15] Nevertheless, it provides ample room for an existential understanding of the human condition as well. Viewed from this perspective, hope can be understood as the only sure path through the twin shoals of dysfunction

---

12. Ten Klooster, *Thomas Aquinas*, 79.

13. Second Vatican Council, "*Gaudium et Spes*," no. 18.

14. *Catechism* 68.

15. *Catechism* 1718.

that are part and parcel of our postmodern existence. According to Monika K. Hellwig, "contemporary Christian spirituality still faces the challenge of the twin temptations of despair and presumption," two temptations against hope that were first articulated by Thomas Aquinas. Hellwig continues: "On the one hand, there is in our society a pervasive despair of finding meaning, purpose, and ultimate satisfaction in human existence . . . Yet it is not only despair but also presumption that constitutes a characteristic contemporary temptation against hope. There are many aspects of contemporary urbanized, industrial society that favor confidence in one's own achievements of wealth, status, and power as the way to total happiness."[16] These are the same root sins that were described in chapter 6.

We are now in a position to examine the compelling story of the anonymous woman with the alabaster jar from chapter 26 of Matthew's Gospel. The details of the story suggest a disciple who has experienced *kenosis*; she has emptied herself of her root sins. The woman's use of the costly oil indicates that her materialism and her sensuality, too, have been set aside for something better. The disciples object to the cost of her extravagant gesture, but she alone knows the true meaning and the true value of the oil and the true meaning and the true value of the moment as well. Her humble approach to Jesus suggests that any worship of self in her, i.e., sinful pride, has been set aside as well. And her willingness to step boldly into the patriarchal environment of a formal dinner party hosted in first-century Israel suggests that she is unconcerned about what others may think and say about her, i.e., sinful vanity. She is poor in spirit, it seems, likely to the point of having mourned her root sins. The anonymous woman is meek as well. She has clearly aligned herself with God's hopes and dreams for her to the extent, in fact, that "what she has done will be spoken of wherever the Gospel is proclaimed." Clearly, the blinders are now off in the case of this remarkable women. We sense that she sees the world as God sees the world, a world very much in need of the healing Jesus promised to all who had eyes to see and ears to hear. We can assume, as well, that she is now "clean of heart" because she has clearly achieved the blessing associated with Matthew's sixth Beatitude: she sees God. Of all those in the room with Jesus, she alone, it seems, has recognized Jesus as the Son of God, hence her use of "perfumed oil," i.e.,

16. Hellwig, "Hope," 513–14.

chrism oil, to anoint him on the crown of his head, thereby acknowledging his status as priest, prophet, and king.

That being said, there is a noticeable difference between the first five of Matthew's Beatitudes and the latter three. We cannot help but sense that those who are clean of heart and those who are peacemakers are truly exceptional. Most of us have surely encountered individuals who are poor in spirit and so, too, the meek and those who hunger and thirst for justice and those who are merciful; but how many of us have encountered anyone whom we would describe as a true friend of God or as a true artist in the journey of faith? And if the clean of heart and peacemakers, too, are so very exceptional, can we still assert that the Beatitudes apply to all of us and that all are called to holiness?

These are legitimate questions. We should keep in mind, however, that the journey of faith so eloquently articulated in Matthew's version of the Beatitudes is more God's work than our own. We cooperate, but the heavy lifting is attributable to God and to God alone. Cleanliness of heart, in particular, is best understood as God's work. In chapter 36 of Ezekiel, God proclaims: "I will sprinkle clean water upon you and cleanse you from your impurities and from all your idols I will cleanse you. A new heart I will give you, and a new spirit I will put within you, and I will remove from your bodies your hearts of stone and give you hearts of flesh" (Ezek 36:25–26). God does the heavy lifting, not us; and this is why we so often echo the words of Psalm 51: "Create in me a clean heart, O God . . ."

Further, the gifts associated with cleanliness of heart seem to be reserved to those who have been set aside for a particular purpose. We have noted that Augustine struggled to align the gifts of the Holy Spirit enumerated by Isaiah with Matthew's Beatitudes, but that conflicting views in this regard persisted well into the late medieval period. A Christological reading of Isaiah's gifts suggests, however, that they pertain, not so much to all or even to some believers, but to Jesus himself: "A shoot shall sprout from the stump of Jesse, and from his roots a bud shall blossom. The spirit of the LORD shall rest upon him: a spirit of wisdom and of understanding, a spirit of counsel and of strength, a spirit of knowledge and of fear of the LORD, and his delight shall be the fear of the LORD" (Isa 11:1–3). This reading refers neither to Israel's leaders nor to faithful Jews more generally. It refers, instead, to a new David, a shoot that will sprout from the stump of Jesse, a particular person recognized by Christians as Jesus. Jesus is the new David upon whom the gifts of the Holy Spirit will descend. A Christological reading of Psalm 24 underwrites this same conclusion: "Who may go up the mountain of the LORD? Who can stand in his holy place? The clean of hand and pure of heart, who has not given his soul to useless things, what is vain. He will receive blessings from the LORD, and justice from his saving God" (Ps 24:3–5). Again, a traditional reading of this liturgical psalm associates it with Jesus.

Paul, too, affirms that the gifts of the Holy Spirit are reserved to some, but not to all: "There are different kinds of spiritual gifts but the same Spirit; there are different forms of service but the same Lord; there are different workings but the same God who produces all of them in everyone. To each individual, the manifestation of the Spirit is given for some benefit" (1 Cor 11:4–7).

This does not mean that the gifts of the Holy Spirit—as we understand them—are not shared or bestowed on Jesus' disciples. Those who are clean of heart—those whom we recognize as friends of God or as artists in the journey of discipleship—seem, however, to have been blessed to an exceptional degree with the gifts of wisdom, understanding, counsel, fortitude, knowledge, piety, and fear of the Lord.

Still further, as rare as they may be, the clean of heart are not unknown to us. Jesus promised the clean of heart that they would see God. In Ignatian spirituality, this is interpreted as "seeing God in all things." The "little way" of Thérèse of Lisieux certainly reflects the gifts of wisdom, piety, and fear of the Lord in a particular way, and so, too, the life of a little-known Carmelite: Brother Lawrence, a monk whose long life spanned the seventeenth century.[17] Brother Lawrence was by no means famous in his own day. On the contrary, he performed the most menial of tasks over the course of his long life of service, first in the monastery kitchen and then as a cobbler. The tasks he performed were hardly the stuff of legend, but Brother Lawrence so enamored his fellow monks that his superior was compelled to write extensively about him after his death. Brother Lawrence's spirituality was oriented to the moment-to-moment celebration of God's presence. This was so not just during his moments of formal prayer but while peeling potatoes, too, and while nailing a new heel onto a boot. Brother Lawrence seemed to his companions to have basked always and everywhere in God's presence, and so was joyful, it seems, even when performing the most lowly of tasks. Indeed, we are told that Brother Lawrence did not see any difference between washing

17. de Beaufort, *The Practice.*

dishes and praying the Liturgy of the Hours in choir. Brother Lawrence truly saw God in all things. Like Thérèse of Lisieux, he was a friend of God. Like Thérèse of Lisieux, he was clean of heart and thus an artist in the journey of faith.

It could be objected that neither Thérèse of Lisieux nor Brother Lawrence can be considered leaders in any conventional sense and thus lie beyond the scope of this text. This reflects too narrow an understanding of leadership, however. We know that purity of heart can affect the world in remarkable ways. Pinckaers used the verb "radiates" to describe this effect and associated this quality of soul with Jesus, who socialized with sinners "in order to radiate upon them and their faults the merciful purity of the love of God, and so heal them."[18] The purity of heart evident in Thérèse of Lisieux and in Brother Lawrence clearly "radiated" in this same way.

Finally, although Matthew's eight Beatitudes certainly reflect a progression in discipleship, they tend to be experienced—more often than not, it seems—in an iterative fashion. Indeed, it is not uncommon to encounter considerable turbulence in our relationship with God over the course of our lifetimes. Further, although the surety and comfort of an abiding friendship with God may elude most of us in this plane of existence, many of us have sensed a particular closeness to God at one or more points in our journeys of faith. These kinds of intense existential encounters—as fleeting as they may be—are not unknown to Christians and to nonbelievers, too. Cleanliness of heart has more in common, it seems, with the kind of "thin places" postulated in Gaelic spirituality than the onset of sudden and permanent enlightenment ascribed, for instance, to the Zen experience of *satori* or to the "one-and-done" acceptance of Jesus as one's savior.

The concept of purity or cleanliness of heart should be of more than eschatological interest to Christians. It is an ideal to which we should all aspire, and hence the need for discernment. The practice of presence is of particular importance in this regard. As detailed above, Thérèse of Lisieux and Brother Lawrence seem to have seen God in all things. They were blessed, indeed!

That being said, we could all too easily dismiss Matthew's sixth Beatitude as something reserved exclusively for the truly holy among us; and, since singleness of heart is so wholly dependent on God's work in

18. Pinckaers, *The Pursuit of Happiness*, 137.

our lives, we could all too easily think of this state of being as something entirely beyond our reach. This conclusion, however, ignores the fact that one must journey through the first five Beatitudes in order to present oneself to God as someone who is entirely open to his hopes and dreams for her; and, for most of us, there is still much work to be done with respect to the five Beatitudes that precede Matthew's pivotal sixth Beatitude.

Formation in moral virtue is essential. Recall the summary of Alasdair MacIntyre's critique of conventional leadership in chapter 5. We may, indeed, be living "beyond our moral means."[19] The missing ingredient is moral virtue understood as the various habitual inclinations or dispositions we harbor that—hopefully—orient us to the good. God's work is certainly essential to the development of moral virtue, but so, too, our cooperation. As Thomas Aquinas put it: "Grace does not destroy nature, but perfects it."[20] Nature, in this context, includes more than our DNA and the temporal, demographic, or cultural circumstances into which we are born. Nature includes our formed orientation to the good or, alternately, to other, less worthy ends.

With respect to Matthew's sixth Beatitude more specifically, we would do well to remember, too, that God is at work in our lives whether we recognize it or not. We should keep in mind, as well, that God intervenes in our lives in subtle ways that may not be discernable to those who are less than fully attentive to his voice. As noted in chapter 7, we can think of the meek among us as those who are attuned to those "thin places" and those "thin moments" in our lives when God may be nudging us in the direction of his hopes and dreams for us.

A manager or nominal leader could argue that this particular Beatitude, i.e., "blessed are the clean of heart," is entirely dispositional and hence of no particular relevance to the kinds of decisions she is challenged to make on a day-to-day basis. This conclusion ignores the fact, however, that Matthew's sixth Beatitude leads directly to his seventh and eighth Beatitudes. The enhanced experience of hope on which cleanliness or singleness of heart rests necessarily leads to action. It cannot be contained. Drawing on the work of Gustavo Gutierrez, Juan Luis Segundo, and Leonardo Boff, Hellwig puts it this way: "These theologies address themselves to the discernment and analysis of the authentic intermediate

19. Pinckaers, *The Pursuit of Happiness*, 515.

20. Aquinas, "Question 1."

objects of hope—those transformations in relationships, values, expectations, and structures of society that are steps in the direction of the full realization of the reign of God among us."[21]

In the following chapter, we will address more specifically the kinds of fundamental transformations to which Hellwig speaks, transformations that are, in fact, the responsibility of true leaders who are also committed disciples of Jesus.

REFLECTION QUESTIONS: "BLESSED ARE THE CLEAN OF HEART"

- How do I understand "cleanliness of heart"? Do I understand it as integrity in faith and hope?

- Have I encountered "cleanliness of heart" in others? When and where? Do I recognize certain exemplars as truly "clean of heart"? How and in what way have I come to recognize them as such?

- Have I experienced moments in my own life in which I can say that I was "clean of heart"? If so, how did I sense God's presence in these moments? If not, what additional work might be required on my part? Do I need to further empty myself of my root sin(s) even to the point of mourning? Do I need to further open myself to God's hopes and dreams for me? Do I need to recognize and respond to others as fellow sons and daughters of God? Do I need to forgive others in order to welcome forgiveness in my own life? Do I need to share God's mercy with others? How can I do so?

- Do I have sufficient faith in God and hope or confidence in his love for me to journey further toward true cleanliness of heart?

- How would my work relationships change if I truly lived a life of integrity in faith and hope? How would my personal relationships change? What new relationships would be required? What old relationships would need to be abandoned?

- How can I better form myself in the virtues of prudence and temperance, both of which are required to engender true cleanliness of heart?

21. Hellwig, "Hope," 513.

Chapter 10

"Blessed Are the Peacemakers" & "Blessed Are They Who Are Persecuted for the Sake of Righteousness"

Early in the morning he arrived again in the temple area, and all the people started coming to him, and he sat down and taught them. Then the scribes and the Pharisees brought a woman who had been caught in adultery and made her stand in the middle. They said to him, "Teacher, this woman was caught in the very act of committing adultery. Now in the law, Moses commanded us to stone such women. So what do you say?" They said this to test him, so that they could have some charge to bring against him. Jesus bent down and began to write on the ground with his finger. But when they continued asking him, he straightened up and said to them, "Let the one among you who is without sin be the first to throw a stone at her." Again he bent down and wrote on the ground. And in response, they went away one by one, beginning with the elders. So he was left alone with the woman before him. Then Jesus straightened up and said to her, "Woman, where are they? Has no one condemned you?" She replied, "No one, sir." Then Jesus said, "Neither do I condemn you. Go, [and] from now on do not sin anymore" (John 8:2–11).

SOME PERCEIVE A CLEAR shift in focus as we move from the first six to the last two of Matthew's Beatitudes. On the surface, at least, we seem to move from the intrapersonal, i.e., the first, second, third, and sixth Beatitudes, and the interpersonal, i.e., the fourth and fifth Beatitudes, to a concern for systems and processes. After all, peacemaking—as we tend to understand the term—can involve whole populations, ideologies of various kinds, iterative stages of negotiation, and hence a broad array of systemic and procedural concerns. The story of the woman about to be so brutally killed in order to provoke a reaction from Jesus reminds us, however, that peacemaking understood as an expression of discipleship is more typically oriented to the needs of persons and communities of persons. This is so even when our peacemaking efforts involve complex systems and time-consuming processes. Jesus' three-year ministry certainly underwrites this view, as does the Thomist personalism of John Paul II and others.

Six aspects of Matthew's seventh and eighth Beatitudes are addressed in this chapter. First, peace should be understood as more than the absence of open conflict. Peacemaking as a defining expression of discipleship pertains, instead, to righteousness understood as the development and nurturing of right relationships or right order. It pertains, as well, to the concept of human flourishing. Matthew's seventh and eighth Beatitudes thus extend on his fourth, i.e., "blessed are they who hunger and thirst for righteousness." Second, "success"—as the world tends to understand the term—cannot serve as the standard against which discipleship is measured. Third, the seventh and eighth Beatitudes follow the first six for a reason. The first six Beatitudes set the stage for peacemaking, including peacemaking efforts that may seem futile or of little importance to the world. Fourth, the various elements of peacemaking—understood here as a defining expression of Christian discipleship—are well articulated in the values and intellectual commitments embodied in Catholic social teaching. Fifth, Jesus is *the* exemplar with respect to peacemaking. Indeed, he is *the* exemplar of servant leadership. Finally, the above analyses hold implications for all Christians, including Christian managers and nominal leaders.

Our understanding of peace as the absence of conflict is undeniably anemic in comparison to the biblical concept of the term. According to Daniel J. Harrington, Matthew's Jesus understood peace to be "*shalom*," God's peace, i.e., the very sharing of God's life with us.[1] This understanding of peace can be further explicated in two senses: first, as right relationship with God and with persons and communities of persons we encounter over the course of our journeys; and second, as human flourishing.

---

1. Harrington, *The Gospel of Matthew*, 79.

The concept of righteousness properly understood as right relationship was initially addressed in chapter 8. Drawing on both Augustine and Aquinas, Ten Klooster affirms that peace, too, "consists in a tranquility of order, and order is the arrangement allotting the proper place to equals and unequals. When everything has its place, there is right order,"[2] notwithstanding the fact that the terms "equal" and "unequal" are dramatically reinterpreted in a Christian moral framework in the light of Jesus' new law of love. Right relationship or right order is thus a constitutive aspect of righteousness as it pertains to peacemaking.

We are drawn ever deeper in this Beatitude, however, to the close connection between Jesus—as he is revealed in the Gospels—and the peace Jesus' disciples are invited to share with others. According to Carol Frances Jegen, Jesus is Emmanuel, "God with us" (Matt 1:23), and hence the embodied peace of God. Jegen cites Paul's Letter to the Ephesians in support of this view:

> Now in Christ Jesus you who once were far off have become near by the blood of Christ. For he is our peace, he who made both one and broke down the dividing wall of enmity, through his flesh, abolishing the law with its commandments and legal claims, that he might create in himself one new person in place of the two, thus establishing peace, and might reconcile both with God, in one body, through the cross, putting that enmity to death by it. He came and preached peace to you who were far off and peace to those who were near, for through him we both have access in one Spirit to the Father. So then you are no longer strangers and sojourners, but you are fellow citizens with the holy ones and members of the household of God, built upon the foundation of the apostles and prophets, with Christ Jesus himself as the capstone. Through him the whole structure is held together and grows into a temple sacred in the Lord; in him you also are being built together into a dwelling place of God in the Spirit (Eph 2:13–22).

Jegen acknowledges that this instruction pertains in a specific way to the divide that separated Jews and gentiles in Paul's day, but argues, nonetheless, that "this text identifies Jesus *as* our peace."[3]

This identification of Jesus with peace is revealed in compelling detail in John's Gospel: "Peace I leave with you; *my peace* I give to you. Not

2. Ten Klooster, *Thomas Aquinas*, 111.
3. Jegen, "Peace," 732. Emphasis added.

as the world gives do I give it to you. Do not let your hearts be troubled or afraid" (John 14:27, emphasis added). In John's Gospel, Jesus promises to restore all of creation to right relationship with God: "I pray not only for them, but also for those who will believe in me through their word, so that they may all be one, as you, Father, are in me and I in you, that they also may be in us, that the world may believe that you sent me. And I have given them the glory you gave me, so that they may be one, as we are one, I in them and you in me, that they may be brought to perfection as one, that the world may know that you sent me, and that you loved them even as you loved me. Father, they are your gift to me. I wish that where I am they also may be with me, that they may see my glory that you gave me, because you loved me before the foundation of the world" (John 17:20–24).

This association of peace with the very person of Jesus was endorsed by a number of the early church fathers, most notably John Chrysostom: "So great a good is peace, as that the makers and producers of it are called the sons of God (Matt 5:9, 45), with reason; because the Son of God for this cause came upon the earth, to set at peace the things in the earth, and those in the heavens."[4] Leo the Great agreed:

> "Blessed are the peace-makers, for they shall be called the sons of God." This blessedness, beloved, belongs not to any and every kind of agreement and harmony, but to that of which the Apostle speaks: "have peace towards God . . ." This peace even the closest ties of friendship and the exactest likeness of mind do not really gain, if they do not agree with God's will . . . They who are in mind always with God, "giving diligence to keep the unity of the Spirit in the bond of peace," never dissent from the eternal law, uttering that prayer of faith, "Thy will be done as in heaven so on earth." These are "the peacemakers," these are thoroughly of *one mind*, and fully harmonious, and are to be called sons "of God and joint-heirs with Christ," because this shall be the record of the love of God and the love of our neighbor, that we shall suffer no calamities, be in fear of no offence, but all the strife of trial ended, rest in God's most perfect peace, through our Lord, who, with the Father and the Holy Spirit, liveth and reigneth for ever and ever. Amen.[5]

---

4. Chrysostom, "Homily III," 25,705.

5. Leo the Great, "Sermon XCV," 38,461. Emphasis added.

The biblical concept of *shalom* understood as righteousness or as "oneness" with God can be further articulated. According to Harrington, true *shalom* means nothing less than the "fullness of God's gifts."[6] This can be understood as an eschatological promise, of course, but recall Aquinas's view that Jesus promised blessings in this plane of existence as well. Jesus did more than just forgive sins; he healed, thereby returning those whom he encountered to right relationship with God, right relationship with themselves, and right relationship with others. The biblical concept of *shalom* thus pertains to human flourishing or *eudemonia* as well, a concept defined in this text as the experience of meaning in one's life. This is the sense in which Jesus can be understood as the definitive answer to the existential questions that confront every one of us. Again, according to the Catechism: "By love, God has revealed himself and given himself to man. He has thus provided the definitive, superabundant answer to the questions man asks himself about the meaning and purpose of his life."[7]

Despite the blessings promised by Jesus, success—as the world tends to understand the term—cannot serve as the standard against which discipleship is measured. Recall a criticism advanced in chapter 3 against Robert Greenleaf's brief on behalf of servant leadership: it is crafted in teleological terms. Greenleaf set the stage for a normative claim in this regard, but backed off in the end, insisting, instead, that servant leadership simply works better than other management theories and models. Despite its more humane trappings, Greenleaf's argument is no less instrumental than the claims advanced in the various managerial language games examined in chapter 2.

This is not how Christian discipleship works, however. This is certainly why Matthew's seventh Beatitude, i.e., "blessed are the peacemakers," is followed by his eighth, i.e., "blessed are they who are persecuted for the sake of righteousness." Suffering can—and often does—attend to peacemaking. In support of this view, the early church fathers pointed to the challenging tasks undertaken by the great prophets of the Jewish scriptures. The prophets's protests against the religious and secular leaders of their own time and place were clearly normative for them. Isaiah, Jeremiah, Ezekiel, and the other great prophets condemned Israel's leaders for worshipping idols and for ignoring the needs of those who lived

6. Harrington, *The Gospel of Matthew*, 79.
7. *Catechism* 68.

on the margins of Jewish society. Indeed, they advocated explicitly on behalf of the *anawim*, a Hebrew word that refers to the poor who seek God's deliverance. Although the deuteronomist editors who contributed so much to the development of the Old Testament canon tended to focus on certain *quid pro quo* elements in God's covenant with the Jewish people, Israel's prophets argued that God should be obeyed simply because God is God. Outcomes and results were largely beside the point for Israel's prophets.

The early church fathers similarly celebrated the ideal of martyrdom, an ever-present reality in the church until the year 313. Writing just prior to the promulgation of Constantine's Edict of Milan, Lactantius (250–320) associated the real possibility of torture and death with Jesus' passion: "If it is virtue not to fear death itself when threatened, and when inflicted to undergo it with fortitude; it follows that the perfect teacher ought both to teach these things by precept, and to confirm them by practice."[8]

Other forms of suffering, including imprisonment and banishment, were lived realities during the great theological controversies of the fourth and fifth centuries as well. The point is that Christian discipleship does not guarantee positive outcomes as the world tends to understand positive outcomes. The Beatitudes promise blessings, but these blessings are not in any sense oriented to instrumental ends. Peacemakers can, in fact, pay a very steep price for their pursuit of righteousness.

Considerable work is needed before the clean of heart are sufficiently formed to engage the world as true peacemakers. According to Augustine, "they are peacemakers in themselves who, by bringing in order all the motions of their soul, and subjecting them to reason—i.e., to the mind and spirit—and by having their carnal lusts thoroughly subdued, become a kingdom of God: in which all things are so arranged, that that which is chief and pre-eminent in man rules without resistance over the other elements, which are common to us with the beasts; and that very element which is pre-eminent in man, i.e., mind and reason, is brought under subjection to something better still, which is the truth itself, the only-begotten Son of God."[9] Indeed, Augustine viewed this pinnacle of formation as a new kind of freedom: "If it is wisdom through which the peacemakers are blessed, inasmuch as they shall be called the children

---

8. Lactantius, "The Divine Institutes," 8,193.
9. Knight, "On the Sermon on the Mount."

of God; let us pray that we may be freed from evil, for that very freedom will make us free, i.e., sons of God, so that we may cry in the spirit of adoption, Abba, Father."[10]

Echoing a turn of phrase noted in the preceding chapter, Pinckaers referred to peacemakers as "artisans of peace."[11] According to Jegen, today's peacemakers can even be thought of as saints. She numbers Mohandas Gandhi, Dorothy Day, Martin Luther King Jr., and Cesar Chavez in this company.[12] Disciples on the journey do not, however, become saints overnight. The journey of discipleship can be a long and winding road. The respective journeys of each of these remarkable individuals seem to have progressed through a conversion process approximating Matthew's eight Beatitudes. Each of them wrestled in one way or another with unhealthy attachments and false idols in their lives. Over time, each of them emptied themselves, even to the point of mourning. They subordinated themselves to a larger purpose in their lives. They were meek. Each of these modern-day saints hungered and thirsted for righteousness, understood as the experience of right relationship. Each of them showered mercy on others, most notably, the *anawim* of the twentieth century. In time, each of them exhibited a singleness of purpose and a personal integrity that attracted others, a personal integrity, in fact, that "radiated" into the world. They were clean of heart; and, in time, each of them emerged as a true artisan of peace. In time, each of them fully integrated peacemaking into their very identities. And in one way or another, each of them suffered for the sake of righteousness. As a result, we recognize them today as prophets and as martyrs, indeed, as children of God or saints.

This is rarified air, to be sure. How many of us would dare aspire to peacemaking understood in this sense of the term? We may believe in peace and we may contribute with our time, talent, and treasure to this or that cause, but how many of us would dare hope to become a true artisan of peace?

We should keep in mind, however, that peacemaking is primarily God's work, not our own. The peace we are called to share is God's peace, i.e., *shalom*. Like all of the blessings associated with the Beatitudes, the particular blessing associated with peacemaking is best understood as a

---

10 Knight, "On the Sermon on the Mount."

11. Pinckaers, *The Pursuit of Happiness*, 162.

12. Jegen, "Peace," 733.

gift. To think otherwise is to stoke the root sin of pride. Indeed, to think otherwise can be understood as a modern-day expression of the pelagian heresy. This is certainly the view of Pope Francis: "Those who yield to this pelagian or semi-pelagian mindset, even though they speak warmly of God's grace, 'ultimately trust only their own powers and feel superior to others because they observe certain rules or remain intransigently faithful to a particular Catholic style . . .' Grace, precisely because it builds on nature, does not make us superhuman all at once. That kind of thinking would show too much confidence in our own abilities . . . Grace acts in history; ordinarily, it takes hold of us and transforms us progressively."[13] All we can do, it seems, is open ourselves to God's hopes and dreams for us and his hopes and dreams for a world greatly in need of healing.

As demanding as the vocation of peacemaking may be, it is, nonetheless, part and parcel of discipleship. We are all disciples on the journey, each of us proceeding in his or her own way. We are all called to holiness by virtue of our baptisms. We should remember, too, that Mohandas Gandhi, Dorothy Day, Martin Luther King Jr., and Cesar Chavez did not start out as peacemakers. Like us, they, too, had to "dabble" in peace for a time. They only emerged as true artisans of peace after years of apprenticeship. Discipleship was every bit as much a journey for them as it is for us.

That being said, only the truly clean of heart can emerge—in time— as peacemakers as the term is defined here. Reflecting on the martyrdom of Polycarp in 155, Christopher A. Hall notes that "everything that the martyrs do is characterized by an austere *single-mindedness* that is typical of the Gospels themselves."[14] Further, the embrace of martyrdom had little to do with the promise of a heavenly reward as such. There is no *quid pro quo* for the clean of heart, it seems. Referencing Origen's thoughts in this regard, Hall observes that the martyrs were in no sense trying to "buy their salvation." Instead, their "hearts are filled with a sense of wonder over the gift God has given them in Christ's salvation and view their martyrdom as a response of love, one similar to Christ's own willingness to embrace his cross in love and obedience to the Father."[15] Like the artisans of peace in our own day, the martyrs of the early church had

13. Francis, *Gaudete et Exsultate,* 28–29.

14. Hall, *Living Wisely,* 33. Emphasis added.

15. Hall, *Living Wisely,* 50.

journeyed a long way prior to their willing embrace of the world's judgment concerning them.

Still further, it will take more than just those whom we recognized as true artisans of peace to radiate God's *shalom* into a hurting world, a world that is riven by division and injustice. Mohandas Gandhi, Dorothy Day, Martin Luther King Jr., and Cesar Chavez mobilized others to the causes they served. Few of us may ever achieve standing as true peacemakers, but we are, nonetheless, presented with opportunities in our own lives to share God's peace with others, both with respect to causes of national and international importance and in the day-to-day encounters we share with others.

Finally, we should not underestimate the potential impacts of the few artisans of peace who are among us. Again, they "radiate" God's peace in a broken world. In a very real sense, they are God's gifts to all of us. An anecdote attributed to Joseph Stalin illustrates this point. When Winston Churchill suggested to Stalin that their ongoing discussions concerning the shape of the postwar world should be broadened to include Pope Pius XII, Stalin responded: "The Pope? How many divisions has he?" Some forty years later, the Soviet Union would collapse due—in no small part—to the prophetic voice and moral courage of a Polish prelate, Karol Wojtyla. Like Mohandas Gandhi, Dorothy Day, Martin Luther King Jr., and Cesar Chavez, John Paul II changed lives in ways that he could not have anticipated when he began his journey. We, too, are challenged to attend to the voices of the prophets among us, both those who are celebrated across the globe and those who are revealed to us in the more narrow confines of our individual journeys.

It should be clear at this point that true peacemaking is about more than whole populations impersonally conceived, ideologies of one sort or another, or iterative stages of high-level negotiations. The missing ingredient is virtue oriented to Christian values and intellectual commitments. Individuals who are steeped in virtue and fully alert to something more than the instrumental ends espoused by the organizations in which they labor can make all the difference. We would do well, therefore, to pick up a thematic thread featured in chapter 8, an argument, in fact, in which right relationships and mercy understood as charity, inner transformation, and forgiveness were identified as essential Christian values and intellectual commitments. These twin packages of values and intellectual commitments are largely oriented to us and to our interpersonal relationships. Something more is required in the case of true peacemaking.

Catholic social teaching can be helpful in this regard. The contemporary expression of this tradition was launched in 1891 in an encyclical written by Pope Leo XIII. *Rerum Novarum* (*Of New Things*) was written to address a number of social problems caused by the industrial revolution and the political changes that had swept across Europe in the latter half of the nineteenth century. It focused on the demeaning working and living conditions of the rapidly expanding working class during a volatile moment in time in which communism, socialism, and anarchy were attracting adherents across Europe. Promulgated some forty years before the social and labor reforms of the New Deal in the United States, *Rerum Novarum* affirmed the inherent, God-given dignity of workers and their families and championed the right of workers to organize.

It is difficult to overestimate what a sea change this document represented. *Rerum Novarum* would be followed by a series of social justice encyclicals over the course of the next century. Each of them built on the ones that preceded it and codified—over time—a coherent, comprehensive, biblically-based, and fully Christian understanding of social justice. And at the Second Vatican Council, the overall trajectory of these several letters was explicitly embraced. In lengthy sessions convened in 1962, 1963, 1964, and 1965, the council fathers abandoned the Church's centuries-long opposition to modernity and democracy. To use Pope John XXIII's celebrated terms for this remarkable turnabout, the Church "opened its windows to the world," i.e., *aggiornamento*, and it did so by "returning to the sources," i.e., *ressourcement*, most notably the patrimony of the Jewish and Christian scriptures and the work of the early church fathers. Catholic bishops and scholars were invited to reclaim the powerful prophetic voice of the Jewish scriptures and the prophetic voice of Jesus as well.

In the fifty-five years since the close of the Second Vatican Council, the various themes embodied in Catholic social teaching have been gathered under seven headings: the life and dignity of the human person; the call to family, community, and participation; rights and responsibilities; the preferential option for the poor; solidarity; the dignity and rights of workers; and care for God's creation.[16]

The hermeneutic key to these several principles—all of which can be understood as non-negotiable values or intellectual commitments—is human dignity. In fact, this first principle is more than just one among

---

16. Pontifical Council for Justice and Peace, *Compendium*.

several such themes. It is foundational to all that follows in Catholic social teaching.

The concept of human dignity has little to do with the capabilities or
capacities with which any particular person is endowed. In the church's
conception of human dignity, even the unborn, the mentally ill, those
about to be executed for heinous crimes, and the terminally ill hold an
inherent dignity that cannot be forfeited. Drawing on the personalist philosophy that animated his vocation, Pope John Paul II thus distinguished
between a "culture of life" and a "culture of death," a culture he perceived
to be endemic in postmodernity.

> The theory of human rights is based precisely on the affirmation
> that the human person, unlike animals and things, cannot be
> subjected to domination by others. We must also mention the
> mentality which tends to equate personal dignity with the ca-
> pacity for verbal and explicit, or at least perceptible, communi-
> cation. It is clear that on the basis of these presuppositions there
> is no place in the world for anyone who, like the unborn or the
> dying, is a weak element in the social structure, or for anyone
> who appears completely at the mercy of others and radically de-
> pendent on them, and can only communicate through the silent
> language of a profound sharing of affection . . . In seeking the
> deepest roots of the struggle between the "culture of life" and the
> "culture of death," we cannot restrict ourselves to the perverse
> idea of freedom mentioned above. We have to go to the heart of
> the tragedy being experienced by modern man: the eclipse of the
> sense of God and of man, typical of a social and cultural climate
> dominated by secularism, which, with its ubiquitous tentacles,
> succeeds at times in putting Christian communities themselves
> to the test. Those who allow themselves to be influenced by this
> climate easily fall into a sad vicious circle: when the sense of
> God is lost, there is also a tendency to lose the sense of man, of
> his dignity and his life; in turn, the systematic violation of the
> moral law, especially in the serious matter of respect for human
> life and its dignity, produces a kind of progressive darkening of
> the capacity to discern God's living and saving presence.[17]

Recall one of the chief criticisms leveled in chapter 5 against certain
rules-based systems of justice, a concern that they are not sufficiently
robust and that their claims on behalf of justice are minimal in nature.
The Christian assertion of the inherent and inviolable nature of each and

---

17. John Paul II, *Evangelium Vitae.*

every person's dignity—regardless of their circumstances—is very robust, indeed, too much so, in fact, for some critics.

The second of these seven principles pertains to family, community, and participation. Christianity is—at its heart—a community-based religion. Its understanding of God as a community of persons and the biblical idea of covenant undergird this key principle. Further, the idea of subsidiarity is embedded in this understanding of family, community, and participation. This discriminating principle holds that nothing should be done at a "higher" level of society that can be more effectively or more appropriately accomplished at a "lower" level. Indeed, the rise of fascism and communism in the twentieth century prompted the Church to think deeply about the limits of its communitarian commitments. The Church thus denounced the extreme centralization of authority implicit in both fascism and communism.

The third principle associated with Catholic social teaching focuses on rights and responsibilities. It, too, is grounded on the idea of covenant. It recalls, as well, the prophets's advocacy on behalf of those who lived on the margins of life in ancient Israel, e.g., widows, orphans, and strangers. The importance of this third principle is best illustrated using two concepts imported into Christianity by way of Judaism: *tzedakah*, the obligation to be charitable; and *tikkun olam*, the obligation to participate in the "healing of the world." As disciples of Jesus, we, too, are obligated to be charitable, and we, too, are obligated to participate in the healing of the world.

Indeed, the expansive nature of the Church's understanding of human rights was revealed in Pope John XXIII's 1963 encyclical *Pacem in Terris*.

> We must first speak of man's rights. Man has the right to live. He has the right to bodily integrity and to the means necessary for the proper development of life, particularly food, clothing, shelter, medical care, rest, and, finally, the necessary social services . . . Moreover, man has a natural right to be respected . . . He has a right to . . . freedom of speech and publication, and freedom to pursue whatever profession he may choose . . . He has the natural right to share in the benefits of culture, and hence to receive a good general education . . . Also among man's rights is that of being able to worship God in accordance with the right dictates of his own conscience, and to profess his religion both in private and in public . . . In the economic sphere, it is evident that a man has the inherent right not only to be given

the opportunity to work, but also to be allowed the exercise of personal initiative in the work he does. A further consequence of man's personal dignity is his right to engage in economic activities suited to his degree of responsibility. The worker is likewise entitled to a wage that is determined in accordance with the precepts of justice. This needs stressing. The amount a worker receives must be sufficient, in proportion to available funds, to allow him and his family a standard of living consistent with human dignity . . . Finally, it is opportune to point out that the right to own private property entails a social obligation as well. Men are by nature social, and consequently they have the right to meet together and to form associations with their fellows. Again, every human being has the right to freedom of movement and of residence within the confines of his own state. When there are just reasons in favor of it, he must be permitted to emigrate to other countries and take up residence there. The fact that he is a citizen of a particular state does not deprive him of membership in the human family, nor of citizenship in that universal society, the common, world-wide fellowship of men . . . As a human person he is entitled to the legal protection of his rights, and such protection must be effective, unbiased, and strictly just."[18]

The contrast to the minimalist and entirely procedural rights enumerated in the Bill of Rights of the Constitution of the United States and in Rawl's theory of justice, for instance, could not be more stark.

The fourth theme of Catholic social teaching, i.e., the preferential option for the poor, employs a turn of phrase that comes from a letter written in 1968 by Pedro Arrupe, the Superior General of Jesuits in South America. It was subsequently picked up by Gustavo Gutierrez, a Dominican priest and theologian, who argued that a "preferential option for the poor" is rooted in both the prophets of the Jewish scriptures and in the New Testament, most notably, in chapter 25 of Matthew's Gospel.

Then the king will say to those on his right, "Come, you who are blessed by my Father. Inherit the kingdom prepared for you from the foundation of the world. For I was hungry and you gave me food, I was thirsty and you gave me drink, a stranger and you welcomed me, naked and you clothed me, ill and you cared for me, in prison and you visited me." Then the righteous will answer him and say, "Lord, when did we see you hungry and feed you, or thirsty and give you drink? When did we see you a

18. John XXIII, *Pacem in Terris*.

stranger and welcome you, or naked and clothe you? When did we see you ill or in prison, and visit you?" And the king will say to them in reply, "Amen, I say to you, whatever you did for one of these least brothers of mine, you did for me." Then he will say to those on his left, "Depart from me, you accursed, into the eternal fire prepared for the devil and his angels. For I was hungry and you gave me no food, I was thirsty and you gave me no drink, a stranger and you gave me no welcome, naked and you gave me no clothing, ill and in prison, and you did not care for me." Then they will answer and say, "Lord, when did we see you hungry or thirsty or a stranger or naked or ill or in prison, and not minister to your needs?" He will answer them, "Amen, I say to you, what you did not do for one of these least ones, you did not do for me." And these will go off to eternal punishment, but the righteous to eternal life (Matt 25:34–46).

The fifth principle associated with Catholic social teaching is solidarity. It builds on the Church's intellectual commitment to human dignity, a commitment that requires action on our part. Given our shared identity as beloved children of the Father, we are obligated to stand with our brothers and sisters in Christ. According to Pope Francis, "the many situations of inequality, poverty, and injustice are signs not only of a profound lack of fraternity, but also of the absence of a culture of solidarity. New ideologies, characterized by rampant individualism, egocentrism, and materialistic consumerism, weaken social bonds, fueling that 'throw away' mentality which leads to contempt for, and the abandonment of, the weakest and those considered 'useless.'"[19] In his 1967 encyclical *Populorum Progressio,* Pope Paul VI drew a similar contrast between our need to live in community and the rampant materialism that economic development seems to generate.

> Each man is also a member of society; hence he belongs to the community of man. It is not just certain individuals but all men who are called to further the development of human society as a whole . . . We are the heirs of earlier generations, and we reap benefits from the efforts of our contemporaries; we are under obligation to all men. Therefore, we cannot disregard the welfare of those who will come after us to increase the human family. The reality of human solidarity brings us not only benefits but also obligations. Man's personal and collective fulfillment could be jeopardized if the proper scale of values were not maintained.

19. Francis, *Fraternity, the Foundation and Pathway.*

The pursuit of life's necessities is quite legitimate . . . But the acquisition of worldly goods can lead men to greed, to the unrelenting desire for more, to the pursuit of greater personal power. Rich and poor alike—be they individuals, families, or nations—can fall prey to avarice and soul-stifling materialism. Neither individuals nor nations should regard the possession of more and more goods as the ultimate objective. Every kind of progress is a two-edged sword. It is necessary if man is to grow as a human being; yet it can also enslave him if he comes to regard it as the supreme good and cannot look beyond it. When this happens, men harden their hearts, shut out others from their minds, and gather together solely for reasons of self-interest rather than out of friendship; dissension and disunity follow soon after. Thus the exclusive pursuit of material possessions prevents man's growth as a human being and stands in opposition to his true grandeur. Avarice, in individuals and in nations, is the most obvious form of stultified moral development.[20]

This fifth principle can be a formidable challenge for individuals and organizations and in the public square, too. This is particularly so given three of its subsidiary principles: integral development, the universal destination of all goods, and the priority of the common good, the last two of which stand in direct opposition to the materialistic mindset now so prevalent in our society and to the libertarian values that undergird so much of our political discourse. According to the *Compendium of the Social Doctrine of the Church*:

The universal destination of goods requires a common effort to obtain for every person and for all peoples the conditions necessary for integral development, so that everyone can contribute to making a more human world in which each individual can give and receive, and in which the progress of some will no longer be an obstacle to the development of others . . . Christian tradition has never recognized the right of private property as absolute and untouchable . . . Private property, in fact, regardless of the concrete forms of the regulations and juridical norms relative to it, is in its essence only an instrument for respecting the principle of the universal destination of goods; in the final analysis, therefore, it is not an end but a means.[21]

---

20. Paul VI, *Populorum Progressio*.

21. Pontifical Council for Justice and Peace, *Compendium*, 76–77.

Note that the Church's understanding of integral development bears a strong resemblance to the articulated moral framework introduced in chapter 5: the good understood as the existential experience of meaning, the moral understood as dignity, and the just understood as opportunity. Note, as well, that the Church's affirmation of social solidarity takes on a sharp edge for organizations and for whole societies when it is read in concert with the preceding principle: the preferential option for the poor.

The sixth principle of Catholic social teaching, i.e., the dignity and rights of workers, can be thought of as a special case of the fifth, i.e., solidarity, but it is particularly salient for managers and nominal leaders who hold some degree of responsibility—at least according to Robert Greenleaf—for the unique journeys of those who report to them. This includes, presumably, any formal and informal associations they may enter into with colleagues and co-workers. This clearly goes beyond the language games associated with human resources management and employment law, which tend to be formal and transactional in nature.

The final principle of Catholic social teaching, i.e., care for God's creation, is also rooted in Scripture, most notably in the idea of sabbath as a day of rest. Echoing the Book of Genesis, this principle holds, too, that all of creation is "good" and hence of intrinsic value. The earth was designed for ends that are more than instrumental *vis-à-vis* the short-term needs of humankind. Further, the obligation to care for God's creation points to the intergenerational nature of our obligations to each other. Stewardship and sustainability are thus privileged over exploitation and a quick return on investment.

We are now in a position to complete the model first introduced in chapter 4 and then modified in chapter 8. See figure 13.

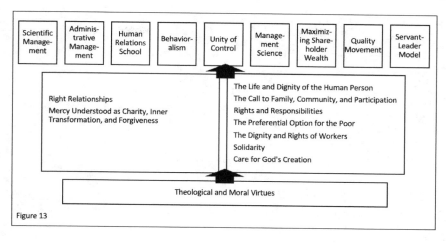

Figure 13

In our final revision, the seven principles of Catholic social teaching complete the taxonomy of values and intellectual commitments. Together, they provide a clear focus for the full exercise of the several Christian theological and moral virtues examined throughout this portion of the text. Together, these Christian values and intellectual commitments can both inform and check managerial decision-making and managerial behavior: a commitment to the engendering of right relationships; mercy understood as charity, inner transformation, and forgiveness; the life and dignity of the human person; the call to family, community, and participation; rights and responsibilities; the preferential option for the poor; solidarity; the dignity and rights of workers; and care for God's creation.

It could be argued that these values and intellectual commitments can no longer be universalized or that their reach is severely circumscribed in what is now a thoroughly secularized world. Although these objections may ring true for some, we must remember that the principles of Catholic social teaching are normative for Christians. They are nonnegotiable for aspiring disciples of Jesus. How and when a particular principle can or should inform decision-making in an organization or in the public square will depend on one or more of three cardinal virtues: justice, i.e., a proper understanding of the way in which life's benefits and burdens should be shared; prudence expressed in *phronesis* or practiced living; and fortitude or courage. That being said, the several principles themselves are not in any sense optional for Christians.

Additionally, we should not discount the extent to which common ground can sometimes be found between those who are guided by the principles of Catholic social teaching and those whose understandings of justice are guided by secular values. Recall, for instance, the five domains of interest articulated in David Held's theory of cosmopolitan governance: the body, social welfare, culture or cultural life, civic associations, the economy, and the organization of violence and coercive relations. There is considerable overlap, in fact, between Held's understanding of justice—which may, like Kant's ethical imperative, harbor a lingering but undisclosed link to our shared Christian patrimony in this regard—and Pope John XXIII's articulation of human rights in *Pacem in Terris*. Peacemaking in our broken world will take a village, and only some of our fellow villagers are likely to be Christian.

As we near the end of this extended reflection on Matthew's version of the Beatitudes, we would do well to remember that Jesus himself is the true exemplar for disciples on the journey, and so our final biblical reflection: the story of his remarkable encounter with the woman who was about to be stoned. As detailed in John's Gospel, Jesus is being baited by a mob that has been cleverly manipulated, it seems, into callously and shamefully using a helpless woman to score a debating point. Instead of entering into the drama and—from the woman's perspective, certainly— the trauma of the moment, Jesus defuses the mob's anger by holding up a rhetorical mirror so that they can see themselves for what they have become: a mob. "Let the one among you who is without sin be the first to throw a stone at her." The anachronistic image of a lightning rod comes to mind, of course. Jesus absorbs the mob's fury and channels it into the ground where it can do no harm. And when the violence of the moment dissipates, Jesus tells the woman: "Go, [and] from now on do not sin anymore." In doing so, Jesus holds up a rhetorical mirror to her as well. She, too, is invited to accept God's mercy and to experience a conversion of heart. Jesus thus moves everyone in this evocative story at least a bit closer to right relationship with God, with themselves, and with others.

This is what peacemakers do, in fact. They help move others ever closer to right relationships with God, with themselves, and with others. They do so in what they say, in what they do, and in their moments of silence, too; and they do so masterfully.

We know the end of the story, of course. Jesus' enemies conspire against him, and he is arrested, tortured, and killed in a most humiliating and cruel fashion. Peacemakers are thus revealed as children of God who may, nonetheless, be subjected to considerable suffering because of their selfless service.

Some may object that this story centers on Jesus, the incarnate second person of the Trinity. "Sure, Jesus handles this encounter well! How could the second person of the Trinity *not* handle it well?" *Babette's Feast*, a remarkable Danish film released in 1987, illustrates how this understanding of peacemaking can be practiced in a very different setting, however; and it demonstrates, too, the connection between peacemaking and the broader journey of discipleship.

The story takes place in the latter half of the nineteenth century in Jutland, a remote region in northern Denmark. The setting is a small village, where the residents lead very simple lives under the direction of a Lutheran pastor. They are pietists who believe that their entire lives should be oriented to God. The pastor has two daughters whom he describes as his "left and right hands." The pastor dies, and the sisters struggle over the course of several decades to minister to their father's flock.

This has proven a difficult task. Over time, divisions have taken root in the small community. Indeed, several disheartening backstories emerge: two women in the congregation have become bitter enemies; two men have cheated each other in business dealings; and an elderly man and woman are beset by guilt over an affair consummated when they were young. The community is old, and its spiritual vitality is drying up. The congregation is in the grip of a slow process of disintegration.

The storyline then moves to 1871. A stranger, Babette, arrives at the daughters's home. She is from Paris, a far-away place viewed by most of the congregants as exotic, foreign, and—worst of all—Catholic. Violence surrounding The Franco-Prussian War and the fall of Napoleon III has claimed Babette's husband and her son, and she is fleeing for her life. Babette agrees to serve the two sisters with no pay. She is provided with room and board in return for her menial labor.

Over time, Babette adopts the simple lifestyle of the community. She cooks for the sisters and for the aged and the infirm in the congregation who have been confined to their homes. Their daily fare is remarkably simple: dried fish, a kind of porridge made out of stale bread, and tea. Babette is never fully embraced as a member of the community, however. She does not talk about her past. And, as much as she is appreciated, she is still a bit suspect because she is French and Catholic.

Fourteen years later, the tiny congregation prepares to celebrate the one hundredth anniversary of their dear pastor's birth. In typical fashion, they plan to do so with prayer, tea, and some simple foods. An unanticipated telegram then arrives. In her prior life, Babette had purchased a lifetime subscription to the French lottery. Unexpectedly, she has won ten thousand francs, an enormous sum. Everyone in the community assumes that Babette will soon leave for Paris to resume her former life. Surprisingly, however, she asks the two sisters to permit her to prepare an authentic Parisian meal in celebration of the centennial of their father's birth. The two sisters reluctantly agree.

As Babette's planning proceeds, the sisters become increasingly anxious. She has imported exotic foods and alcohol from Paris, all of which is viewed as decadent and sinful. It is even described as a "witch's feast." One of the sisters experiences nightmares involving the devil and the fires of hell. The sisters assemble the small community to share their fears. Everyone agrees that they have to go through with the dinner because of their deep appreciation for all that Babette has done for them, but they promise each other that they will not talk about the food or their experience of dining together. They will participate, but they will not let the sheer excess of the occasion draw them in.

The storyline then turns to the dinner itself. It is a transformative experience, in fact, an experience in which the community members are reminded of all they have long valued in each other. Broken relationships are mended, and the community is given new life. The elaborate dinner is thus revealed as a kind of eucharist.

At the very end of the story, Babette is revealed as having been feted in her former life as the most renowned chef in Paris, a true culinary artist. We learn, too, that she has spent the entire ten thousand francs on this one dinner. Further, Babette has no intention of leaving the community in which she had lived for fourteen years. Indeed, Babette is revealed as a Christ-like peacemaker who has restored a broken and dying community to life.

Babette is a peacemaker because she elected—over the course of many years—not to enter into the drama and the trauma that had beset the congregation she served. She entered into the life of the community, but always maintained a certain distance. She honored the values of the tiny community she served, but her core values and intellectual commitments were always anchored elsewhere.

Babette can also be understood as a servant-leader. Again, "the servant-leader is servant first . . . It begins with a natural feeling that one wants to serve, to serve *first*. Then conscious choice brings one to aspire to lead. The person is sharply different from one who is *leader* first, perhaps because of the need to assuage an unusual power drive or to acquire material possessions."[22] In her menial labor, Babette brought healing to the members of the tiny community she served; and, when an opportunity presented itself, she spent all that she had acquired, i.e., her time, her talent, and her treasure, on a single event that engendered the full restoration of right relationships among those whom she served.

Still further, Babette is revealed as a true artist. As affirmed in the preceding chapter, those who are clean of heart exhibit a certain grace, a certain way of being in the world that we associate with the moral virtues of prudence and temperance. This did not just happen in Babette's case, however. Over the course of fourteen years, Babette mourned the loss of her prior, ostensibly rich life. She was poor in spirit. Babette opened herself to God's hopes and dreams for her, hopes and dreams that she could not have anticipated when she was celebrated as a renowned chef in Paris. She was meek. Babette's eyes had been opened to the hunger and thirst for reconciliation in the small, insulated community that had provided a home for her, a community in which she had extended God's mercy and healing to all whom she served. Finally, Babette was clean of heart. There was an integrity in Babette that was truly remarkable, and she radiated this integrity to all whom she encountered. She was a true artisan of peace.

There is still another way to understand Babette, however. Peacemakers are promised that they "will be called children of God." This suggests that we may need to rethink certain references in the Gospels to children. Consider the interpretation typically associated with a particular story featured in all three of the synoptic Gospels. "Children were brought to him that he might lay his hands on them and pray. The disciples rebuked them, but Jesus said, 'Let the children come to me, and do not prevent them; for the kingdom of heaven belongs to such as these.' After he placed his hands on them, he went away" (Matt 19:13–14).

We often think of this story as an endorsement of an uncritical or naive form of faith; but there is another way to understand it. Unless they have suffered extreme abuse, children know they are loved. They demand unconditional love, in fact, and express themselves in no uncertain terms when it is not showered upon them. Like children, the clean of heart and peacemakers know they are loved. Those who have journeyed through the first six Beatitudes know that their struggles are no match for God's love for them. They bask in an abiding love that they

22. Greenleaf, *Servant Leadership*, 27.

are compelled to share with others. Drawing on Thomas Aquinas's reflections in this regard, Anton Ten Klooster notes: "Those who go the way of the 'peacemakers' merit the happiness of being called 'children of God.' This discourse on meritorious action is placed within the context of the life of grace."[23] Babette, it seems, knows that she is loved by God, and she is compelled to share this love with all whom she encounters. Babette is not just an artisan of peace; she is a child of God as well.

The ending of *Babette's Feast* is thus noteworthy. As her guests leave the banquet so lavishly hosted on their behalf, they stop to gather around the town well. They grasp each other's hands and then circle slowly around the well singing a simple song that they had evidently sung as children. They have been reminded by Babette that they, too, are children of God.

Could the presence of a true peacemaker—as the term is understood here—have made a difference in the tragedies recounted in chapter 4: the Tuskegee syphilis study, the Ford Pinto scandal, the Nestlé infant formula controversy, the space shuttle *Challenger* disaster, and the clergy sexual abuse scandal that has so plagued the Catholic Church over the course of the last thirty years? To answer this question, recall, first, the distinction drawn between management on the one hand, narrowly defined in this text as the responsibility for and performance of any one or more of several organizational or societal functions in a manner oriented to ends external to the manager, and leadership on the other, understood here as the balanced exercise of these same responsibilities in service to a broader array of stakeholders in a manner constrained by the leader's internalized virtues and informed by values and intellectual commitments drawn from a larger belief system, but oriented, nonetheless, to ends sanctioned by the organization or by society. And recall, second, the normative nature of the several Christian values and intellectual commitments detailed in chapter 8 and in this chapter, too. We can expect that true peacemakers who have been fully habituated to the theological and moral virtues and who are fully cognizant of and fully committed to the robust set of Christian values and moral commitments detailed above would have been well positioned to resist the myopic tunnel vision and stress that contributed so much to each of these tragic events, the same kind of myopic tunnel vision and stress, in fact, that contributes to so

---

23. Ten Klooster, *Thomas Aquinas*, 74.

much dysfunction in so many of our contemporary organizations each and every day.

We could expect, too, that leaders in the public square, leaders who have been fully formed as genuine artisans of peace, would be well positioned to contribute in positive ways to our public discourse. The contentious fare now imposed upon us is governed for the most part, it seems, by an insatiable hunger for political advantage and the exigencies of public polling. This has not served us well. Virtue should matter more and so, too, the values and intellectual commitments to which the virtues of our political leaders—to the extent they exist—should be oriented.

The exercise of this kind of leadership—in contemporary organizations of all kinds and in the public square, too—can be thought of as a kind of ongoing and reflexive theological reflection. Some trace this concept to the Second Vatican Council and to Pope John XXIII's sense that the Church of his day needed to better "read the signs of the times," a critique, in fact, that found expression in the see-judge-act method subsequently attributed to Bernard Lonergan and Cardinal Joseph Cardijn.[24] "Seeing," in this context, pertains to the full comprehension of the lived reality of an individual or a community; "judging" requires a broader analysis of the situation at hand and the development of options in this regard; and "acting" denotes the execution of concrete steps designed to address the matter.

James D. and Evelyn Eaton Whitehead recommend a particular approach to theological reflection, a strategy that may be of use here.[25] Modified just slightly, this strategy engages three distinct "conversation partners": first, any particular concern, imperative, or objective that may be of consequence to the organization or to society; second, the Christian tradition, for our purposes, the rich mix of Christian values and intellectual commitments detailed above; and third, any relevant context and history pertaining to the imminent concern and any impacts, constraints, or opportunities that could come into play for a wide variety of stakeholders. See figure 14.

24. Sands, "Cardinal Cardijn's See-Judge-Act."
25. Whitehead and Whitehead, *Method in Ministry*, 5.

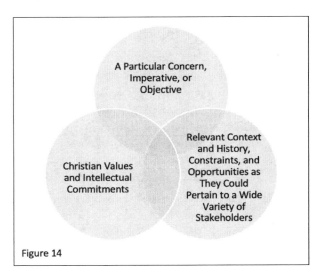

A Particular Concern, Imperative, or Objective

Christian Values and Intellectual Commitments

Relevant Context and History, Constraints, and Opportunities as They Could Pertain to a Wide Variety of Stakeholders

Figure 14

At its best, this kind of theological reflection can generate new insights and possibilities for action through what Patricia O'Connell Killen and John DeBeer call a process of "correlation."[26] This approach to theological reflection may be of particular use to Christians who aspire to leadership for three reasons: first, it inserts an explicit consideration of Christian values and intellectual commitments into the decision-making process; second, it expressly considers implications a decision could hold for individuals and for communities of individuals, thus inserting moral thinking based on a personalist perspective into the conversation; and, third, it takes the interests of a broad range of stakeholders into consideration.

As attractive as this version of theological reflection may be, it cannot be viewed as a technique *per se*. It is more descriptive than normative in nature. This is simply how artisans of peace think, in fact; this is their way of being in the world. This kind of thinking is second nature for those who have journeyed through the Beatitudes as accomplished disciples of Jesus. Knowing when and how to employ this kind of thinking depends on the extent to which a leader has embraced the theological and moral virtues; it requires deeply ingrained habits of heart and mind. And discerning what should be done in any particular situation—in terms of the organization's instrumental objectives on the one hand and a full consideration of what the good, the moral, and the just might require on the other—requires wisdom, another gift of the Holy Spirit in which

26. Killen and DeBeer, *The Art of Theological Reflection*, 127–28.

disciples of Jesus who hold responsibilities in the secular world can be formed over time.

REFLECTION QUESTIONS: "BLESSED ARE THE PEACEMAKERS" AND "BLESSED ARE THEY WHO ARE PERSECUTED FOR THE SAKE OF RIGHTEOUSNESS"

- Do I recognize certain exemplars as true peacemakers? Who and in what way have I come to recognize them as such?

- Do I recognize the voice of prophets in my work relationships, in my family, and in other relationships I share? In what ways do these voices appeal to me? In what ways are they inconvenient? What uncomfortable truths do the prophets in my life speak?

- Am I frequently drawn into the drama and trauma of everyday life in the organizations with which I am associated, in my family, or in the exercise of other duties and responsibilities? Do I tend to add to or to dampen this experience of drama and trauma?

- Have I been presented with opportunities to serve as a peacemaker or a prophet? How did I respond? Did I spurn these roles in favor of other roles on the job, in my family, and in other relationships I share?

- Which, if any, of the seven principles of Catholic social teaching have I fully incorporated into my life? How so? With which of these principles do I struggle? Why?

- Am I prepared to accept the slings and arrows that can accompany both the role of the peacemaker and the role of the prophet?

- How can I better form myself in the virtues of fortitude, and justice, and prudence, all of which are required for a sustained life of peacemaking?

Chapter 11

An Exemplar

Blessed is the man who does not walk
in the counsel of the wicked,
Nor stand in the way of sinners,
nor sit in company with scoffers.
Rather, the law of the LORD is his joy;
and on his law he meditates day and night.
He is like a tree
planted near streams of water,
that yields its fruit in season;
Its leaves never wither;
whatever he does prospers.
But not so are the wicked, not so!
They are like chaff driven by the wind.
Therefore, the wicked will not arise at the judgment,
nor will sinners in the assembly of the just.
Because the LORD knows the way of the just,
but the way of the wicked leads to ruin (Ps 1).

THE ROLE VIRTUE ORIENTED to Christian values and intellectual commitments can play in our lives is alluded to in the very first psalm. This gateway to the psalter is especially fitting if we think of virtue oriented to the Christian *kerygma* as a kind of law—the law of love, in fact—written not on the mind but on the human heart. The key contrast is between a person artfully re-imagined as a tree whose roots are planted near running water on the one hand and an unthinking tumbleweed blown this way and that by the exigencies of the moment on the other. With respect to our purposes, a manager or nominal leader who lacks virtue is all too likely to succumb to temptation, to instrumental myopia, to tunnel vision, or to stress at the very moment when authentic leadership is most needed, authentic leadership that enjoys ready access to the flowing waters of virtue.

Is this image achievable in real life? Or is it just an ideal, an appealing but unattainable aspiration? Exemplars can be helpful in addressing these kinds of questions. In this context, an exemplar can be thought of as someone with whom we can identify who has successfully integrated virtue into her life. In a religious context, we often think of saints as exemplars. After all, saints are men and women who demonstrably lived as God wanted them to live. They show us the way.

Many of the greatest saints in the Catholic and Orthodox traditions can seem impossibly remote, however. Most of them are far removed from our time and place. As a result, we sometimes struggle to identify with the great saints of our religious traditions. Further, their memories are often occluded by devout hagiography. Their failings and their doubts are smoothed over in the accounts available to us. And many of them lived and labored in ecclesial settings. At first glance, at least, the monastery, the cloister, and the cathedral seats of bishops seem to have little to do with the contemporary boardroom, the management suite, or the shop floor.

For these several reasons, Dag Hammarskjöld is introduced here as an exemplar who may be more accessible to today's managers and nominal leaders. As we shall see, Hammarskjöld's personal and professional journeys intersected to a considerable extent. He was a man of virtue, and he was a leader in the sense detailed in this text: an individual who understood his professional role as the balanced exercise of a full complement of managerial responsibilities oriented, nonetheless, to a broad set of stakeholders in a manner constrained by his internalized virtues and informed by values and intellectual commitments drawn from a larger belief system—in this instance, a deeply integrated set of Christian values and intellectual commitments—but oriented, nonetheless, to ends sanctioned by the organization he served.

We will first examine Hammarskjöld's familial and professional lives, his philosophical orientation, and the surprising nature of his spiritual journey. This will be followed, in turn, by a brief reflection on

Matthew's eight Beatitudes and how each of them is reflected in Hammarskjöld's life.

On April 1, 1953, Dag Hammarskjöld was announced as Trygve Lie's successor as Secretary General of the United Nations. This came as something of a shock to much of the world, so much so, in fact, that his selection was widely interpreted as a political compromise. The Western powers and the Soviet Union had failed to agree on a candidate until Hammarskjöld's name was proposed. Indeed, many expected him to serve as little more than a short-term caretaker. According to Brian Urquhard, one of Hammarskjöld's closest associates at the United Nations: "They thought they'd got a safe bureaucratic civil servant, and they got Hammarskjöld instead. It will never happen again; nobody's ever going to make that mistake twice."[1]

This is not to say that Hammarskjöld was unqualified. Prior to his selection, he had served as Vice-Minister of Sweden's Foreign Service, the highest office then open to a member of Sweden's bureaucracy. Hammarskjöld had previously served with distinction in a number of progressively responsible positions, including a key role in the administration of the Marshall Plan following the defeat of Nazi Germany. Nevertheless, he was largely unknown to the world's leaders prior to his appointment to the United Nations's highest administrative office.

Hammarskjöld was born on July 29, 1905, as the youngest of four sons. He came from a distinguished family that had long enjoyed close ties to both the national government and the Lutheran Church in Sweden. Hammarskjöld was devoted to his mother, Agnes, but experienced a somewhat distant relationship with his father, Hjalmar, a formal man who had served briefly as Sweden's prime minister in 1914. In a 1954 contribution to *This I Believe*, a radio program hosted by Edward R. Murrow, Hammarskjöld shared this remembrance: "From generations of soldiers and government officials on my father's side I inherited a belief that no life was more satisfactory than one of selfless service to your country—or to humanity. This service required a sacrifice of all personal interests, but likewise the courage to stand up unflinchingly for your convictions. From scholars and clergymen on my mother's side, I inherited a belief that in the radical sense of the Gospels, all men were equals as children of God, and should be met and treated by us as our masters in God."[2]

---

1. Lipsey, *Hammarskjöld*, 117.
2. Lipsey, *Hammarskjöld*, 178.

Hammarskjöld was a bright and hardworking student who would go on to pursue a degree in economics. He was considered an exceptional athlete and would remain an avid outdoorsman and skier over the course of his life. Hammarskjöld never married and lived at home until he was forty. According to his biographers, he seems to have shied away from intimate relationships. Still, he enjoyed an extensive and varied network of friends in Sweden and later in New York. Hammarskjöld's intellectual interests were both wide and deep and included the arts, literature, theatre, and theology. He was widely viewed as a highly cultured and brilliant man.

According to Hammarskjöld biographer Henry P. Van Dusen, "the 'profile' which emerged from inquiries [upon the surprise announcement of his selection as Secretary General] showed a Swedish civil service aristocrat, gifted administratively, unobtrusive rather than flamboyant, a brilliant technician, an executant rather than a political leader, and, some feared, a compromiser rather than a fighter,"[3] in short, a manager. What the world got instead was a bold leader. In no uncertain terms, Hammarskjöld asserted the United Nation's autonomy in the face of Senator Joseph McCarthy's efforts to intimidate the organization and its leaders.[4] In 1956, he initiated what was then widely dismissed as a futile outreach to Communist China.[5] Also in 1956, Hammarskjöld engineered an unprecedented intervention in the Suez Canal Crisis, an initiative that led to the creation of a United Nations Emergency Force. In 1958, he played a leading role in negotiations among the Arab states during crises in Lebanon and Palestine. United Nations "observers" were then used for the first time. In the late 1950s, Hammarskjöld proved a persuasive advocate on behalf of the recently de-colonialized nations in Africa and Asia. In 1960, he successfully resisted a Soviet effort to unseat him.[6] The Soviet Union's insistence on a "troika" leadership structure had been cynically advanced to undermine Hammarskjöld's authority and influence. And he launched a bold diplomatic effort in war-torn Congo in 1961, an intervention that would cost him his life when the aircraft in which he was flying was shot down by partisans on September 18, 1961.

3. Van Dusen, *Dag Hammarskjöld*, 11.
4. Van Dusen, *Dag Hammarskjöld*, 128.
5. Lipsey, *Hammarskjöld*, 210–36.
6. Lipsey, *Hammarskjöld*, 445–52.

Our chief interest here is not so much Hammarskjöld's professional accomplishments, however, as it is the extent to which his spiritual life informed his professional decision-making and behavior. We are fortunate, in fact, to have several windows into Hammarskjöld's inner life. In his *This I Believe* appearance, Hammarskjöld recalled a youthful encounter with Albert Schweitzer, who was then celebrated across the globe for his search for the "historical Jesus" and for his remarkable life of service. Hammarskjöld's personal journal *Vägmärken*, i.e., "Trail Marks," was posthumously published as *Markings* in 1963. It consists of some six hundred entries typed over the course of a forty-year period. We know, too, of his devotion to Thomas à Kempis's *Imitation of Christ*, a spiritual classic, which he kept at this bedside. Hammarskjöld even carried it with him on his last trip to Congo. We also know of his close relationship with Martin Buber toward the end of his life. According to Van Dusen, the renowned author of *I and Thou* served as Hammarskjöld's "principal tutor" in his last few years of life.[7] In fact, Hammarskjöld was working on a Swedish translation of Buber's classic text when he died.

When *Markings*'s existence was revealed shortly after Hammarskjöld's death, some undoubtedly expected an unflinching psychological profile. The raw material for an exposé of this kind was certainly there: a doting mother, an austere father, high expectations, a traditional religious upbringing, and a dearth of intimate relationships. This is not what Hammarskjöld's journal or any of the other windows into his inner life reveal, however. Hammarskjöld's biographers are agreed on this point. We find, instead, a journey of Christian discipleship, a journey that was largely hidden from the world during Hammarskjöld's lifetime. As one friend reported, "he was surrounded by companions who for the most part were spiritually and religiously unawakened, and to whom he had to speak in another language—a language foreign to his soul."[8] According to Van Dusen, this engendered "habits of reticence regarding things of the spirit."[9]

Two aspects of Hammarskjöld's spiritual journey are especially noteworthy for our purposes. First, he seems to have experienced a crisis of faith in the years leading up to his appointment as General Secretary. The depth of his despair during this time period is evident in a journal

---

7. Van Dusen, *Dag Hammarskjöld*, 204.

8. Van Dusen, *Dag Hammarskjöld*, 41.

9. Van Dusen, *Dag Hammarskjöld*, 41.

entry from 1952: "What I ask for is absurd: that life shall have a meaning. What I strive for is impossible: that my life shall acquire a meaning. I dare not believe, I do not see how I shall ever be able to believe: that I am not alone."[10]

It seems that Hammarskjöld then underwent a religious conversion of sorts. Some three months prior to his appointment as Secretary General, he experienced something akin to the "leap of faith" described by the nineteenth-century Danish philosopher Søren Kierkegaard,[11] a leap of faith Hammarskjöld interpreted in terms of risk. Hammarskjöld described this experience in 1961, just four months before his death: "I don't know who—or what—put the question, I don't know when it was put. I don't even remember answering. But at some moment I did answer Yes to Someone—or Something—and from that hour I was certain that existence is meaningful and that, therefore, my life in self-surrender had a goal. From that moment I have known what it means 'not to look back,' and 'to take no thought of the morrow.'"[12]

Second, this conversion experience was not to any particular liturgical tradition, to any established collection of dogma, or to a prescriptive morality of any kind. Hammarskjöld's leap of faith was triggered, it seems, by a personal apprehension of God in the guise of a very human Jesus who has risked everything for the love of the Father. According to Gustaf Aulén, Hammarskjöld's spiritual biographer, his "starting point [was] Jesus' risky choice of self-sacrifice—for the sake of others. Risk is crucial; if the choice had not been a risky one, Jesus would not have been a human being among other human beings and his 'commandment' could not have had the compelling force it now possessed."[13] Further, "(faith) in God [for Hammarskjöld] means primarily a very personal, existential relationship, not an assent to fixed doctrines. Statements about God—so far as they can be articulated—are statements about the God who makes himself known in the relationship of faith without thereby ceasing to be a mystery."[14]

This conversion experience seems to have begun in 1951 with an extended reflection on Jesus:

10. Hammarskjöld, *Markings*, 86.

11. Kierkegaard, "Concluding Scientific Postscript," 195–96.

12. Hammarskjöld, *Markings*, 205.

13. Aulén, *Dag Hammarskjöld's White Book*, 89.

14. Aulén, *Dag Hammarskjöld's White Book*, 30.

A young man, adamant in his committed life. The one who was nearest to him related how, on the last evening, he arose from supper, laid aside his garments, and washed the feet of his friends and disciples—an adamant young man, alone as he confronted his final destiny . . . He had assented to a possibility in his being, of which he had had his first inkling when he returned from the desert . . . If God required anything of him, he would not fail. Only recently, he thought, had he begun to see more clearly, and to realize that the road of possibility might lead to the cross . . . Well, then, the last evening. An adamant young man: "Know ye what I have done to you? . . . And now I have told you before it comes to pass . . . . One of you shall betray me . . . Wither I go, ye cannot come . . . Will'st thou lay down thy life for my sake? Verily I say unto thee: the cock shall not crow . . . My peace I give unto you . . . That the world may know that I love the Father, and as the Father gives me commandment, even so I do . . . Arise, let us go hence." Is the hero of this immortal, brutally simple drama in truth "the Lamb of God that taketh away the sins of the world"? Absolutely faithful to a divined possibility—in that sense the Son of God, in that sense the sacrificial Lamb, in that sense the Redeemer. A young man, adamant in his commitment, who walks the road of possibility to the end without self-pity or demand for sympathy, fulfilling the destiny he has chosen—even sacrificing affection and fellowship when the others are unready to follow him—into a new fellowship.[15]

We hear in this reflection an echo of Albert Schweitzer's search for the very human Jesus of history and Thomas à Kempis's counsel as well: "Rest your thoughts on Christ's Passion."[16] We sense, too, the longing for an I-Thou encounter that would, in time, draw Hammarskjöld to Martin Buber.

Two questions thus follow. First, can Hammarskjöld's journey be considered existential as the term was defined chapter 3? And second, can Hammarskjöld's journey be considered Christian? Each will be addressed in turn.

Recall from chapter 3 that existential philosophers and theologians collectively posit a universal "drive for meaning" and, further, that we associated this drive with the calling to servant leadership. In the view of existential philosophers and theologians, this "drive for meaning" is

15. Hammarskjöld, *Markings*, 68–69.

16. à Kempis, *Imitation of Christ*, 65.

prompted—more often than not—by one or more of the five realities that together define the human condition. One, the prospect of suffering and death and a nagging sense of life's absurdity prompt a degree of dread or *angst* in reflective human beings. Two, the creation or discovery of meaning is fundamental to who we are as persons. Three, meaning entails the whole person, not just a particular aspect or dimension of a life. Four, the existential understanding of meaning can only be achieved at the personal level; it cannot be imposed from without. And five, meaning is oriented to the future.

Each of these realities was part and parcel of Hammarskjöld's spiritual journey. Two, in particular, will be examined here. Most importantly, death and the "limit conditions" of suffering that so concern existential philosophers and theologians were never far from Hammarskjöld's mind. He personally witnessed two suicides and struggled to make sense of them in his journal. According to one of his biographers, "nearly a third of the 'markings' and half the pages in [the years 1945–49] comment upon 'death.'"[17] Further, he would meditate on a traditional Swedish hymn, *Snart Stundar Natten*, i.e., "Night Approaching Now," every New Year's Eve. As explained by Van Dusen, this melancholy hymn is "a meditation on the transience of life and its final verse declares an anticipation and grateful welcome of death: 'How vain the worldling's pomp and show. How brief his joys and pleasures! The night approaches now, and lo! We leave all earthly treasures.'"[18] At least once in 1952, Hammarskjöld is thought to have considered suicide.[19] And in 1957, he wrote: "In the last analysis, it is our conception of death which decides our answers to all the questions life puts to us."[20]

Indeed, Hammarskjöld anguished over life's apparent meaninglessness in the several years prior to his conversion experience in early 1953. The years 1950 through 1952 were particularly difficult, it seems. At the peak of his professional career in Sweden, Hammarskjöld was stricken by a profound sense of despair. According to Van Dusen: "those years witnessed the depths of his inner despondency verging on despair. It was then that he experienced the most acute phase of self-questioning and self-accusation, of solitariness and dejection, a long twilight and black

17. Van Dusen, *Dag Hammarskjöld*, 66.
18. Van Dusen, *Dag Hammarskjöld*, 71.
19. Van Dusen, *Dag Hammarskjöld*, 74.
20. Hammarskjöld, *Markings*, 160.

midnight, the 'Dark Night of the Soul,' which continued until a wholly unforeseen and unexpected burst of dawn shortly before sudden elevation to climactic responsibilities at the United Nations transported him to a new world and a new life."[21] According to Aulén, he was nearly consumed by an oppressive sense of meaninglessness during this troubled time.[22]

Existentialism's orientation to the future was also central to Hammarskjöld's reflections. According to Martin Heidegger, "the future must . . . win itself, not from a present, but from the inauthentic future."[23] He described this orientation to the future as "thrownness."[24] In Sartre's view, "I project myself toward the future in order to merge with that which I lack."[25] "I no longer *am* my past, but I am thematizing it."[26] According to Karl Jaspers, "truth lies in the future."[27] And like Heidegger and Tillich, Rudolf Bultmann defined authenticity in terms of an orientation to the future: "In inauthentic existence, man understands himself in the available world. In authentic existence, he understands himself in the unavailable future."[28]

Hammarskjöld was inexorably driven, it seems, into the future. As we shall see, this drive manifested itself in a hunger for recognition in the 1930s and 1940s. During his crisis years, Hammarskjöld hungered for a sense of meaning and purpose. And from 1953 onward, he hungered to serve. Following his conversion experience, Hammarskjöld was driven to serve.

That being said, Hammarskjöld remained an unrelenting self-critic until his untimely death, a scold, in fact, who could sometimes anguish over his perceived shortcomings. An entry in 1958 is telling in this regard: "The pure, simple self at the hour of waking—and the first thing it sees—its grotesque image in the distorting mirror of yesterday."[29]

The overall trajectory of Hammarskjöld's journal entries after 1952 reflects a heightened sense of responsibility for the future. In Van Dusen's

---

21. Van Dusen, *Dag Hammarskjöld*, 68.

22. Aulén, *Dag Hammarskjöld's White Book*, 21.

23. Heidegger, *Being and Time*, 310.

24. Heidegger, *Being and Time*, 135.

25. Sartre, *Being and Nothingness,* 85.

26. Sartre, *Being and Nothingness*, 221.

27. Jaspers, *Reason and Existenz*, 104.

28. Bultmann, "Hermeneutics and Theology," 251.

29. Hammarskjöld, *Markings*, 164.

estimation, Hammarskjöld's mature "faith shows forth three principal elements; the intimate presence of the living God, the example of Jesus, and the imperative of duty."[30] These several elements "thematized" the present and the future at the expense of the past. Hammarskjöld recognized, too, that the creation or discovery of meaning for ourselves and for others is fundamental to who we are as persons. In 1950, he concluded: "To become free and responsible. For this alone was man created, and he who fails to take the Way which could have been his shall be lost eternally."[31]

Although Hammarskjöld's journey can be considered existential—and hence universal—can it be considered religious? It is important to note, first, that Roman Catholics do not hold a monopoly on virtue and neither do Christians more generally. Again, the Catholic Church affirms that all are called to holiness. Still, Hammarskjöld did not attend religious services on a regular basis. He did not hold membership in any congregation or publicly associate himself with any denomination. Indeed, Hammarskjöld rarely shared anything about his religious or spiritual views with anyone, in part, his biographers believe, because he did not want to be exclusively associated with the West in the eyes of some non-Christian heads of state and governments.

Nevertheless, Karl Rahner's understanding of the term "anonymous Christian" seems appropriate in this instance. This turn of phrase has proven somewhat controversial both for non-Catholic Christians who understand their faith in dogmatic or confessional terms and for some non-Christians who believe it to be dismissive of their own beliefs. In fact, the terms "anonymous Christian" and "anonymous Christianity" testify to the sheer breadth of Rahner's conception of the *missio Dei*, i.e., God's mission in the world: "What 'anonymous Christianity' signifies, first and foremost, is that interior grace which forgives man and gives him a share in the Godhead even before baptism."[32] An anonymous Christian can thus be understood as a person of "faith"—writ large—whose way of being in the world is habitually guided by virtue and the truths of her faith as she understands them. Whether we consider Hammarskjöld to have been an unconventional Christian, a paradigmatic Christian, or an anonymous Christian, his life certainly embodied key elements of this expansive understanding.

30. Van Dusen, *Dag Hammarskjöld*, 193.
31. Hammarskjöld, *Markings*, 14.
32. Rahner, "Anonymous Christianity," 165.

We are now in a position to evaluate the extent to which Dag Hammarskjöld's life reflects the journey of faith unfolded in Matthew's version of the Beatitudes. In chapter 6, we examined the first two Beatitudes: "blessed are the poor in spirit" and "blessed are they who mourn." The twin concepts of root sin and self-emptying or *kenosis* were introduced. To a considerable extent, we relied on the teachings of the early church fathers in exploring these themes.

Hammarskjöld certainly understood the concept of root sin, very likely through the cherished lens of Thomas à Kempis's *Imitation of Christ*. According to à Kempis, "we have all been born with a fierce, self-centered desire for success, status, and pleasure that clashes with our longing for God."[33] Hammarskjöld accepted, as well, the challenge we all face in emptying ourselves of root sin even to the point of mourning. In doing so, he clearly followed à Kempis: "When a person becomes filled with sorrow and regret for his sins, then the whole world looks different to him. A good person finds reason enough for mourning and weeping, for whether he thinks of himself or of his neighbor, he knows that no one lives without hardships in this life. And the more closely he examines himself the more he grieves. The grounds for our just grief and remorse are our faults and sins."[34]

Hammarskjöld's overriding concern in his spiritual life—his root sin, if you will—can best be described as vanity, a persistent failing we understand theologically as the idolatrous worship of what others think and say about us. Aulén described this ever-present temptation in Hammarskjöld as "self-centeredness,"[35] but this is clearly too broad a term. Self-centeredness can pertain either to pride, i.e., the worship of self, or to vanity. Even though Hammarskjöld rarely used the term "vanity," he clearly recognized his core vulnerability for what it was and understood how it differed from pride.[36] A journal entry from 1941 or 1942 makes this clear: "The Straight Road—to live for others in order to save one's soul. The Broad—to live for others in order to save *one's self-esteem*."[37] This theme emerged again in a 1950 journal entry: "Your contempt for your fellow human beings does not prevent you, with a well-regarded

33. à Kempis, *Imitation of Christ*, 41.

34. à Kempis, *Imitation of Christ*, 52.

35. Aulén, *Dag Hammarskjöld's White Book*, 16.

36. Hammarskjöld, *Markings*, 92.

37. Hammarskjöld, *Markings*, 14. Emphasis added.

self-respect, from trying to win their respect."[38] He leveled this severe accusation against himself again in 1952: "Reason tells me that I am bound
to seek my own good, seek to gratify my desires, win power for myself
and admiration from others. And yet I 'know'—know without knowing—that in such a perspective, nothing could be less important. A vision
in which God is."[39]

The apparent ease with which Hammarskjöld accomplished so
many assignments over the course of his youth and in his professional
life, too, could certainly have lent itself to arrogance or pride, but—by all
accounts—it did not. Instead, Hammarskjöld was tormented, it seems, by
a thorough apprehension of his susceptibility to an inordinate hunger for
recognition and praise.

Hammarskjöld acknowledged, too, the pressing need to empty himself of his obsession over the good opinion of others *if* he was ever to experience meaning in life. According to W. H. Auden, the celebrated poet
who contributed an introduction to *Markings*: "Hammarskjöld knew exactly what his problem was—if he was not to go under, he must learn how
to forget himself and find a calling in which he could forget himself—and
knew that it was not in his own power to do so."[40] Hammarskjöld knew
that he was in need of *kenosis*, and he recognized Jesus as an exemplar in
this regard. According to Aulén, "Hammarskjöld sees Jesus in contrast to
his own faltering position as one who shrinks from 'accepting criticism.'
Inquiries which had already entered his mind now became actualized in
a new light; he seems to have heard the voice of Jesus as a severe accusation directed at himself."[41]

In chapter 7, we focused on Matthew's third Beatitude: "blessed are
the meek." We defined meekness as an unequivocal orientation to God's
hopes and dreams.

According to Aulén, the concepts of *kenosis* or self-surrender on
the one hand and self-realization on the other were opposite sides of
the same coin for Hammarskjöld: "The first word describes the action
negatively; the second, positively. These two attitudes are intimately connected with each other—in the *yes* to God. The yes means saying no to the
self, self-surrender; but it means at the same time saying yes to yourself,

38. Hammarskjöld, *Markings*, 41.
39. Hammarskjöld, *Markings*, 83.
40. Hammarskjöld, *Markings*, xv.
41. Aulén, *Dag Hammarskjöld's White Book*, 52.

self-realization."[42] As Hammarskjöld himself put it: "Out of myself as a stumbling block, into myself as fulfillment."[43] Similarly, "in order for the eye to perceive color, it must divest itself of all colors."[44]

Indeed, Hammarskjöld viewed *kenotic* self-surrender as a prerequisite for a life-giving encounter with God: "Only when you descend into yourself and encounter the Other, do you then experience goodness as the ultimate reality—united and living—*in* him and *through* him."[45] Aulén, an accomplished Lutheran theologian, explained Hammarskjöld's conversion experience as a kind of transparency "to the divine light" in which he served "as a 'lens' through which the light shines. Every tendency to self-centeredness robs the lens of its transparency. Self-effacement, therefore, is a condition antecedent to the transparency of the lens."[46]

Further, Hammarskjöld experienced this self-surrender to God's hopes and dreams for him as a kind of freedom, indeed, as a "freedom from self-concern."[47] He concluded in 1953 that "he who has placed himself in God's hand stands free *vis-à-vis* men: he is entirely at his ease with them, because he has granted them the right to judge."[48] He recognized, however, that this freedom can only be sustained by habit, that is, by a sustained formation in virtue: "You dare your Yes—and experience a meaning. You repeat your Yes—and all things acquire a meaning. When everything has a meaning, how can you live anything but a *Yes*."[49]

This freedom implies, of course, a high level of trust in God. This is the sense in which Kierkegaard referred to true conversion as a leap of faith. Risk is involved. Indeed, this is the sense in which Hammarskjöld echoes Viktor Frankl in affirming that a life-sustaining sense of meaning can be realized in any setting, in Frankl's case, even in a Nazi concentration camp. According to Hammarskjöld, "we are not permitted to choose the frame of our destiny. But what we put into it is ours."[50] Further, "has life a meaning? Seek by daring to take the leap into unconditional

---

42. Aulén, *Dag Hammarskjöld's White Book*, 65.

43. Hammarskjöld, *Markings*, 152.

44. Hammarskjöld, *Markings*, 127.

45. Hammarskjöld, *Markings*, 165.

46. Aulén, *Dag Hammarskjöld's White Book*, 102.

47. Aulén, *Dag Hammarskjöld's White Book*, 67.

48. Hammarskjöld, *Markings*, 90.

49. Hammarskjöld, *Markings*, 125.

50. Hammarskjöld, *Markings*, 55.

obedience . . . You will find that, thus subordinated, your life will receive from Life all its meaning, irrespective of the conditions given you for its realization."[51]

In chapter 8, we moved from the intrapersonal focus of the first three Beatitudes to the interpersonal orientation of the fourth and fifth: "blessed are they who hunger and thirst for righteousness" and "blessed are the merciful." We reframed righteousness in terms of right relationship and expanded our everyday understanding of mercy to include the need to welcome God's forgiveness and the need to forgive others.

Hammarskjöld seems to have exhibited a profound respect and concern for individuals, regardless of their position or rank. He is remembered for having visited every one of the thirty-five hundred staff members who worked at the United Nations within a month of his arrival.[52] They were reported at the time to be deeply dispirited by a host of controversies. As we might expect, his time-consuming gesture was well-received. According to Ralph Bunche, one of Hammarskjöld's closest associates at the United Nations, "his relations with his close collaborators were easy, friendly, and informal, and always on a first-name basis. There was nothing formidable about him; he not only tolerated but seemed to relish views at odds with his own. His greatest weakness in administration was found precisely in the fact that he usually could not be hard when personal situations demanded it because of an underlying soft-heartedness."[53]

In his dealings with others, Hammarskjöld exhibited what can be described as a personalist commitment to the engendering of right relationships. His commitment in this regard is affirmed, for instance, in a journal entry from 1956: "It is better for the health of the soul to make one man good than 'to sacrifice oneself for mankind.'"[54] Further, "the end of all political effort must be the wellbeing of the individual in a life of safety and freedom."[55] This is a key sense in which Hammarskjöld anticipated Robert Greenleaf's work.

Hammarskjöld seems to have recognized, too, that a leader cannot truly appreciate the other as an autonomous person of inestimable value

---

51. Hammarskjöld, *Markings*, 130.

52. Van Dusen, *Dag Hammarskjöld*, 110.

53. Van Dusen, *Dag Hammarskjöld*, 111.

54. Hammarskjöld, *Markings*, xx.

55. Hammarskjöld, *Dag Hammarskjöld*, 324.

unless she has, first, confronted the debilitating effects of root sin and thereby opened herself to God's hopes and dreams for her. As was noted in chapter 8, the road to the third Beatitude can only be traveled through the first two. A journal entry from 1956 makes this clear: "He who can totally sweep clean the chalice of himself can carry the inborn nature of others to its fulfillment."[56] Further, this commitment to the other requires mercy manifested as forgiveness, both of oneself and others, a lesson Hammarskjöld undoubtedly learned from à Kempis: "A patient person undergoes a great and wholesome cleansing, who while bearing injuries grieves more for the evil of others than for his own wrongs; who gladly prays for his enemies, and who forgives them; who does not shrink from asking forgiveness from others; who is more easily moved to compassion than to anger; who remains disciplined; and who directs every part of his life to his quest for God."[57]

In chapter 9, we turned to Matthew's sixth Beatitude: "blessed are the clean of heart." The living saints among us were described as artisans, as individuals who had been well formed or steeped in virtue over time. At the same time, it was observed that the aspiring disciple's journey is an iterative process characterized by moments of great joy and setbacks as well.

Hammarskjöld certainly experienced moments of ecstatic joy or what the great mystics he revered referred to as an experience of oneness with God or with God's hopes and dreams for them. A journal entry from 1956 affirms this: "In his hand, every moment has its meaning, its greatness, its glory, its peace, its coherence. From this perspective, to 'believe in God' is to believe in yourself, as self-evident, as 'illogical,' and as impossible to explain: if I can be, then God *is*."[58] An ease—indeed, an artistry—is revealed in this and other such entries. Consider the following, for instance: "To be single-hearted is to experience reality, not in relation to ourselves, but in its sacred independence. It is to see, judge, and act from the point of *rest* in ourselves. Then, how much disappears, and all that remains falls into place."[59] As Aulén explains, the connection between "single-heartedness" and "rest" may have been a direct one for Hammarskjöld since "single-hearted" can be translated as

---

56. Hammarskjöld, *Markings*, 134

57. à Kempis, *Imitation of Christ*, 57.

58. Hammarskjöld, *Markings*, 127.

59. Hammarskjöld, *Markings*, 174. Emphasis added.

"simple-hearted" in Swedish.[60] Hammarskjöld would sometimes explain this "rest" in terms of a certain self-forgetfulness or oblivion: "Be grateful as your deeds become less associated with your name, as your feet ever more lightly tread the earth."[61]

That being said, Hammarskjöld could never free himself entirely from his addiction to the good opinion of others. He could be "thin-skinned" and sensitive to criticism.[62] According to Aulén, "page after page in *Markings* shows that—through the last prayer of the final year—this faith was constantly at battle. It was a faith at battle with the risks of returning chaos and ever threatening self-centeredness,"[63] a failing we have defined here as vanity. Note, for instance, a journal entry from 1955: "So, once again, you chose for yourself—and opened the door to chaos. The chaos you become whenever God's hand does not rest upon your head." Speaking of himself, but in the third person: "When his attention is directed beyond and above, how strong he is, with the strength of God who is within him because he is in God. Strong and free, because his self no longer exists."[64]

Over time, however, Hammarskjöld exhibited a moral resilience—even in the face of setbacks—that had been absent during his crisis years. A journal entry in 1956 makes this clear: "Uneasy, uneasy, uneasy—why? Because—anxious for the good opinion of others, and jealous of the possibility that they may become 'famous,' you have lowered yourself to wondering what will happen in the end to what you have done and been . . . *Bless your uneasiness as a sign that there is still life in you.*"[65] And in 1957, he admitted that "the intense blaze of your anxiety reveals to what a great extent you are still fettered, still alienated from the One. However, don't worry about this or anything else, but *follow the Way of which you are aware, even when you have departed from it.*"[66]

In chapter 10, we turned to the final two of Matthew's eight Be-atitudes: "blessed are the peacemakers" and "blessed are they who are persecuted for the sake of righteousness." We observed that peace—as

---

60. Aulén, *Dag Hammarskjöld's White Book*, 68.

61. Hammarskjöld, *Markings*, 146.

62. Hammarskjöld, *Markings*, 133.

63. Aulén, *Dag Hammarskjöld's White Book*, 145.

64. Hammarskjöld, *Markings*, 104.

65. Hammarskjöld, *Markings*, 137. Emphasis added.

66. Hammarskjöld, *Markings*, 154. Emphasis added.

Jesus understood the term—involves more than the mere absence of hostilities. Further, we acknowledged the fleeting nature of success as the
world understands the term.

Hammarskjöld was widely hailed as a peacemaker, of course. For the
most part, he relied on private diplomacy, which he sometimes described
as "preventive diplomacy"[67] or "midwifery."[68] This, again, demonstrates
his personalist orientation to others. Hammarskjöld was respected by
those with whom he negotiated, and his good intentions and the discre-
tion he exhibited in sensitive moments were deeply appreciated.

Hammarskjöld worked tirelessly to defuse tensions in the world. In
doing so, he seems to have followed the example of Jesus in his encounter
with a mob determined to stone an adulterous woman. Hammarskjöld
knew, it seems, that the mercy so desperately needed in the world would
require forgiveness at a deep and abiding level, the very forgiveness he
himself had received: "Forgiveness breaks the chain of causality because
he who 'forgives' you—out of love—takes upon himself the consequences
of what you have done. Forgiveness, therefore, always entails a sacrifice.
The price you must pay for your own liberation through another's sacrifice is that you in turn must be willing to liberate in the same way, irrespective of the consequences to yourself."[69]

At the same time, Hammarskjöld could be bold in pursuing his
agenda and in asserting the United Nation's prerogatives. At critical points
over the course of his tenure as Secretary General, he demonstrated a
level of self-assurance that was unanticipated at the time of his appointment. In 1958, he was adamant in this regard: "Within the limits thus set,
however, I believe it to be the Secretary General's duty to use his office
and, indeed, the machinery of the organization to its utmost capacity
and to the full extent permitted at each stage by practical circumstances.
On the other hand, I believe it is in keeping with the philosophy of the
Charter that the Secretary General should be expected to act also without
such guidance, should this appear to him necessary in order to help in
filling any vacuum that may appear in the systems which the Charter and
traditional diplomacy provide for safe-guarding of peace and security."[70]

67. Lipsey, *Hammarskjöld*, 422.

68. Van Dusen, *Dag Hammarskjöld*, 137.

69. Hammarskjöld, *Markings*, 197.

70. Van Dusen, *Dag Hammarskjöld*, 133.

Nevertheless, Hammarskjöld had come to accept the likelihood that his efforts would lead—in time—to naught. This acceptance was clearly assuaged to a considerable extent, however, by his confidence in God's ultimate victory. In a 1954 address to the second assembly of the World Council of Churches, Hammarskjöld pointed specifically to Matthew's Gospel in affirming this view:

> In the Sermon on the Mount it is said that we should take no thought of the morrow "for the morrow shall take thought for the things of itself. Sufficient unto the day is the evil thereof." Can anything seem farther from the practical planning, the long-term considerations typical of political life? And yet—is this not the very expression of the kind of patience we must all learn to show in our work for peace and justice? Mustn't we learn to believe that when we give this work, daily, what it is in our power to give, and when, daily, we meet the demands facing us to all the extent of our ability, this will ultimately lead to a world of greater justice and good will, even if nothing would seem to give us hope of success or even of progress in the right direction.[71]

In the end, Hammarskjöld recognized that it was not his understanding of peace or the world's understanding, for that matter, that was at stake. It was God's peace. In 1956, he expressed this view in prayer:

> Hallowed be Thy name,
> *not mine,*
> Thy kingdom come,
> *not mine,*
> Thy will be done,
> *not mine*
> Give us peace with Thee
> Peace with men
> Peace with ourselves
> And free us from all fear.[72]

Indeed, Hammarskjöld associated his own efforts with the suffering servant, Jesus: "He who has surrendered himself to it knows that the Way ends on the Cross—even when it is leading him through the jubilation of Gennesaret or the triumphal entry into Jerusalem."[73] A journal entry

71. Hammarskjöld, *Markings*, 61.

72. Hammarskjöld, *Markings*, 142.

73. Hammarskjöld, *Markings*, 91.

posted on Good Friday in 1956 makes this same point: "The third hour. And the ninth. They are here. And now. They are now! 'Jesus will be in agony even to the end of the world. We must not sleep during that time' (Pascal). We must not—And for the watcher in the far-off present—also present in his contact with mankind among whom, at every moment, Jesus dies in someone who has followed the trail marks of the inner road to the end; love and patience, righteousness and humility, faith and courage, stillness."[74]

In fact, Hammarskjöld viewed each setback as a kind of "little death," a little dying that was integral, nonetheless, to discipleship. In 1957, he asked: "Why, then, weep at this little death? Take it to you—quickly—with a smile die this death, and become free to go further—one with your task, your whole you of the moment."[75]

According to Aulén, Hammarskjöld viewed "sacrifice as self-surrender to others within the framework of one's own vocation. But precisely in the self-surrender is to be found the only authentic self-realization. This self-surrender demands readiness to accept the full consequences of service to others—even the consequences of death."[76] Hammarskjöld may have drawn some comfort in this regard from Thomas à Kempis: "To be able to endure feeling rejection and loneliness, to continue on in humility, and not to think that you deserve far better is a real blessing, especially if you can feel this way for the honor of God, and if you do so willingly."[77]

What then can we say of Dag Hammarskjöld as a disciple of Jesus and as a leader? To use Karl Rahner's terminology, we can understand him, first, as an "anonymous Christian." Hammarskjöld's religious commitments were entirely hidden from the world during his lifetime. They were certainly unconventional. Nevertheless, Hammarskjöld journeyed along a privileged path, a way fully laid out for disciples of Jesus in Matthew's Beatitudes. After years of struggle, Hammarskjöld achieved a true poverty of spirit, it seems, even to the point of mourning his failings. Following a period of inner struggle, he surrendered himself to God's purposes in his life. In the spiritual sense of the term, he was meek. This enabled Hammarskjöld, in turn, to see the world more nearly as God sees

74. Hammarskjöld, *Markings*, 126.

75. Hammarskjöld, *Markings*, 158.

76. Aulén, *Dag Hammarskjöld's White Book*, 65.

77. à Kempis, *Imitation of Christ*, 73.

it. He hungered and thirsted for righteousness. He sought to engender right relationships among his colleagues, among those with whom he negotiated, and in the world more broadly. Hammarskjöld also recognized the need for mercy expressed, first and foremost, as forgiveness. Although he never seems to have been entirely at ease with himself, Hammarskjöld certainly enjoyed moments of great clarity, moments in which he experienced cleanliness of heart as a true blessing. Finally, Hammarskjöld engendered peace when and where he could and accepted willingly, it seems, the consequences for doing so.

Hammarskjöld can also be considered a servant-leader. Again, "the servant-leader is servant first . . . It begins with a natural feeling that one wants to serve, to serve *first*. Then conscious choice brings one to aspire to lead. The person is sharply different from one who is *leader* first, perhaps because of the need to assuage an unusual power drive or to acquire material possessions."[78] It took some time for Hammarskjöld to achieve this identity. By the time he accepted his appointment as Secretary General of the United Nations, however, he was every bit a servant-leader.

We can say, too, that he was a leader as the term is defined in this text. Hammarskjöld understood his professional role as the balanced exercise of a full complement of managerial responsibilities oriented to a broad set of stakeholders in a manner constrained by his internalized virtues and fully informed by values and intellectual commitments drawn from a larger belief system—in this instance, a deeply integrated set of Christian values and intellectual commitments—but focused on ends sanctioned by the organization he served. Hammarskjöld clearly understood leadership in this way. To be effective, leadership must be more than blind acquiescence to the instrumental ends of the organization one serves. In a 1955 commencement address, Hammarskjöld affirmed this view in no uncertain terms: "International service requires of all of us first and foremost the courage to be ourselves. In other words, it requires that we should be true to none other than our ideals and interests—but these should be such as we can fully endorse after having opened our minds, with great honesty to the many voices of the world."[79]

Among his biographers, Henry Van Dusen, in particular, associated this understanding of leadership with Hammarskjöld: "What, if any, is the meaning of Hammarskjöld's spiritual pilgrimage and its outcome

78. Greenleaf, *Servant Leadership*, 27.

79. Hammarskjöld, *Dag Hammarskjöld*, 80–81.

for each of us? The answer is to be discovered at the two poles around which every human life revolves—and which Hammarskjöld himself was so fond of distinguishing as the 'private' and the 'public servant'—in his case, behind and beneath and within both of which . . . in the most intimate and continuous interrelation with both—at once a reflection, a mirror of the 'public servant' and the 'private man' and at the same time the determinative prime mover of each—was the 'inner person,' known only to himself, the real Dag Hammarskjöld."[80]

80. Van Dusen, *Dag Hammarskjöld*, 128.

Chapter 12

Implications for Key Societal Institutions and Practices

Woe to you, scribes and Pharisees, you hypocrites. You pay tithes of mint and dill and cummin, and have neglected the weightier things of the law: judgment and mercy and fidelity. [But] these you should have done, without neglecting the others. Blind guides, who strain out the gnat and swallow the camel! Woe to you, scribes and Pharisees, you hypocrites. You cleanse the outside of cup and dish, but inside they are full of plunder and self-indulgence. Blind Pharisee, cleanse first the inside of the cup, so that the outside also may be clean. Woe to you, scribes and Pharisees, you hypocrites. You are like whitewashed tombs, which appear beautiful on the outside, but inside are full of dead men's bones and every kind of filth. Even so, on the outside you appear righteous, but inside you are filled with hypocrisy and evildoing (Matt 23:23–28).

W E ARE OFTEN DRAWN to organizational or societal solutions when we read about the kinds of organizational failures described in chapter 4. We quickly turn to strategy or technique. We focus our attention on this or that legal or organizational remedy. We look for deterrents of one kind or another, prophylactics that can protect us, the organizations we serve, key stakeholders, and the larger community from the greed, the tunnel vision, and the stress that can so easily corrupt decision-making in organizations and in the public square. And there is certainly a place for the law, professional standards, oversight mechanisms of various kinds, checks and balances, collaborative decision-making, detailed protocols, and the intentional foregrounding of philosophical and religious ideals. They all have their place.

We would do well to remember, however, that the law proved ineffective in preventing the scandals that engulfed Worldcom, Enron, Arthur Anderson, Lehman Brothers, and so many other private sector firms over the course of the last several decades. The Hippocratic Oath did not derail the decades-long Tuskegee syphilis study. Ford Motor Company has a mission statement and a vison statement, both of which promise customer satisfaction, but the verdict in the Pinto scandal was celebrated, nonetheless, as a great success. Nestlé's corporate structure is designed to ensure oversight, but local decisions in the case of the firm's infant formula products still contributed to the deaths of an untold number of infants in developing countries across the globe. Engineering teams and detailed protocols failed to prevent the launch of the space shuttle *Challenger* on that very cold morning in January 1986. And the sexual abuse scandals of the last thirty years have undermined—to a devastating extent—the Catholic Church's credibility as a moral agent.

The unexamined factor in many such situations, it seems, is the inner makeup of the individuals who render decisions or model behaviors in the organizations in which they serve, whether in the private sector, the public sector, or the nonprofit sector. And the missing ingredient with respect to the inner makeup of some who serve in managerial or leadership capacities, it seems, is virtue oriented to values and intellectual commitments external to the instrumental ends espoused by the organizations they serve. Again quoting Paul J. Wadell, "virtue is a characteristic way of behavior which makes both actions and *persons* good and which also enables one to fulfill the purpose of life."[1] Virtue is an engrained or habituated way of being in the world.

So where do we find virtuous leaders? At the organizational or societal level, how do we promote the need for virtue oriented to external values and intellectual commitments in managers and nominal leaders? How do we engender Christian virtues oriented to Christian values and Christian intellectual commitments in aspiring disciples of Jesus who labor in secular organizations? And how can we hope to do any of this in a world that is being de-Christianized at a rapid pace?

Much of this work can only be pursued at the individual level, of course. We have noted the need for a rich prayer life and for spiritual

1. Wadell, "Virtue," 998. Emphasis added.

direction. We have also affirmed the primacy of one's identity as a Christian over one's role a manager or nominal leader. We do not cultivate virtue in order to achieve material or reputational success. Notwithstanding Robert Greenleaf's qualified view in this regard, professional success is beside the point. We further affirmed that all are called to holiness and that this calling is a 24/7/365 proposition. A disciple of Jesus is not free to park or bracket her identity as a Christian when she steps into the boardroom or the management suite or onto the shop floor. The heavy lifting of formation is undertaken and sustained by individuals both in their personal relationships with God and in the stances they assume *vis-à-vis* the world.

This is not to say that a number of institutional, societal, and cultural influences are unimportant. They are. Jesus acknowledged this in his vitriolic condemnation of the Pharisees and the scribes in the pericope that opens this chapter. The Pharisees represented the oppressive moral authority of Israel's religious elite, just as the scribes served as the bare remnant of Israel's independent governing structure. In our own day, family, the legal system of the society in which we live, the codes of conduct of certain professional associations, politics, the media, and any number of other factors can exert powerful influences on an individual's moral development.

Inertia can play a role, too. According to Charles Taylor, certain generalized notions of benevolence drawn from Christianity have been carried over into our increasingly secular world, and this has taken place, for the most part, in an uncritical fashion. Unconsciously merged with the constitutional order we have inherited, these notions of benevolence now serve as a kind of civil religion, a social regulator of sorts that has become increasingly attenuated in recent decades. This is why some moral philosophers, including Charles Taylor and Alasdair MacIntyre, think we may now be "living beyond our moral means."[2] Interestingly, Dag Hammarskjöld shared this concern:

> A student of the growth of human rights through the ages will recognize its close relationship to the development of tolerance inspired by intellectual liberalism or, perhaps more often, by ethical concepts of religious origin. Attempts are made to link the development of human rights exclusively to the liberal ideas which broke through to predominance in the Age of Enlightenment. However, to do so means to me to overlook the historical

2. Taylor, *Sources of the Self,* 515.

background of those ideas. It means also cutting our ties to a source of strength that we need in order to carry the work for human rights to fruition and to give to those rights, when established, their fitting spiritual content.[3]

Three traditional sources of authority, in particular, have long played regulatory roles with respect to the promotion and cultivation of virtue. Although their effectiveness in this regard has been undermined to a considerable extent in recent decades, religion, academia, and certain political norms have long been associated with the promotion and cultivation of virtue. Each will be examined in turn.

Religion is on the ropes in the United States. According to the Pew Research Center, "65 percent of American adults describe themselves as Christians when asked about their religion, down 12 percentage points over the past decade. Meanwhile, the religiously unaffiliated share of the population, consisting of people who describe their religious identity as atheist, agnostic, or 'nothing in particular,' now stands at 26 percent, up from 17 percent in 2009."[4] It is now clear that the United States is following a path blazed in recent decades by Europe. Still, it appears that many in the United States still sense a need for a life-giving and life-sustaining spirituality. According to the Pew Research Center, some 27 percent of adults now say they think of themselves as spiritual, but not religious, up 8 percentage points over the course of the last five years.[5]

These anomalous findings suggest that the existential questions posed in *Gaudium et Spes* remain salient for many of us: again, "What is humanity? What is the meaning of suffering, evil, death, which have not been eliminated by all of this progress? What is the purpose of these achievements, purchased at so high a price? What can people contribute to society? What can they expect from it? What happens after this earthly life has ended?"[6] Not surprisingly, given its anthropological or ontological roots, an existential hunger for the experience of meaning persists.

At the same time, it is clear that religion—at least as it is perceived by the religiously unaffiliated and the poorly catechized—fails to satisfy or promise the experience of meaning so many of us seek. For many, religion—narrowly construed as liturgical practice, as the affirmation of

3. Hammarskjöld, *Dag Hammarskjöld,* 131.

4. Pew Research Center, "In US, Decline of Christianity."

5. Pew Research Center, "More Americans Now Say."

6. Second Vatican Council, "*Gaudium et Spes,*" no. 18.

certain dogmatic truths, or as morality narrowly framed as adherence to the Decalogue and to Church teaching on abortion, human sexuality, and end-of-life issues—fails to satisfy this existential yearning. A slight modification of an old but reliable joke makes this point: "A liturgist, a systematic theologian, and a moral theologian walked into a crowded bar . . . And no one noticed." In the West, it seems, fewer and fewer people are noticing. This should be profoundly disturbing to those among us who find solace in the affirmation that "by love, God has revealed himself and given himself to man. He has thus provided the definitive, super-abundant answer to the questions man asks himself about the meaning and purpose of his life."[7]

Even more problematic are those who have been so wounded or anesthetized by our culture that the kinds of existential questions posed above are no longer salient. Recall from chapter 5 that the term "reification" is used by some scholars to describe the superficial experience of life many believe to be endemic in our world. Individuals are increasingly defined in terms of the things they own, and human existence has, thereby, been "commodified." Sartre attributed this kind of existence to bad faith. "One *puts oneself* in bad faith as one goes to sleep and one is in bad faith as one dreams. Once this mode of being has been realized, it is as difficult to get out of it as to wake oneself up; bad faith is a type of being in the world, like waking or dreaming, which by itself tends to perpetuate itself, although its structure is of the *metastable* type."[8]

Alienation lies at the opposite end of this spectrum of unfulfilled living. According to Allen Wood, "[to be alienated] is to be separated from one's own essence or nature; it is to be forced to lead a life in which that nature has no opportunity to be fulfilled or actualized. In this way, the experience of 'alienation' involves a sense of a lack of self-worth and an absence of meaning in one's life."[9] This is, perhaps, the "quiet desperation" in which Henry David Thoreau believed so many of us experience our lives.

We can add to this menagerie of discontent all those who subscribe to the postmodern assertion that all historical narratives are contrived, hegemonic, and oppressive, failing to recognize, of course, that postmodernism is itself a narrative construct.

7. *Catechism* 68.

8. Sartre, *Being and Nothingness*, 3.

9. Wood, *Alienation*, 22.

In fact, the institutional Church has little or no access to those who consider themselves to be spiritual but not religious, to those who no longer see the point of any religion or spirituality, or to those who think of religion as but one ideology among so many others. As a result, the institutional Church has little or no access to those who are unaware of the Church's rich tradition pertaining to the theological and moral virtues or to its core values and intellectual commitments. This should be of concern to those who take seriously the "great commission" proclaimed at the very end of Mathew's Gospel: "Go, therefore, and make disciples of all nations, baptizing them in the name of the Father, and of the Son, and of the holy Spirit, teaching them to observe all that I have commanded you" (Matt 28:19–29).

This is not to dismiss the enduring value of liturgical order, faithfulness to the Church's dogmatic pronouncements, or the need for moral clarity in addressing life issues. In terms of evangelization, however, none of these three expressions of church life—as faithful to the tradition and as life affirming as each of them may be for some believers—is likely to attract seekers to discipleship or to awaken the disaffected among us to the Good News of the Father's love for all of creation. Further, none of these three expressions of church life—in and of themselves—is likely to engender the wisdom or the courage managers and nominal leaders need to think, act, and live as moral agents in the organizations they serve. To fulfill the imperative of the great commission, the Church will need to meet people in the various "places" in which they find themselves. In some instances, they are spiritual, but not religious. In others, they have been morally anesthetized by a culture that disdains transcendent values. And in still others, they are alienated from any number of contemporary institutions, including the Church, even to the point of cynical disdain.

As a first step in this direction, the church will need to accelerate its efforts to restore its credibility on moral issues, credibility squandered so shamefully in the sexual abuse scandals of the last three decades. Some progress has been made in this regard, but the ground to be recovered is substantial.

Further, the Church will need to craft its appeal in positive terms. Those who are disaffected from the Church and those who do not perceive any need for a deeper faith life will simply not respond to browbeating or to shaming. Pope Francis's view in this regard is to the point: "One of the more serious temptations which stifles boldness and zeal is a defeatism which turns us into querulous and disillusioned pessimists, 'sourpusses.' Nobody can go off to battle unless he is fully convinced of victory beforehand. If we start without confidence, we have already lost half the battle and we bury our talents."[10] Recall Aquinas's argument that the ultimate goal in the spiritual life is happiness, and not just the promised happiness of heaven. We are invited to happiness in this life, too. Over the course of our spiritual journeys, we may well be emptied—voluntarily or involuntarily—of our unhealthy attachments, our idols, and our sins to the point of mourning. This is for a purpose, however. We are invited to make room for something more, indeed, for something better. And this should be cause for great joy!

As important as these steps may be, however, they simply set the stage for an appeal based on the kinds of questions posed in *Gaudium et Spes*, questions that can best be answered in the person of Jesus. To be clear, these questions are existential rather than dogmatic in nature. According to Karl Rahner, Jesus often had to remind his listeners of their essential humanity *before* he could proclaim the Good News of the Father's love to them. In exasperation at times, Jesus would challenge those who attended to his voice: "Anyone who has ears to hear ought to hear" (Mark 4:23). Questions must precede answers, however, and so, the need to awaken the disaffected and the disengaged to the fundamental questions that should be of the utmost importance to all of us. This is the sense in which Rahner defined "man as the one who listens to God in history."[11] We must first be awakened to the *need* to listen to God before we can fully open ourselves to doing so. Acknowledging that we now live in mission territory, Anthony Gittins makes a similar point. He notes that "children have to be trained, to be *made* human."[12] They have to be provided with ears to hear.

Awakening individuals to the need for a lifelong journey of conversion is no easy task, however. Challenging the disengaged and the disaffected with the need to pursue a more authentic experience of meaning in their lives can be daunting. Nevertheless, doing so can itself be an expression of discipleship. According to Rahner:

> If man is consciously aware of who he is and what he is making of himself in his own freedom, the chance that he will succeed in this self-achievement of his and arrive at a radical self-fulfillment

10. Francis, *Evangelii Gaudium*, 85.
11. Rahner, "Theology and Anthropology," 42.
12. Gittins, *Ministry at the Margins*, 66.

is greater than if he merely possesses and fulfils his own humanity at a merely inert and unconscious level. Hence the conscious self-realization of a hitherto anonymous Christianity brought about by missionary preaching implies on the one hand the achievement of a more radical dimension of responsibility and on the other a greater chance of this Christianity interiorly bestowed by grace being brought to its fullness in all dimensions precisely as an explicit Christianity and in a state of radical freedom.[13]

In this sense, Rahner's concept of "anonymous Christianity" can be understood as a kind of non-sectarian and non-dogmatic belief system that, nonetheless, acknowledges the universal hunger for the experience of meaning in our lives. In fact, the articulated moral framework presented in chapter 5, i.e., the good, the moral, and the just understood, respectively, as the experience of meaning, a respect for the dignity of all persons, and opportunity, may provide a working definition for Rahner's concept of the "anonymous Christian." An anonymous Christian accepts her responsibility to discover or create meaning in her life through the full exercise of her creative gifts, through the development of loving relationships with others, through a deep appreciation for the incomparable beauty of our engraced world, and through the courageous stance she assumes *vis-à-vis* life's challenges. Further, an anonymous Christian recognizes and celebrates the inherent dignity of every human being. Still further, she works in various settings to create opportunities in which others—most notably the poor and disadvantaged among us—can experience meaning in their own lives. In an organizational setting, this operational framing of Rahner's concept of the "anonymous Christian" can also serve as an apt description of servant leadership.

This is not to say that a commitment to an existential moral framework of this kind is preferable to truths revealed in the Christian tradition. According to Rahner, "religion in particular—this authentic relationship to God the absolute, all-supporting and all-saving mystery of existence—is not just a particular area of human existence but rather at once its original and once more all-unifying unity."[14] That being said, many of us must first be awoken to the salience of the existential questions that should confront all thinking persons, before we can evaluate any of the particular belief systems our pluralistic world presents to us as possible answers. A steadfast belief in God and a committed life of discipleship are the preferred

13. Rahner, "Anonymous Christianity," 177.
14. Rahner, "Being Open to God," 4–5.

alternatives to which we are all called. Rahner recognized, however, that we live in a world of competing belief systems.[15] For this reason, dialogue is required, the kind of dialogue that can be pursued most effectively from within the more generalized moral framework implied in the overarching existential question: What is the purpose of this life?

We are called in this particular time and place—a time and place in which the Church is viewed with considerable suspicion—to engage others in the contexts of their own unique belief systems, as poorly defined and opaque as some of them might be. As Rahner put it, this will require Christian evangelization "on a modest and inconspicuous scale."[16]

Nevertheless, we should not be afraid to affirm our conviction that the Christian response to the overarching existential questions noted above is preferable to all other responses. We must give others ears to hear, but the Gospel message must be proclaimed as well. If we are successful, the seeds of this message will fall on fertile ground and germinate, if not immediately, then, perhaps, at some later point in time.

Indeed, we would do well to think of conversion as a three-part process, the first of which involves the awakening of ourselves and others to the need to assume responsibility for our unique spiritual journeys. The second part pertains to the proclamation of the Gospel. And the third addresses the journey of discipleship itself, the primary focus of part II of this text. See figure 15.

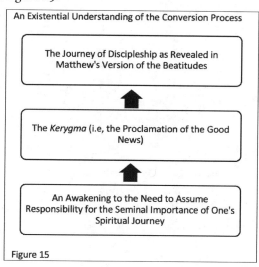

Figure 15

15. Rahner, "Reflections on Dialogue," 34.

16. Rahner, "Christian Living," 13.

Institutions of higher learning, too, have long played a prominent role in promoting virtue oriented to alternative sets of values and intellectual commitments. This includes values and intellectual commitments that are both Christian and civic in nature. This traditional function of education can be traced back to the Academy founded by Plato in 387 BCE. Indeed, formation for leadership was widely viewed as a primary function of higher education through the mid-twentieth century.

Much has changed in this regard, however. The demand for more and more courses in many of our professional academic programs has eviscerated general education course offerings across the nation. Over time, the kinds of courses in which the existential questions noted above and virtue and core values can be explored have been reduced to a bare minimum. Further, postmodernists are now overrepresented in the faculties of the arts and the social sciences in many of our colleges and universities. As a result, a not insignificant number of today's general education courses focus less on the great existential questions, virtue, and personal and civic values than on the "deconstruction" of the intellectual patrimony of the West. This is not to say that critique of this kind has no place in the curriculum. It certainly does, but the pressing need to form young people—the pressing need to give them ears to hear and eyes to see—remains as well. In truth, we have yet to balance the ongoing need to critique our culture and our institutions on the one hand and the obligation to form character and consciences on the other.

This development is not entirely new. In the nineteenth century, John Henry Newman (1801–90) decried calls for the liberal arts to be abandoned in English institutions of higher learning. In his seminal work *The Idea of a University* (1852), Newman rejected a vocation-oriented program of instruction in favor of a curriculum designed to promote true formation and the development of leaders. The threat is certainly more acute now, however, in an increasingly de-Christianized West. Indeed, the academy's virtual abandonment of the field in this regard can be viewed as a repudiation of its historic mission. In response to this disconcerting trend, distinguished scholars such as Thomas Ehrlich,[17] Robert Bringle,[18] and their respective colleagues have promoted various curricula and pedagogies, all of which are intended to promote civic

17. Ehrlich, *Civic Responsibility*.
18. Bringle et al., *Colleges and Universities*.

engagement. Still, those who support robust general education programs appear to be swimming upstream against a very strong current.

In a curriculum that truly promoted personal formation and preparation for authentic leadership, students would be confronted over and over again with the radical freedom that defines human existence and the limit conditions—including death—that haunt all of us. Further, students would be challenged to choose one or more preferred belief systems and then to defend their choices. A variety of options, e.g., philosophical, religious, aesthetic, political, and scientific, could be explored in this way; and a uniquely Christian understanding of the human person should certainly be included among them. Finally, students would be counseled against the hazards of easy and false choices with respect to the commitments they make in this regard.

This essential work could be advanced in any number of classroom and co-curricular settings. Aside from well-designed and well-taught courses in comparative moral philosophy and social justice, this duty to form students could be expressed in various approaches known in higher education circles as "high impact practices." This includes learning communities in which faculty in different academic disciplines link their course assignments in order to promote learning objectives that cut across the curriculum; sequenced general education courses; personal reflections on service-learning projects; and capstone courses designed to integrate a student's experiences over the course of her first several years of study using a thought-provoking set of questions, for instance: How do I experience meaning in my life? How do I hope to experience meaning after I graduate? What obligations do I have to others? How do I anticipate that these obligations will evolve over time? And to what extent have my answers to these questions been informed by my college experience?

For Christian institutions of higher learning, the watering down of our general education programs in favor of more and more courses in this or that professional program is particularly worrisome. The challenge can be framed, in fact, as a matter of institutional identity. Further, re-centering the missions of Christian institutions of higher learning around the obligation to evangelize students in the three-step process described above would undoubtedly hold implications that go well beyond the classroom. Faculty should be challenged to assume collective responsibility for their institution's general education programs; and, most importantly, boards of trustees and senior administrators should re-think what it means for an institution to be Christian. The choice between a nominal Christianity and a dogmatically sanctioned Christian identity is a false one. Again, students must first be awakened to the moral obligation to assume responsibility for their own unique spiritual journeys. Only then could we hope that some of them will open themselves to the *kerygma*, the Good News that is Jesus; and only then, in turn, could we hope that some of them will embrace the rigors of a lifelong journey of discipleship.

Further, this threefold conversion process should be understood as more than a private affair involving the intellect and the heart. It holds implications for the larger community, too. According to Gittens, "authentic Christian spirituality is expressed in the daily living out of the conviction that God is a loving creator who initiates, sustains, and restores and mends relationships . . . Far from producing a privatized spirituality or even a religion of pious observances, such an attitude calls us all to a radical engagement with the world, with social justice, and with the rest of humanity."[19] For students who hope to serve as true leaders, a sophisticated understanding of the world will thus be needed and so, too, a sophisticated understanding of the various language games of contemporary management theory and practice. This, too, is the essential but sometimes forgotten work of higher education.

The extent to which we are vulnerable to political demagoguery has now been amply demonstrated over the course of several election cycles. Given this, our politics are important as well. As citizens, we are formed to a considerable extent—for good or ill—in the public square. This can be a real challenge for committed disciples of Jesus. As noted in chapter 5, an explicit appeal to religious values and intellectual commitments is unlikely to find purchase in pluralistic societies that are becoming ever more diverse and secular in nature.

There is more to the public square than politics, of course; nevertheless, elections are the crucible in which the public's temper and its aspirations are most clearly revealed. Because of this, we would do well to reframe our election campaigns in at least three ways, three ways that may hold some potential to foreground certain civic virtues, virtues that were once taken for granted as part and parcel of our political patrimony. Unfortunately, this is no longer the case. As the last thirty years have demonstrated, civic virtue can no longer be assumed.

---

19. Gittins, *Called to Be Sent*, 48.

First, we would do well to distinguish between certain threshold issues on the one hand and the standard mix of policy concerns around which our political discourse typically revolves on the other. The following questions touch on foci that should precede the sharing of any particular public policy position in a debate setting. "Do you believe that all votes are equal in value?" "Should we make it easier to vote or more difficult?" "What obligations do we have to each other as citizens?" "How do you understand your obligations to those who voted for you or will vote for you?" "How do you understand your obligations to others with whom you disagree?" "Why do you want to serve in public office?"

Second, we would do well to focus more explicitly on character issues as we evaluate candidates for public office and officeholders, too. Elected officials are voted into office to make decisions and to model behavior. To this end, virtue matters! Key questions in this regard could include the following: "How do you understand personal and civic virtue?" "What kinds of decisions do you find to be difficult and why?" "Have you ever had to make a decision that mitigated against your electoral, personal, or professional interests?" "Do you have core beliefs or values that guide your decision-making?" "What is the source of these core beliefs or values?" "From whom do you seek wisdom?" "How would you describe the political philosophy that informs your public policy judgments?" (Something along these line was attempted in back-to-back interviews with candidates John McCain and Barack Obama hosted by Pastor Rick Warren during the 2008 presidential campaign.)

These first two ways of reframing public discourse do not speak specifically to religious virtues or to religious values and intellectual commitments. Nevertheless, individual responses could reference these sources of wisdom and so bring them into conversation with other belief systems. Further, these kinds of fundamental questions assume certain moral commitments to which we would all do well to subscribe, something akin, in fact, to the articulated moral framework examined in chapter 5, a moral framework in which human beings are understood as meaning-seeking beings, in which the good is understood as the experience of meaning, in which the moral is understood as the full recognition of the dignity that inheres in all persons regardless of their circumstances, and in which the just is understood as opportunity.

Third, we would do well to be more disciplined in the way we evaluate truth claims advanced in public discourse. Jürgen Habermas, a pragmatist whose work was examined in chapter 5, can be helpful in this regard. He argues that four distinct kinds of truth claims are typically advanced in the public square: empirical truth claims, normative truth claims, expressive truth claims, and aesthetic truth claims.[20] Habermas argues, further, that different warrants or evaluation criteria should attend to each of these categories of truth claims. An empirical truth claim is either objectively true or untrue and should be confirmed as such. Policy positions are often framed as empirical truth claims. A belief or action embedded in a normative truth claim is deemed appropriate or inappropriate by the audience to which it is directed. Appeals to rights and duties are often framed as normative truth claims. An expressive truth claim is determined to be authentic or inauthentic, again, by the audience to which it is directed. Claims that go to the core of the audience's identity are often framed in this way. And an aesthetic truth claim can be affirmed as beautiful, i.e., aesthetically pleasing, or not beautiful. Appeals to patriotism or to an idealized past are often crafted in this way.

According to W. C. Booth and his colleagues, a warrant should include three elements to be effective: a description of the evidence being offered, a description of the kind of claim that follows from that evidence, and a stated or implied connection between the two.[21] Holding elected officials and candidates for office accountable for the kinds of truth claims they advance and for the applicability of the warrants they employ in each instance could go a long way toward resolving the muddle so many of us encounter in today's public discourse.

These general prescriptions assume, of course, an electorate that is knowledgeable and capable of critical thought, candidates for public office who are committed, first, to the vitality and wellbeing of the public square and the electoral process itself, and media and other intermediaries and gatekeepers interested in something more than raw controversy or the daily vicissitudes of tracking polls.

Imagine, instead, three debates in every election cycle involving candidates for high office. The first would focus exclusively on the kinds of threshold issues detailed above; the second on matters of character, including questions and answers pertaining to virtue, values, and intellectual commitments; and the third on the candidates's public policy positions. Public policy positions examined through the alternative lenses of the several language games noted in chapter 5, i.e., rules-based constructs

20. Habermas, *The Theory*, 23.
21. Booth et al., *The Craft of Research*, 113.

of one kind or another, utilitarianism, libertarianism, and pragmatism, will always be important. As we know so well, however, there is more to the story. Again, virtue matters!

This reflection could be viewed as discouraging. There is so much work to be done, and our institutional and cultural resources are not as strong or resilient as they have been in the past. We should remember, however, that Christian discipleship should not be oriented *per se* to results as much of the world understand results. As the example of Jesus and the teachings of the early church fathers affirm, faithful discipleship can lead to suffering and martyrdom.

We would do well to remember, too, that faithful disciples are guided in their efforts by the Holy Spirit. We do not labor alone. Even a few leaders whose efforts are informed by deeply engrained and fully habituated sets of moral virtues, all of which are oriented to Christian values and intellectual commitments, can have a profound influence on the organizations they serve and in the public square, too. Jesus' parable of the sower and the seeds is relevant in this regard. "A sower went out to sow. And as he sowed, some seed fell on the path, and birds came and ate it up. Some fell on rocky ground, where it had little soil. It sprang up at once because the soil was not deep, and when the sun rose it was scorched, and it withered for lack of roots. Some seed fell among thorns, and the thorns grew up and choked it. But some seed fell on rich soil, and produced fruit, a hundred or sixty or thirtyfold. Whoever has ears ought to hear" (Matt 13:3–9).

Appendix 1

Table of Management "Language Games"

	Focus or Unit of Analysis	Goals and Objectives	Signature Methods and Techniques	Strengths or Enduring Value	Key Criticisms
Frederick Taylor and Scientific Management:	The Task	• Job Simplification • Task Efficiency • The Profitability of the Firm	• Time-and-Motion Studies • Job Simplification • Standard Operating Procedures • Close Supervision	• Job Analysis • Workplace Design • The "Seedbed" for Other Theories and Models in the "Efficiency Movement"	• A Narrow Focus on Job Tasks • A Truncated Understanding of Worker Motivation • Little Interest in Social Concerns
Henri Fayol and Luther Gullick and Administrative Management Theory:	• Managerial Functions • Organizational Structure	• Singleness of Purpose • Conformance to Policy	• Policy • Clear Lines of Authority • The Promise of Career Advancement	• Simplicity • The Promise of Rational Order	• A Static Conception of the Organization • An Instrumental View of Workers • Little Interest in Informal Networks
Elton Mayo et al. and the Human Relations Movement:	• Worker Motivation • The Inter-relationships of Workers and Their Supervisors	• Job Satisfaction • Productivity	• Action Research • Team Building • Job Design/ Enrichment • Coaching • Improved Communications • Conflict Resolution	• A Corrective to Prior Theories and Models • Organizational Development	• A Perceived Lack of Scientific Rigor • An Instrumental View of Workers
Herbert Simon and Behavioralism:	Decision-making that "Satisfices"	• Purpose • Efficiency	• Experimental and Quasi-experimental Designs • The Quantitative and Qualitative Methods of Research Employed in the Social Sciences	• A Focus on Decision-making • Testability	• The Separation of the Academic Study of Management from Practice • Limited Applicability in "Complex" Settings • An Internally Focused Moral Framework

	Focus or Unit of Analysis	Goals and Objectives	Signature Methods and Techniques	Strengths or Enduring Value	Key Criticisms
Peter Drucker and Unity of Focus:	• Chief Executive Officers • Practices that Promote Effective Decision-making	• Organizational Effectiveness • Results	• Management-by-Objectives • Strategic Planning	• Easily Understood • A Focus on Planning	• Lack of Precision • Lack of Empirical Support • Failure of MBO • Instrumental View of Workers
Robert McNamara and Management Science:	Decision-making Pertaining to Particular Products, Processes, and Initiatives	The Optimized Use of Resources to Achieve Pre-determined Objectives	• Operations Research • Systems Thinking • Program Budgeting	• Analytic Rigor • The Integration of Analysis, Planning, and Budgeting	• Unwieldy Budgets • Sub-optimization • Uncritical Acceptance of Goals • "Loss of Touch" with the Product, Process, or Initiative
Milton Friedman and the Maximization of Shareholder Wealth:	Asset Valuation	The Maximization of Shareholder Wealth	• Financial Compensation Packages • Deregulation • Leveraged Buyouts	• Easily Understood • Easily Communicated • Easily Measured	• Little Reflection on Philosophical Premises • A Thin Moral Framework • Little Concern for the Community or Society • Mixed Results • Inappropriate Use in the Public Sector
W. Edwards Deming, Joseph M. Juran _et al._ and the Quality Movement:	• Work Processes • Quality Infrastructure, i.e., Planning, Control, and Improvement	• Customer Satisfaction • Conformance to Specifications	• Continuous Improvement • Process Control • Teams • Quality Award and Certification Programs	• A Sustained Focus on Work Processes • A Commitment to Customer Satisfaction • A Concern for the "Meaning" of Work	• An Instrumental View of Workers • A Disconnect with Strategic Focus and Planning
Robert Greenleaf and Servant Leadership:	• The Servant-leader • Those Affected by the Servant-leader	Human Flourishing	• Deep Listening • Persuasion • A _Primus Inter Pares_ Leadership Style • A Tolerance for Imperfection • Love	• Appeal to the "Wisdom Literature" • Meaning as a Key Motivator • A Broad Focus	• An Appeal to Results • Lack of Direction for Balancing Claims • No Prescription for Developing Servant-leaders

Appendix 2

Reflection Questions

CHAPTER 6: "BLESSED ARE THE POOR IN SPIRIT" AND "BLESSED ARE THEY WHO MOURN"

- Do I understand faith as a preliminary response to an invitation that addresses my fundamental orientation to the experience of meaning?

- Do I understand the role that root sin, i.e., materialism and sensuality, pride, and vanity, play in my life?

- Have I committed myself to *kenosis* or self-emptying in this regard?

- Where do I look for wisdom in confronting the day-to-day struggles I face with respect to my root sin(s)?

- What steps do I need to take to be more fully formed in the virtues of fortitude, prudence, and temperance, all of which are required in the struggle against root sin?

- What might this mean in terms of my work, key relationships in my life, and the challenges I face on a day-to-day basis? What new behaviors or disciplines will be required? What deep-seated behaviors will need to be abandoned?

CHAPTER 7: "BLESSED ARE THE MEEK"

- Do I experience hope as a fervent desire for a deep and abiding relationship with God?

- What practices in my life are oriented to the development of a relationship with God and to knowing God's hopes and dreams for me and his hopes and dreams for those with whom I journey? Am I faithful to these practices?

- What new practices and disciplines in this regard may be needed for me to better discern God's hopes and dreams for me?

- How do I sense God's presence in my life?

- What steps do I need to take in order to be more fully formed in the virtue of prudence, which is essential to discerning God's hopes and dreams for me?

- Do I have a sense of what God is asking of me now in terms of my work, key relationships in my life, and the challenges I face on a day-to-day basis? If not, have I truly emptied myself of my root sin(s) and so opened myself to God's hopes and dreams for me? Further, what can I do to engender a better sense of what God may be asking of me at this point in my journey?

- Am I prepared for the sacrifices that God's hopes and dreams for me and for those with whom I journey might require?

CHAPTER 8: "BLESSED ARE THEY WHO HUNGER AND THIRST FOR RIGHTEOUSNESS" AND "BLESSED ARE THE MERCIFUL"

- How do I view others in my life? Do I see them primarily as opportunities or as obstacles or constraints? Do I see them as "things" valued primarily for their "handiness" to me? Or do I recognize them as fellow sons and daughters of God?

- If I struggle in this regard, have I truly emptied myself of my root sin(s) and so opened myself to God's hopes and dreams for me?

- Where in my life do relationships need to be mended? In and among those with whom I work? In and among those who are impacted directly or indirectly by my work? In my family? In my church? In my community? In the world?

- How do I understand my time, talent, and treasure? Do I see them as gifts from God, all of which should be ordered to the common good? If not, have I emptied myself sufficiently of my own root sin(s) and so opened myself to God's hopes and dreams for me in this regard?

- How do I understand "mercy"? Is it mine to give or is it better understood as God's mercy, which I am invited to share with others?

- How am I in need of forgiveness? What acts of mercy do I hope for?

- Who in my work relationships, in my personal relationships, and in my many other relationships in the world needs forgiveness? How am I challenged to shared God's mercy with them? What will this require of me?

- How can I better form myself in the virtues of fortitude, justice, and prudence so that I can be ever more faithful in sharing God's mercy with others?

CHAPTER 9: "BLESSED ARE THE CLEAN OF HEART"

- ✤ How do I understand "cleanliness of heart"? Do I understand it as integrity in faith and hope?

- ✤ Have I encountered "cleanliness of heart" in others? When and where? Do I recognize certain exemplars as truly "clean of heart"? How and in what way have I come to recognize them as such?

- ✤ Have I experienced moments in my own life in which I can say that I was "clean of heart"? If so, how did I sense God's presence in these moments? If not, what additional work might be required on my part? Do I need to further empty myself of my root sin(s) even to the point of mourning? Do I need to further open myself to God's hopes and dreams for me? Do I need to recognize and respond to others as fellow sons and daughters of God? Do I need to forgive others in order to welcome forgiveness in my own life? Do I need to share God's mercy with others? How can I do so?

- ✤ Do I have sufficient faith in God and hope or confidence in his love for me to journey further toward true cleanliness of heart?

- ✤ How would my work relationships change if I truly lived a life of integrity in faith and hope? How would my personal relationships change? What new relationships would be required? What old relationships would need to be abandoned?

- ✤ How can I better form myself in the virtues of prudence and temperance, both of which are required to engender true cleanliness of heart?

CHAPTER 10: "BLESSED ARE THE PEACEMAKERS" AND "BLESSED ARE THEY WHO ARE PERSECUTED FOR THE SAKE OF RIGHTEOUSNESS"

- Do I recognize certain exemplars as true peacemakers? Who and in what way have I come to recognize them as such?

- Do I recognize the voice of prophets in my work relationships, in my family, and in other relationships I share? In what ways do these voices appeal to me? In what ways are they inconvenient? What uncomfortable truths do the prophets in my life speak?

- Am I frequently drawn into the drama and trauma of everyday life in the organizations with which I am associated, in my family, or in the exercise of other duties and responsibilities? Do I tend to add to or to dampen this experience of drama and trauma?

- Have I been presented with opportunities to serve as a peacemaker or a prophet? How did I respond? Did I spurn these roles in favor of other roles on the job, in my family, and in other relationships I share?

- Which, if any, of the seven principles of Catholic social teaching have I fully incorporated into my life? How so? With which of these principles do I struggle? Why?

- Am I prepared to accept the slings and arrows that can accompany both the role of the peacemaker and the role of the prophet?

- How can I better form myself in the virtues of fortitude, and justice, and prudence, all of which are required for a sustained life of peacemaking?

Bibliography

à Kempis, Thomas. *Imitation of Christ*. Translated by William C. Creasy. Notre Dame, IN: Ave Maria Press, 1989.

Ackerman, Bruce A. *Social Justice in the Liberal State*. New Haven, CT: Yale University Press, 1980.

Ambrose. "On the Duties of the Clergy, NPNF2-10." In *From Nicene and Post-Nicene Fathers*, edited by Philip Schaff, translated by H. Romestin, 35,685-873. London, UK: Catholic Way, 2014.

———. "On the Duties of the Clergy." In *Nicene and Post-Nicene Fathers*, edited by Philip Schaff, translated by H. Romestin. London, UK: Catholic Way, 2014.

Aquinas, Thomas. "First Part, Question 1." In *The Summa Theologiæ of St. Thomas Aquinas*, translated by the Fathers of the English Dominican Province, 2nd ed., 1920. https://www.newadvent.org/summa/1001.htm.

———. "First Part of the Second Part, Question 2." In *The Summa Theologiæ of St. Thomas Aquinas*, translated by the Fathers of the English Dominican Province, 2nd ed., 1920. http://www.newadvent.org/summa/2002.htm.

———. "First Part of the Second Part, Question 68." In *The Summa Theologiæ of St. Thomas Aquinas*, translated by the Fathers of the English Dominican Province, 2nd ed., 1920. https://www.newadvent.org/summa/2068.htm.

———. "Things that Are Contained in the New Law." In *The Summa Theologiæ of St. Thomas Aquinas*, translated by the Fathers of the English Dominican Province, 2nd ed., 1920. https://www.newadvent.org/summa/2108.htm.

———. "Question 1." In *The Summa Theologiæ of St. Thomas Aquinas*, translated by the Fathers of the English Dominican Province, 2nd Edition, 1920. https://www.newadvent.org/summa/1001.htm.

Arendt, Hannah. *The Human Condition*. Chicago, IL: University of Chicago Press, 1998.

Augustine. *The Confessions*. Translated by Maria Boulding. New York, NY: Vintage, 1997.

———. "Of Holy Virginity, NPNF1-14." In *Nicene and Post-Nicene Fathers*, edited by Philip Schaff, translated by C. I. Cornish, 15,129-70. London, UK: Catholic Way, 2014.

———. "Our Lord's Sermon on the Mount, NPNF1-06." In *Nicene and Post-Nicene Fathers*, edited by Philip Schaff, translated by William Findlay, 17,788-950. London, UK: Catholic Way, 2014.

Aulén, Gustaf. *Dag Hammarskjöld's White Book: An Analysis of Markings*. Philadelphia, PA: Fortress, 1969.

Axel, Gabriel, dir. *Babette's Feast*. Copenhagen, Denmark: Nordisk Film, 1987.

Barry, William A. *Spiritual Direction and the Encounter with God*. Mahwah, NJ: Paulist, 2004.

Bentham, Jeremy. *An Introduction to the Principles of Morals and Legislation.* 1789. https://www.earlymoderntexts.com/assets/pdfs/bentham1780.pdf.

Bernstein, Richard J. *Beyond Objectivism and Relativism.* Philadelphia, PA: University of Pennsylvania Press, 1983.

Bevans, Stephen B., and Roger P. Schroeder. *Prophetic Dialogue: Reflections on Christian Mission Today.* Maryknoll, NY: Orbis, 2011.

Booth, W. C., G. G. Colomb, and J. M. Williams. *The Craft of Research.* Chicago, IL: The University of Chicago Press, 1995.

Bringle, Robert G., Richard Games, and Edward A. Malloy. *Colleges and Universities as Citizens.* Needham Heights, MA: Allyn and Bacon, 1999.

Buber, Martin. *I and Thou.* New York, NY: Touchstone, 1970.

Buckley, Michael J. "Discernment of Spirits." In *The New Dictionary of Christian Spirituality,* edited by Michael Downey, 274–81. Collegeville, MN: Liturgical Press, 1993.

Bultmann, Rudolf. "Hermeneutics and Theology." In *The Hermeneutics Reader: Texts of the German Tradition from the Enlightenment to the Present,* edited by Kurt Mueller-Vollmer, 241–55. New York, NY: Continuum, 1992.

Business Roundtable. "Our Commitment." https://opportunity.businessroundtable. org/ourcommitment/.

Calvin, John. "Prefix to the Fourth Edition, 1581." In *Institutes of the Christian Religion,* translated by Thomas Norton. https://www.biblestudytools.com/history/calvin-institutes-christianity/book1/prefixed-to-the-fourth-edition-1581.html.

Cassian, John. "Second Conference of Abbot Moses, NPNF2–1." In *Nicene and Post-Nicene Fathers,* edited by Philip Schaff, translated by Edgar C. S. Gibson, 37,314–39. London, UK: Catholic Way, 2014.

Catechism of the Catholic Church. Vatican: Libreria Editrice Vaticana, 1997.

Chapman, Lawrence Arthur. "Fathers of the Church." *Catholic Encyclopedia.* https://en.wikisource.org/wiki/Catholic_Encyclopedia_(1913)/Fathers_of_the_Church.

Chrysostom, John. "A Commentary on the Gospel of St. Matthew, Homily XV Matt. V. 1, 2." In *Nicene and Post-Nicene Fathers,* edited by Philip Schaff, translated by George Prevost, 22,388–413. London, UK: Catholic Way, 2014.

———. "Homilies of St. John Chrysostom, A Commentary on the Acts of the Apostles, Homily XLIV, NPNF1–11." In *Nicene and Post-Nicene Fathers,* edited by Philip Schaff, 23,701–09. London, UK: Catholic Way, 2014.

———. "The Homilies of St. John Chrysostom on the Gospel of St. John: Homily XXXIII, John IV. 21, 22, NPNF1–14." In *Nicene and Post-Nicene Fathers,* edited by Philip Schaff, 26,521–29. London, UK: Catholic Way, 2014.

———. "Homily Concerning Lowliness of Mind and Commentary on Philippians I. 18, NPNF1–09." In *Nicene and Post-Nicene Fathers,* edited by Philip Schaff, 21,638–52. London, UK: Catholic Way, 2014.

———. "Homily III Colossians I, NPNF1–13." In *Nicene and Post-Nicene Fathers,* edited by Philip Schaff, 25,698–707. London, UK: Catholic Way, 2014.

———. "On the Epistle to the Hebrews, Homily XII, NPNFI-14." In *Nicene and Post-Nicene Fathers,* edited by Philip Schaff, translated by Frederick Gardiner, 27,063–074. London, UK: Catholic Way, 2014.

Clement of Alexandria. "The Stromata or Miscellanies, ANF02." In *Nicene and Post-Nicene Fathers,* edited by Philip Schaff, 4,2203–76. London, UK: Catholic Way, 2014.

Cocoș, Florentina. "Case Study 04 Ford Pinto." https://www.scribd.com/presentation/229945440/Case-Study-04-Ford-Pinto.

Covey, Stephen. "Foreword." In *Servant Leadership: A Journey into the Nature of Legitimate Power and Greatness*, by Robert Greenleaf, 1–13. Mahwah, NJ: Paulist Press, 1977.

de Beaufort, Joseph. *The Practice of the Presence of God.* Translated by Jonathan Wilson-Hartgrove. Brewster, MA: Paraclete, 2012.

De Unamuno, Miguel. *Tragic Sense of Life.* Translated by J. E. Crawford Flitch. New York, NY: Dover, 1954.

Deming, W. Edwards. *Out of the Crisis.* Cambridge, MA: MIT Press, 2018.

Denning, Steven. "The Origin of the 'World's Dumbest Idea.'" *Forbes.com*, June 26, 2013. https://www.forbes.com/sites/stevedenning/2013/06/26/the-origin-of-the-worlds-dumbest-idea-milton-friedman/#8448efb870e8.

Doohan, Helen. "Beatitude(s)." In *The New Dictionary of Christian Spirituality*, edited by Michael Downey, 78–83. Collegeville, MN: Liturgical Press, 1993.

Dowie, Mark. "Pinto Madness." *Mother Jones,* September/October 1977. https://www.motherjones.com/wp-content/uploads/v2n8_sept1977-pinto.pdf.

Drucker, Peter F. *Concept of the Corporation.* New York, NY: Routledge, 1993.

———. *The Effective Executive: The Definitive Guide to Getting the Right Things Done.* New York, NY: HarperCollins, 2006.

———. *The Practice of Management.* New York, NY: HarperBusiness, 1982.

Ehrlich, Thomas. *Civic Responsibility and Higher Education.* Phoenix, AR: Oryx, 2000.

Fayol, Henri. *General and Industrial Management.* Translated by Constance Storrs. 1949. https://archive.org/details/in.ernet.dli.2015.13518/page/n11/mode/2up.

Festenstein, Matthew. *Pragmatism & Political Theory.* Chicago, IL: The University of Chicago Press, 1997.

Feigenbaum, Armand V. *Total Quality Control, Third Edition.* New York, NY: McGraw-Hill, 1983.

Foote, Philippa. *Virtues and Vices.* Oxford, UK: Oxford University Press, 2002.

Fourtner, A. W., C. R. Fourtner, and C. F. Herreid. "Bad Blood: A Case Study of the Tuskegee Syphilis Project." *National Center for Case Study Teaching in Science.* https://sciencecases.lib.buffalo.edu/cs/files/2-bad_blood.pdf.

Francis, Pope. *Fraternity, the Foundation and Pathway to Peace.* January 1, 2014. http://www.vatican.va/content/francesco/en/messages/peace/documents/papa-francesco_20131208_messaggio-xlvii-giornata-mondiale-pace-2014.html.

———. *Gaudete et Exsultate, On the Call to Holiness in Today's World.* Huntington, IN: Our Sunday Visitor, 2018.

———. *Evangelii Gaudium, The Joy of the Gospel.* Vatican: Libreia Editrice Vaticana, 2013.

Frankl, Viktor E. *Psychotherapy and Existentialism.* New York, NY: Washington Square, 1967.

Friedman, Milton. "The Social Responsibility of Business Is to Increase Its Profits." *New York Times*, September 13, 1970.

Geertz, Clifford. *The Interpretation of Cultures.* New York, NY: Basic, 1973.

Gittins, Anthony J. *Called to Be Sent: Co-Missioned as Disciples Today.* Liguori, MO: Liguori/Triumph, 2008.

———. *Ministry at the Margins: Strategy and Spirituality for Mission.* Maryknoll, NY: Orbis, 2007.

Greenleaf, Robert. *Servant Leadership: A Journey into the Nature of Legitimate Power and Greatness*. Mahwah, NJ: Paulist Press, 1977.

Gregory the Great. "Epistle XVIII, NPNF2–12." In *Nicene and Post-Nicene Fathers*, edited by Philip Schaff, translated by James Barmby, 38,819–26. London, UK: Catholic Way, 2014.

Gryna, Frank M., ed. *Juran's Quality Control Handbook, Fourth Edition*. New York, NY: McGraw-Hill, 1988.

Gullick, Luther. "Notes on the Theory of Organization." In *Classics of Public Administration*, edited by Jay M. Shafritz and Albert C. Hyde, 80–89. Fort Worth, TX: Harcourt Brace, 1992.

Habermas, Jürgen. *The Theory of Communicative Action: Reason and the Rationalization of Society*. Boston, MA: Beacon, 1984.

Halberstam, David. *The Reckoning*. New York, NY: William Morrow, 1986.

Hall, Christopher A. *Living Wisely with the Church Fathers*. Downers Grove, IL: InterVarsity, 2017.

Hammarskjöld, Dag. "Extract from Statement on UN Operations in the Congo Before the Security Council, 17 October 1960." In *Dag Hammarskjöld, Servant of Peace: A Selection of His Speeches and Statements*, edited by Wilder Foote, 319–24. New York, NY: Harper & Row, 1962.

———. *Markings*. New York, NY: Vintage Spiritual Classics, 2006.

Harrington, Daniel J. *The Gospel of Matthew*. Collegeville, MN: Liturgical Press, 2007.

Harrison, Neil. *Nestlé Alimentana S. A.–Infant Formula (Abridged)*. Cambridge, MA: Harvard Business School, 1990.

Hearing before the Subcommittee on Science, Technology, and Space of the Committee on Commerce, Science, and Transportation, 99th Cong., 2nd Session, 1986. "Investigation of the *Challenger* Accident." https://www.govinfo.gov/content/pkg/GPO-CRPT-99hrpt1016/pdf/GPO-CRPT-99hrpt1016.pdf.

Heidegger, Martin. *Being and Time*. Albany, NY: State University of New York Press, 1996.

Held, David. *Democracy and the Global Order: From the Modern State to Cosmopolitan Governance*. Stanford, CA: Stanford University Press, 1995.

Hellwig, Monika K. "Hope." In *The New Dictionary of Christian Spirituality*, edited by Michael Downey, 506–15. Collegeville, MN: Liturgical Press, 1993.

Hobbes, Thomas. *Leviathan*. https://oll.libertyfund.org/titles/hobbes-leviathan-1909-ed.

Hungerman, Daniel M. "Substitution and Stigma: Evidence on Religious Competition from the Catholic Sex-Abuse Scandal." National Bureau of Economic Research Working Paper No. 17589. 2011. https://www.nber.org/papers/w17589.pdf.

International Commission on English in the Liturgy. "A Homily on Ezekiel by Gregory the Great." In *Liturgy of the Hours According to the Roman Right IV*, 1365. New York, NY: Catholic Book Publishing, 1975.

———. "On Pastors by Augustine." In *Liturgy of the Hours According to the Roman Right IV*, 1366. New York, NY: Catholic Book Publishing, 1975.

Irenaeus. "Against Heresies." In *Nicene and Post-Nicene Fathers*, edited by Philip Schaff, 774–1,305. London, UK: Catholic Way, 2014.

Janis, Irving, and Leon Mann. *Decision-Making: A Psychological Analysis of Conflict, Choice, and Commitment*. New York, NY: Free Press, 1977.

Jaspers, Karl. *Reason and Existenz*. New York: NY: Noonday, 1955.

Jegen, Carol Frances. "Peace." In *The New Dictionary of Christian Spirituality*, edited by Michael Downey, 732–34. Collegeville, MN: Liturgical Press, 1993.

John Jay College of Criminal Justice. "The Nature and Scope of Sexual Abuse of Minors by Catholic Priests and Deacons in the United States, 1950–2000." 2004. http://www.bishop-accountability.org/reports/2004_02_27_JohnJay_revised/2004_02_27_John_Jay_Main_Report_Optimized.pdf.

John of the Cross. *The Collected Works of St. John of the Cross*. Translated by Kieran Kavanaugh and Otilio Rodriguez. Washington, DC: ICS, 1991.

John Paul II, Pope. *Christifideles Laici, The Lay Members of Christ's Faithful People*. Boston, MA: Pauline, 1988.

———. *Code of Canon Law*. Washington, DC: Canon Law Society of America, 1984.

———. *Evangelium Vitae*. 1995. http://www.vatican.va/content/john-paul-ii/en/encyclicals/documents/hf_jp-ii_enc_25031995_evangelium-vitae.html.

John XXIII, Pope. *Pacem in Terris*. 1963. http://www.vatican.va/content/john-xxiii/en/encyclicals/documents/hf_j-xxiii_enc_11041963_pacem.html.

Joint Declaration on the Doctrine of Justification by the Lutheran World Federation and the Catholic Church. 1999. https://www.lutheranworld.org/sites/default/files/2020/documents/joint_declaration_2019_en.pdf.

Jung, C. J. *Modern Man in Search of a Soul*. New York, NY: Harcourt Brace, 1933.

Justin. "Dialogue of Justin, Philosopher and Martyr, with Trypho, a Jew." In *Nicene and Post-Nicene Fathers*, edited by Philip Schaff, 499–678. London, UK: Catholic Way, 2014.

Kant, Immanuel. *Groundwork of the Metaphysic of Morals*. Translated by H. J. Paton. New York, NY: Harper, 1964.

Kaufman, Herbert. *The Forest Ranger: A Study in Administrative Behavior*. Washington, DC: Resources for the Future, 1967.

Keith, Kent M. *The Case for Servant Leadership*. South Orange, NJ: Center for Servant Leadership, 2008.

Kierkegaard, Søren. "Concluding Scientific Postscript." In *The Essential Kierkegaard*, edited by Howard V. Hong and Edna H. Hong, 187-251. Princeton, NJ: Princeton University Press, 2000.

Killen, Patricia O'Connell, and John DeBeer. *The Art of Theological Reflection*. New York, NY: Crossroad, 2002.

Klingwell, Mark. *A Civil Tongue: Justice, Dialogue, and the Politics of Pluralism*. University Park, PA: The Pennsylvania State University Press, 1995.

Knight, Kevin. "On the Sermon on the Mount." *New Advent*. https://www.newadvent.org/fathers/1601.htm

Kübler-Ross, Elisabeth, and David Kessler. *On Grief and Grieving: Finding the Meaning of Grief Through the Five Stages of Loss*. New York, NY: Scribner, 2005.

Lactantius. "The Divine Institutes, ANFO7." In *Nicene and Post-Nicene Fathers*, edited by Philip Schaff, 7,939–8,484. London, UK: Catholic Way, 2014.

Leo the Great. "Sermon XCV, A Homily on the Beatitudes, St. Matt. v.9, NPNF2–12." In *Nicene and Post-Nicene Fathers*, edited by Philip Schaff, 38,461–86. London, UK: Catholic Way, 2014.

Lindblom, Charles E. "The Science of 'Muddling Through.'" In *Classics of Public Administration*, edited by Jay M. Shafritz and Albert C. Hyde, 224–35. Fort Worth, TX: Harcourt Brace, 1992.

Lipsey, Roger. *Hammarskjöld: A Life*. Ann Arbor, MI: University of Michigan Press, 2016.

Lohfink, Gerhard. *Jesus of Nazareth: What He Wanted, Who He Was*. Collegeville, MN: Liturgical Press, 2012.

―――. *No Irrelevant Jesus: On Jesus and the Church To*day. Collegeville, MN: Liturgical Press, 2014.

Lowery, Daniel. "Self-Reflexivity: A Place for Religion and Spirituality in Public Administration." *Public Administration Review* 65 (2005) 324–34.

Loyola, Ignatius of. *The Spiritual Exercises*. Translated by Elder Mullan. Lexington, KY: First Rate, 2016.

Luther, Martin. "The Creation, a Critical and Devotional Commentary on Genesis." In *Project Gutenberg's Commentary on Genesis, Vol. I*. Translated by John Nicholas Lenker. Minneapolis MN: Lutherans in All Lands, 1904. https://www.gutenberg. org/files/48193/48193-h/48193-h.htm.

MacIntyre, Alasdair. *After Virtue*. Notre Dame, IN: University of Notre Dame Press, 2007.

McNamara, Robert S. *In Retrospect: The Tragedy and Lessons of Vietnam*. New York, NY: Vintage, 1995.

Marcuse, Herbert. *One-Dimensional Man*. Boston, MA: Beacon Press, 1964.

Maslow, Abraham H. "A Theory of Human Motivation." In *Classics of Public Administration*, edited by Jay M. Shafritz and Albert C. Hyde, 129–37. Fort Worth, TX: Harcourt Brace, 1992.

Mayo, Eldon. *The Social Problems of an Industrial Civilization*. 1945. https://archive. org/details/socialproblemsofoomayo/page/n5/mode/2up.

McCarthy, Thomas. "Translator's Introduction." In *The Theory of Communicative Action: Reason and the Rationalization of Society*, by Jürgen Habermas, vii–xxxix. Boston, MA: Beacon, 1984.

McCloskey, Deirdre N. *The Bourgeois Virtues: Ethics for an Age of Commerce*. Chicago, IL: The University of Chicago Press, 2006.

Meier, John P. *A Marginal Jew: Mentor, Message, and Miracles*. New York, NY: Doubleday, 1994.

Mishel, Lawrence, and Julia Wolfe. "CEO Compensation Has Grown 940% Since 1978." Economic Policy Institute, August 14, 2019. https://www.epi.org/publication/ceo-compensation-2018/.

Newman, John Henry. *The Idea of a University*. Princeton, NJ: Yale University Press, 1996.

Niebuhr, H. Richard. *Christ & Culture*. New York, NY: HarperOne, 1996.

Nozick, Robert. *Anarchy, State, and Utopia*. New York, NY: Basic, 1974.

O'Connell, Laurence J. "Vocation." In *The New Dictionary of Christian Spirituality*, edited by Michael Downey, 1,009–10. Collegeville, MN: Liturgical Press, 1993.

Paul VI, Pope. *Populorum Progressio*. 1967. http://www.vatican.va/content/paul-vi/en/ encyclicals/documents/hf_p-vi_enc_26031967_populorum.html.

Pegis, Anton C., ed. *Introduction to St. Thomas Aquinas*. New York, NY: The Modern Library, 1948.

Pew Forum on Religion & Public Life. "Faith in Flux: Changes in Religious Affiliation in the US, 2009." April 27, 2009. https://www.pewforum.org/2009/04/27/faith-in-flux/.

Pew Research Center. "In US, Decline of Christianity Continues at Rapid Pace: An Update on America's Changing Religious Landscape." October 17, 2019. https://www.pewforum.org/2019/10/17/in-u-s-decline-of-christianity-continues-at-rapid-pace/.

———. "More Americans Now Say They're Spiritual but Not Religious." September 6, 2017. https://www.pewresearch.org/fact-tank/2017/09/06/more-americans-now-say-theyre-spiritual-but-not-religious/.

Pinckaers, Servais. *The Pursuit of Happiness—God's Way: Living the Beatitudes.* Eugene, OR: Alba House, 1998.

———. *The Sources of Christian Ethics.* Washington, DC: The Catholic University of American Press, 1995.

Pontifical Biblical Commission. "The Interpretation of the Bible in the Church." In *The Bible Documents: A Parish Resource,* 131–96. Chicago, IL: Liturgical Publications, 2001.

Pontifical Council for Justice and Peace. *Compendium of the Social Doctrine of the Church.* Washington, DC: United States Conference of Catholic Bishops, 2005.

Porter, Michael E. *Competitive Strategy: Techniques for Analyzing Industries and Competitors.* New York, NY: Free Press, 1980.

Presidential Commission on the Space Shuttle *Challenger* Accident. "Report to the President, June 6, 1986." https://sma.nasa.gov/SignificantIncidents/assets/rogers_commission_report.pdf.

Rahner, Karl. "Anonymous Christianity and the Missionary Task of the Church." In *Theological Investigations: Confrontations II,* translated by David Bourke, XII.161–78. New York, NY: Seabury, 1974.

———. "Being Open to God as Ever Greater." In *Theological Investigations: Further Theology of the Spiritual Life,"* translated by David Bourke, VII.25–46. New York, NY: Seabury, 1977.

———. "Christian Living Formerly and Today." In *Theological Investigations: Further Theology of the Spiritual Life I,* translated by Karl H. Kruger and Boniface Kruger, VII.3–24. New York, NY: Seabury, 1974.

———. "The Dignity and Freedom of Man." In *Theological Investigations: Man in the Church,* translated by Karl H. Kruger, II.235–64. Baltimore, MD: Helicon, 1963.

———. "The Experiment with Man." In *Theological Investigations: Writings of 1965–67,* translated by Graham Harrison, IX.1–13. New York, NY: Seabury, 1972.

———. "Intellectual Honesty and Christian Faith." In *Theological Investigations: Further Theology of the Spiritual Life I,* translated by David Bourke, VII.3–16. New York, NY: Seabury, 1977.

———. "On Christian Dying." In *Theological Investigations: Further Theology of the Spiritual Life I,* translated by David Bourke, VII.285–93. New York, NY: Seabury, 1977.

———. "Proving Oneself in Time of Sickness." In *Theological Investigations: Further Theology of the Spiritual Life I,* translated by David Bourke, VII.275–84. New York, NY: Seabury, 1977.

———. "Reflections on Dialogue within a Pluralistic Society." In *Theological Investigations: Concerning Vatican Council II,* translated by Karl H. Kruger and Boniface Kruger, VI.31–42. New York, NY: Seabury, 1974.

———. "The Scandal of Death." In *Theological Investigations: Further Theology of the Spiritual Life I,* translated by David Bourke, VII.140–44. New York, NY: Seabury, 1977.

———. "The Sin of Adam." In *Theological Investigations: Confrontations I,* translated by David Bourke, XI.247–62. New York, NY: Seabury, 1974.

———. "Theology and Anthropology." In *Theological Investigations: Writings of 1965–67,* translated by David Bourke, IX.28–45. New York, NY: Seabury, 1977.

———. "Theology of Freedom." In *Theological Investigations: Concerning Vatican Council II,* translated by Karl H Kruger and Boniface Kruger, VI.178–96. New York, NY: Seabury, 1974.

———. "Thoughts on the Possibility of Belief Today." In *Theological Investigations: Later Writings,* translated by Karl H. Kruger, V.3–22. Baltimore, MD: Helicon, 1966.

Rawls, John. *A Theory of Justice.* Cambridge, MA: Harvard University Press, 1971.

Rolheiser, Ronald. *The Holy Longing: The Search for Christian Spirituality.* New York, NY: Doubleday, 1999.

Rorty, Richard. *Consequences of Pragmatism.* Minneapolis, MN: University of Minnesota Press, 1982.

———. *Contingency, Irony, and Solidarity.* New York, NY: Cambridge University Press, 1989.

———. *Philosophy and the Mirror of Nature.* Princeton, NJ: Princeton University Press, 1979.

Sandel, Michael J. *Justice.* New York, NY: Farrar, Straus, and Giroux, 2009.

Sands, Justin. "Article Introducing Cardinal Cardijn's See-Judge-Act as an Interdisciplinary Method to Move Theory into Practice." *Religions,* April 14, 2018.

Sartre, Jean-Paul. *Being and Nothingness: A Phenomenological Essay on Ontology.* New York: NY: Washington Square, 1984.

Schön, Donald, A. *The Reflective Practitioner: How Professionals Think in Action.* New York, NY: Basic Books, 1983.

Second Vatican Council. "*Gaudium et Spes*: Pastoral Constitution on the Church in the Modern World." In *Vatican Council II: The Basic Sixteen Documents,* edited by Austin Flannery, 163–282. Northport, NY: Costello, 2007.

———. "*Lumen Gentium*: Dogmatic Constitution on the Church." In *Vatican Council II: The Basic Sixteen Documents,* edited by Austin Flannery, 1–95. Northport, NY: Costello, 2007.

Senge, Peter. *The Fifth Discipline: The Art and Practice of the Learning Organization.* New York, NY: Doubleday, 1990.

Senior, Donald, ed. *The Catholic Study Bible.* London, UK: Oxford University Press, 2006.

———. *Jesus: A Gospel Portrait.* Mahwah, NJ: Paulist Press, 1992.

———. *Matthew.* Nashville, TN: Abingdon, 1998.

Simon, Herbert A. *Administrative Behavior.* New York, NY: Free Press, 1997.

Stone, Oliver, dir. *Wall Street.* Los Angeles, CA: 20th Century Fox, 1987.

Taylor, Charles. *Sources of the Self: The Making of the Modern Identity.* Cambridge, MA: Harvard University Press, 1989.

———. *A Secular Age.* Cambridge, MA: Harvard University Press, 2007.

Taylor, Frederick Winslow. *The Principles of Scientific Management*. 1911. strategy. sjsu.edu/www.stable/pdf/Taylor,%20F.%20W.%20(1911).%20New%20York,%20Harper%20&%20Brothers.pdf.

Ten Klooster, Anton. *Thomas Aquinas on the Beatitudes: Reading Matthew, Disputing Grace and Virtue, Preaching Happiness*. Leuven, Belgium: Peeters, 2018.

Tertullian. "Of Patience, ANF03." In *Nicene and Post-Nicene Fathers*, edited by Philip Schaff, translated by S. Thelwall, 3,967–87. London, UK: Catholic Way, 2014.,

Tillich, Paul. *The Courage to Be*. New Haven. CT: Yale University Press, 1980.

United States Conference of Catholic Bishops. "Charter for the Protection of Children and Young People." 2011. https://www.usccb.org/offices/child-and-youth-protection/charter-protection-children-and-young-people.

———. *Create in Me a Clean Heart: A Pastoral Response to Pornography*. 2015. https://www.usccb.org/issues-and-action/human-life-and-dignity/pornography/upload/Create-in-Me-a-Clean-Heart-Statement-on-Pornography.pdf#:~:text=The%20document%20Create%20in%20Me%20a%20Clean%20Heart%3A,the%20USCCB%20at%20its%20November%202015%20General%20Meeting.

Van Dusen, Henry P. *Dag Hammarskjöld: The Man and His Faith*. New York, NY: Harper Colophon, 1967.

Wadell, Paul J. "Virtue." In *The New Dictionary of Christian Spirituality*, edited by Michael Downey, 997–1,007. Collegeville, MN: Liturgical Press, 1993.

Waldo, Dwight. *The Administrative State*. New York, NY: Holmes & Meier, 1984.

Weber, Max. "Bureaucracy." In *Classics of Public Administration*, edited by Jay M. Shafritz and Albert C. Hyde, 51–56. Fort Worth, TX: Harcourt Brace, 1992.

Wedgeworth, Steven. "John Calvin and the Tradition of the Church Fathers." *The Calvinist International*, May 3, 2013. https://calvinistinternational.com/2013/05/03/john-calvin-and-the-tradition-of-the-church-fathers/

Whitehead, James D., and Evelyn Eaton Whitehead. *Method in Ministry: Theological Reflection and Christian Ministry*. Lanham, MD: Sheed & Ward, 1995.

Williams, Thomas D. "What is Thomistic Personalism." *Alpha Omega* VII (2004) 163–98.

Wojtyla, Karol. *Sign of Contradiction*. New York, NY: Seabury, 1977.

Wood, Allen. "Alienation." In *The Oxford Companion to Philosophy*, edited by Ted Honderich, 21–22. New York, NY: Oxford University Press, 1995.

Name Index

Subject Index

academia, see "institutions higher learning"

action research, 35

administrative management theory, 26–27, 30–35, 38, 40, 47, 54–55, 66, 112

agape, see "love"

aggiornamento, 228

allegorical analysis, 114

American Telephone and Telegraph, 60

anarchy, 228

anawim, 9, 58, 81, 92, 224–25

angst, 20, 68, 124, 150, 164, 251

anonymous Christianity, 253, 262, 272

anonymous woman with the alabaster jar, 210, 213

anti–essentialism, 123

apathy, 82

apostolic tradition, 104, 142–43, 145, 149, 156, 172

appreciative inquiry, xiv–xv, 16, 28, 55, 150

apprenticeship, 208, 226

Arianism, 145

Army Air Forces, 43

Arthur Anderson, 49, 226

artist, 209–10, 214–16, 225–27, 238–39, 258

asset valuation, 47, 61

authenticity, 20, 69, 71, 73–74, 76, 97, 106, 126, 136, 164–65, 186, 201, 217, 237, 245, 252, 262, 271–72, 275–76, 278

autonomous choice, see "freedom"

Babett's Feast, 236–40

bad faith, 269

beatitudes, x, xiii, xv, 9, 77, 81, 106, 135–58, 173, 180, 184, 191, 198–99, 202, 206, 212, 214, 224–25, 235–36, 242, 246, 262,

first beatitude: the poor in spirit, 154–55, 160–66, 168, 170–72, 176, 180–81, 190–91, 206–7, 207–8, 210, 213–14, 238, 254, 262

second beatitude: they who mourn, 159, 166–73, 180, 184, 190, 207, 210, 254

third beatitude: the meek, 155, 175–87, 190, 207–8, 210, 214, 217, 255

fourth beatitude: they how hunger and thirst for righteousness, xiv, 155, 190–92, 207, 210, 214, 220, 239, 257

fifth beatitude: the merciful, 111, 138, 140, 144, 154–55, 190, 192–200, 202–3, 207, 211, 214, 216, 225, 227, 229, 235–36, 239, 257–58, 260, 263

sixth beatitude: the clean of heart, 205–18, 224–26, 238–39, 258

seventh beatitude: peacemakers, 138, 155, 195, 208, 211, 214, 219–42, 259–61, 263

eighth beatitude: they who are persecuted for the sake of righteousness, 158, 211, 223, 259

behavioralism, 27, 36–38, 42, 111

behaviorism or operating modeling, 27

Bill of Rights, 112–13, 119, 231

303